BEFORE THE NATION

BEFORE THE NATION

MUSLIM–CHRISTIAN COEXISTENCE AND ITS DESTRUCTION IN LATE OTTOMAN ANATOLIA

NICHOLAS DOUMANIS

OXFORD

UNIVERSITY PRESS

OXFORD
UNIVERSITY PRESS

Great Clarendon Street, Oxford, OX2 6DP,
United Kingdom

Oxford University Press is a department of the University of Oxford.
It furthers the University's objective of excellence in research, scholarship,
and education by publishing worldwide. Oxford is a registered trade mark of
Oxford University Press in the UK and in certain other countries

British Library Cataloguing in Publication Data

Data available

Library of Congress Cataloging in Publication Data

Data available

ISBN 978–0–19–954704–3

Printed in Great Britain by
MPG Books Group, Bodmin and King's Lynn

I wish to dedicate this book to four generations of women to whom I owe everything: my late grandmother Kalliroi, my mother Kokona (Connie), my wife Helen, and my daughter Daphne.

Contents

List of Abbreviations

CUP   Committee for Union and Progress

IMRO International Macedonian Revolutionary Organization

KMS   *Kentro Mikrasiatikon Spoudon* (Centre for Asia Minor Studies)

FO   Foreign Office

PRO   Public Records Office

WO   War Office

Note on Place Names, Terms, and Transliterations

For the most part I have favoured place names familiar to Greek Orthodox subjects at the time (e.g. 'Alatsata' rather than 'Alaçatı', and 'Kios' rather than 'Gemlik'), and those familiar to English-speaking readers, such as 'Constantinople' and 'Smyrna' rather than 'Istanbul' and 'Izmir'. However, towns better known to readers by their Turkish names have been retained, such as 'Trabzon' rather than 'Trapezounta', and 'Safranbolu' rather than 'Safranopolis'. I have also avoided using Greek names of towns that were not in common use at the time, such as Halikarnassos (Bodrum) and Neapolis (Nevşehir).

I also refer to numerous villages that were described by refugees or western consular staff, but which can no longer be identified with confidence. Some of these villages were completely abandoned in 1922 and never reoccupied, while others have since been given names that bear little or no resemblance to names given in the sources. Where possible, I have tried to identify these villages by their current Turkish names (e.g. Tzaitzouma-Çaycuma), but where this is not possible I have retained the names given in the sources.

Terms familiar by their English spellings have been preferred to Turkish or Ottoman terms (e.g. 'pasha' rather than 'paşa', and 'hodja' rather than 'hoca'), but lesser-known terms are given in Turkish (e.g. 'Hıdırellez' rather than 'Hidir Iles' or 'Khidr'). With Greek transliterations I have generally followed conventions in recent times observed in Classics and Ancient Greek history, whereby words and place names in common English usage remain unchanged (e.g. 'St George' rather than 'Aghios Giorgos', 'Rhodes' rather than 'Rodhos'), but less familiar words are transliterated to appear more 'Greek'. Thus the Greek 'k' is preferred to the Latin 'c' (example, Nikomedia rather than Nicomedia), while a name like 'Demetrius' is rendered as 'Dimitrios'.

Preface

In 1962, after a forty-year absence, Dimitris Maoutsidis returned to his homeland to see it once more while he was still able to travel. The Greek term for homeland, *patrida* (πατρίδα, literally 'fatherland'), can mean 'country' or nation, but for the average twentieth-century Greek migrant it really referred to the ancestral town or village, where kinfolk were buried, where community signified a moral environment, and where the locality was replete with physical sites (churches, chapels, graveyards, brooks, mountains) that embodied meanings and elicited memories. Maoutsidis' *patrida* happened to be Çakılköy in Turkey, although he knew it as Michaniona, one of many Greek Orthodox villages near Bandırma on the southern shoreline of the Sea of Marmara. In late Ottoman times, Michaniona was home to 1,500 or 1,600 Orthodox Christians,[1] but it had since been inhabited by ethnic Pomaks, Muslims whose homelands had been somewhere in the Rhodope mountain region in Greece's far north, or perhaps on the Bulgarian side of the border. Dimitris and the Pomaks were born within an intensely multiethnic empire, where difference was normative, and where coexistence was both a practical and ethical consideration.[2] The Pomaks received him warmly at the local coffeehouse, where he was moved to stand and say a few words:

> Dear patriots, I've been gone from Michaniona for forty years but have not forgotten her. I always had in my mind the desire to return to kiss the soil of my fatherland. Now I am happy that one of my life's dreams has been fulfilled.

As he spoke he became visibly emotional, 'as did the Pomaks, who now remembered Greece. One of them gave me a sheep as a gift. I could not take it with me, so we feasted on it.'[3] The mixed gendered ascription of *fatherland* as also *motherland*—he had not forgotten 'her'—simply reinforced the fact that homeland was deemed the primary moral space and site of identity.

Dimitris and the Pomaks had been victims of modern state formation. To be more specific, their lives were ruined by the great 'unmixing of peoples' during the period 1912–24, when millions of subjects of the Ottoman Empire were forcibly repatriated or killed in order to make way for more ethnically coherent nation-states.[4] They could empathize with each other's plight and understand each other's grievances. The occasion even allowed for at least one subtle, albeit subversive, political gesture. Dimitris described the Pomaks as *patriotes* because they were of the same locality, and perhaps even as a gesture of common victimhood and humanity. As Greek and Turkish nationals, they were not supposed to like each other, or welcome each other as fellow countrymen, or sympathize with each other's fate. For a brief moment, these former Ottomans slipped back into an old intercommunal mode. With speeches, the shedding of tears, and the feast that followed, Greek and Turkish nationals demonstrated they could still behave as if they were members of the same community. The Pomaks honoured Dimitris by providing all the normal courtesies to a returning 'local', which they did in an appropriately heartfelt manner. Such moments had a way of exposing the limits of the nation's hegemony.

A complicating factor, however, were the silences, or what was *not* said. Much of what happened at this homecoming could be read as veiled criticism of nationalism, and a censuring of the political elites who mobilized Christians against Muslims and Turk against Greek. Yet at no stage did Dimitris or the Pomaks actually criticize states or elites directly. The easiest explanation would be to attribute that silence to fear, for Greeks and Turks lived under regimes that acted punitively against most forms of dissent, and certainly did not tolerate criticism of the nation-state, its heroes, and its history. However, it was also probably the case that the parties had moral reservations. For they were also now members of national 'communities' that had appropriated all the idioms and values of an organic community (unity, family, honour), and which demanded the same unquestioning loyalty. Dimitris was a local but he was also Greek, as much as the Pomaks were now Turks. Each regarded it shameful to openly criticize their own national community in the company of 'strangers', and each did not wish to insult the other by impugning the reputation of their 'national' community. The occasion probably involved a continuous shifting of boundaries, as the values of community and intercommunality on the one hand, and those of the nation on the other, were constantly being negotiated.

The effects of nation building at the grass roots level were evidently complex. During the first half of the twentieth century, in central and eastern Europe and in Anatolia, nation building tended to be an extremely violent process that killed millions and traumatized many more, and yet the nation usually managed to impose its moral authority. Dimitris and the Pomaks in Michaniona/Çakılköy were community people *and* nationals, *patriotes* and *xenoi* (ξένοι, strangers). They resented the pain caused by nationalism and yet not only did they come to terms with it, they embraced most of its premises. Ordinary people in Greece and Turkey found ways to balance the contradictory values of nation and community, of being flag-waving patriots who treat the nation's enemies as their enemies, and of being communal actors who treat these 'enemies' to local norms of hospitality. Anthropologists dealing with modern Greece have identified and studied a number of binaries that Greeks have sought to reconcile in social life, such as the tension between the idea of Greece as European and Western, and the Greece which is more familiar with the Balkans, Turkey, and the Middle East.[5] Another is the discord between 'History' as the story of the nation and its interests, and the 'histories' or personal struggles of ordinary life.[6] For Dimitris and the Pomaks, the catastrophic consequences of nation building at the local level had to be reconciled somehow with the fact that they were also proud of their national histories.

Although the critical issues that arise from anthropology are of relevance here, this book is essentially a study in history, and its priorities are focused particularly on what the testimonies of people like Dimitris can actually tell us about the non-national or proto-national past. Much of what follows seeks to recover that past through the use of popular or social memory, of people who later became 'nationalized' to varying degrees, but who were perplexed by, and unresponsive to, the nation's initial callings. The story of Dimitris' return illustrates the point that the local and the national are difficult to disentangle, and yet it is also important to try and de-centre the nation, given that it has implicated itself everywhere and in everything. Its universal claims extend to the past, determining, to take one example, that the nineteenth century was the 'age of nationalism' when in fact most Europeans and Ottomans at the time were unfamiliar with it and its symbols.[7] To see that past in its own terms it is important to wade through the nation's retrospectively ascribed distortions and anachronisms and appreciate the world that Dimitris and the Pomaks once knew. Apart from the last chapter, which deals with the political violence that marked the conclusion of Ottoman history, the focus here is on the identities, relationships, and routines that the nation sought to supplant. That was a very different world indeed.

The research for this project was funded by several grants and sabbaticals from the University of Newcastle, the University of Sydney, and my current institution, the University of New South Wales. The project was also supported by two fellowships: an Australian Research Council Fellowship and a Stanley J. Seeger Fellowship at Princeton. Anyone who has been a guest of the Program in Hellenic Studies at Princeton is bound to note the warm hospitality of its director, Dimitri Gondicas. I also wish to note the support of the Ford Foundation, which funded two workshops on the theme of religious accommodation at Columbia University and the Netherlands Institute of Advanced Study, and the organizer, Wayne te Brake of State University of New York at Binghamton. I am indebted to two institutions in Athens. The British School at Athens is wonderful for studying any period of Greek history, and an exceptionally pleasant place to stay. For the purposes of this research project, the Centre for Asia Minor Studies in Plaka has been essential. I wish to thank its dedicated staff, particularly the archive's curator, Barbara Kontogiannis.

Many individual scholars gave me inspiration and encouragement. In alphabetical order they are Karen Barkey, Vahdet Çankaya, David Christian, Richard Clogg, Nick Dallas, Margaret Housepian Dobkin, Tom Gallant, Renée Hirschon, Aslı Iğsız, Kostas Katsapis, Heath Lowry, Mark Mazower, Theodosis Nikolaidis, Ayşe Ozil, Penelope Papailias, and Aron Rodrigue. My old friends Dirk Moses, Nick Eckstein, and Jim Masselos influenced my thinking over numerous curries and barbequed *souvlakia*, while Geoff Nathan and Chrissie Verevis did the same over coffee outside the Morven Brown building. Milan Voykovic gave me the benefit of his wisdom (and biting sarcasm) by e-mail. For their warm hospitality and long conversations on things Greek or ethnographic, I am indebted to Philip Carabott, Efi Gazi, Neni Panourgia, Connie Sutton, Antonio Lauria Pericelli, Margaret Poulos, Xenia, and Yanis Varoufakis. Petro Alexiou and the redoubtable George Hatzikosmidis gave me the benefit of their expertise, as did John Gesouras, Nick Pappas, and David Sutton, each of whom went above and beyond the call of duty by reading and commenting on the entire penultimate draft. I am forever in their debt. Max Harcourt and David Christian have had an enormous influence on the kind of history I write, and I sorely miss our long conversations. I have also been lucky enough to enjoy the support of three of the sharpest minds in the history profession, Richard Bosworth, Antonis Liakos, and Martyn Lyons, each of whom gave me the impression that I was onto something. That this work was written at all has much to do with Christopher Wheeler of Oxford University Press, whose gentle prodding and good humour encouraged me to get it done. Thanks also to Gail Eaton, and to the Press's Stephanie Ireland, Emma Barber, and Elizabeth Stone for their stellar work. Then there are the 'civilians' who were good for morale: Steve, Vanessa, Nick, and Stella, two uncles called 'Manoli' (one in Kos, the other in San Souci), my Pontic 'in-laws' Giorgos and Despina, and my father, Iakovos, or Jack as he is known in the new country.

Introduction

Intercommunality, Everyday Life, and Social Memory

Everyday life consists of the little things one hardly notices in time and space . . . The event is, or is taken to be, unique; the everyday happening is repeated, and the more often it is repeated the more likely it is to become a generality or rather a structure. It pervades society at all levels, and characterises ways of being and behaving which are perpetuated through endless ages.[1]

Fernand Braudel

In those days nothing ever happened [between Christians and Muslims], *the community was peace loving. From my father I heard that one time, one of them* [the Muslims] *killed someone and the police came from Vourla* [Urla]. *The killer was seized and put in jail. That was that.*[2]

Maria Birbili of Giatzilari

Jerry: *What's the show about?*
George: *It's about nothing!*
Jerry: *What, no story?*
George: *Who says you gotta have a story?*
...
Jerry: *I think you may have something there.*[3]

Larry David and Jerry Seinfeld

In some senses the study of intercommunality is indeed about nothing, in that it refers to a mode of living designed to negate conflict or 'events'. It refers to the accommodation of difference between cultural, ethnic, or religious communities that happened to occupy the same street, neighbourhood, village, or rural environ. These living arrangements were conducted in a spirit of neighbourliness, and underscored by routine practices, social bonds, and shared values. Intercommunality was one important reason why many former Ottoman Greeks and Turks remembered the decades preceding the Balkan Wars as a *belle époque*. It was a time when the two communities claimed that they 'got on well', which in turn meant that they could pursue such essential basic tasks as working, raising families, and social engagements with clearer minds. As one researcher noted about his interview with a former Ottoman subject about this *belle époque*: 'We were talking about a peaceful time when they, too, had a life that was settled and nice.'[4] To date, historians have not given much regard to these nostalgic traditions of coexistence, and yet it is surely the case that social order within multiethnic societies was predicated on such forms of accommodation between communities, much as it was on state mechanisms.[5] The present study regards this nostalgia for an Ottoman *belle époque* as an invitation to investigate the ways in which peaceful and constructive engagement was maintained between communities.

Intercommunality served several purposes. First, it was conceived as a prophylactic against the kinds of conflicts that could be anticipated between different communities living in close proximity, or which had to share spaces and resources. All parties were mindful of the *potential* for such conflicts, for personal disputes to escalate into communal conflict, and were consequently more vigilant in securing prevention. Secondly, each group could appreciate the importance of cooperation for social order and common prosperity. Collaboration was necessary for many aspects of local life, such as managing bazaars, organizing religious festivals, determining grazing rights, and water access. Thirdly, Ottoman Muslims, Christians and Jews wished to live within a convivial and pleasant local environment, and most of these communities preferred to participate in joint recreational activities and even religious celebrations. These shared experiences had the effect of solidifying social bonds across communal divisions. Fourthly, each community had an interest in upholding the reputation of the locality, which meant that Muslims and Christians often behaved as if they were one organic community. And finally, and perhaps most importantly, each community saw intercommunality as a way of preserving boundaries. Cultural groups are defined by their boundaries, and in Ottoman times it was important that the sensibilities and interests of the other community were observed, particularly gender boundaries.

In other words, intercommunality was designed to produce the kind of history that Hegel likened to a blank page.[6] It militated against the possibility of 'events', which are the grist of conventional historical writing and story telling, and yet for Fernand Braudel, who famously compares events to the mere surface disturbances of the tides of history, it was the kind of routines and habits that were found in intercommunal living that were of real historical import.[7] In the Ottoman Empire, Christians and Muslims accommodated each other out of habit, good will, and practical necessity, which together constituted a 'generality' or 'structure' that characterized 'a way of being'. However, as Braudel says of everyday phenomena, the practices of intercommunal engagement were taken for granted and rarely noted in the sources.[8] Another reason why modern historians in particular have been unable to 'see' intercommunality is because, as Eric Wolf once put it, they continue to see 'nations, societies, or cultures with the qualities of internally homogenous and externally distinctive and bounded objects'.[9] To understand the workings of multiethnic societies it is critical to see these entities as internally heterogeneous and less bounded, and to reduce the attention normally given to those moments of rupture (riot, pogrom, revolution, war), which were historically uncommon and which amplified and overstated differences.

The paradox of coexistence

Before beginning to discuss intercommunality in late Ottoman Anatolia, more ground clearing is required since the very nature of this study and its premises will probably seem to many observers to be absurd, such as the mere suggestion that the nostalgic reminiscences of ordinary people could at all be trusted or indeed say anything of value about such a large historical question as Ottoman societal stability. Just as bizarre, it seems, is the very idea of the late Ottoman Empire as a place where Muslims and non-Muslims lived in harmony. After all, the empire did indeed experience a rise in intercommunal violence over the course of the nineteenth century, as happened in the Levant in the middle decades and in eastern Anatolia from the 1870s.[10] The Armenian Genocide and the brutal sectarian violence that wracked the empire between the Balkan Wars and the Greek–Turkish War (1919–22) would seem to confirm that ethnic animosities had been brewing between Muslims and Christians for quite some time.

And yet how does one explain the fact that until 1912, much of the empire was flourishing and stable, particularly western Anatolia and the Levant. Indeed, at the dawn of the twentieth century, the empire could boast a series of growing and intensely polyphonic port cities, from Salonica to Beirut and down to recently Ottoman Alexandria, each of which attained new found prosperity in a modernizing international economy.[11] Although not altogether free of communal or ethnic tensions, these centres were much better known for their splendour and cosmopolitan spirit.[12] Inter-communal tensions did indeed rise during the nineteenth century, but as the historian Donald Quataert explains, 'inter-Ottoman group relations during most of Ottoman history were rather good relative to the standard of the age'.[13] He concedes that the stresses of modern political and economic change certainly did affect communal relations, yet the forms of accommodation that were characteristic of the normal workings of Otto-man society appeared to persist in most provinces.[14] The sectarian conflicts that rocked the Levant in the middle decades of the nineteenth century did not prevent the renewal of cross-communal ties after tensions cooled, and as late as 1908, Christians, Jews, and Muslims throughout the Levant were celebrating a revolution that promised equality and a new spirit of brother-hood.[15] In other words, the empire and its multiethnic order demonstrated a capacity for adapting to a world experiencing intense change at all levels.[16] Whereas historians have been more attuned to noticing the occasional rup-tures that seemed to anticipate the catastrophes that ensued after 1912, it would be more interesting to explain why so much of the empire, including its 'hopelessly' mixed port cities, maintained social stability in an age of rampant political, social, and economic change.

Before the Nation sheds light on the nature of coexistence by considering Greek Christian experiences. The book is not a history of the Greek Orthodox community, or of what was known within the Ottoman Empire as the *millet-i Rum* (the Roman community).[17] There is no attempt here to appraise the standard themes, such as the community's internal political and ecclesiastical conflicts, the fortunes of its financial and commercial interests, or how its leaders responded to Ottoman reform and regime changes. The book does, however, seek to explain why so many Greek Orthodox Chris-tians stayed in Anatolia, despite its large Muslim majority, and why so many migrated *to* Anatolia from the Kingdom of Greece and other parts of the empire. Why did these Anatolian Greeks claim that they 'lived well with the Turks', given the terrible violence of the final years?

The lack of intercommunal tension was cause for surprise for observers, even in the nineteenth century. Such was the case of prying Western travel-lers, who frequented these areas in great number and published their impressions in vivid detail. They were often struck by the fact that Christians and Muslims seemed to be more at ease in each other's company than were Armenians with Greek Orthodox Christians or Anatolian Turks with Circassians, Pomaks, or Albanian Muslims. Interestingly, intercommunal relations was not a subject that could distract travellers from the region's archaeology or the aspects of the Near East that normally excited Westerners: its exoticism, rankness, backwardness, and the merits of its women, most of whom were hidden from public view. They were also obsessed with ethnic character traits: were Greeks more cunning than the Armenians? Why did Turks seem so much friendlier than their received image? Why were they surprisingly hospitable to missionaries and yet completely unreceptive to their message? Whose women were more beautiful? Which ethnic group was better suited for the modern age? And why did these 'races' appear to coexist peacefully? Having journeyed on horseback through much of Anatolia, the adventurer Fred Burnaby, wrote:

> Great harmony existed between the Turks and Christians. Whenever I dined with an Armenian there were always Mohammedans present. When I visited a Turk's house, I generally found Armenians among the visitors.[18]

Twenty or so years later, the archaeologist William Ramsay, who had a much more intimate feel for Anatolia than Burnaby, and who went on to write numerous books on the region, concluded that the worst he encountered was some mild bigotry:

> Even among the Greek villagers I might in the same way say that I saw few signs of hatred for the Turks, and never among those who spoke only Turkish . . . It was almost as rare an experience to hear in a Greek village expressions of hatred to Mohammedans in general, as vice versa. Once in 1883, I found a Greek bakal (keeper of a small retail shop or general store) who had started trade in Islam-Keui. As he was turning away from a group of Turks to show me something, he muttered in a low voice 'abominations of Turks' (misémata Toúrkôn). But this was a solitary instance in my experience; and his words may have been caused by his unfortunate business experience, for trade, even in a large village like Islam-Keui, was very flat.[19]

In his vivid portrait of eastern entrepôts, including Smyrna, the historian Philip Mansel describes Babel-like societies in which bigotries, nationalisms, and occasional sectarian violence were part of the heady cocktail or elixir of coexistence. What fascinated outsiders more was the fact that Muslims and non-Muslims also appeared to find it pleasurable to be in each other's company, and to enjoy private functions and public celebrations together.

'Greeks visited Jewish districts when illuminated for Purim', writes Mansel, and 'Muslim districts when illuminated for Bairam'. During carnival season, the city's many Christian groups held celebrations of various kinds, and 'every class joined in'. These occasions might have been fuelled by chauvinist rivalry, but the fact remains that mutual involvement in the city's festive occasions was part of the local habitus.[20] The same was true throughout Anatolia, including the villages. It was also common among village peasants to celebrate weddings, circumcisions, and baptisms by inviting friends and notables of other faiths.

These practices arguably say much more about the nature of the Ottoman Empire than the sectarian riots in the Levant or eastern Anatolia, and about the functioning of empires per se. As historians and social scientists have shifted the focus recently from nation to empire, the question of cultural difference and social order has come more firmly into focus. What is clear is that cultural complexity required deliberative state responses, and that imperial integration entailed 'varying and changing emphases on coercion, rewards, structural transformation, cooption and accommodation'.[21] Historians have typically treated the topic as a top-down matter. Of the Ottoman Empire and its dealing of non-Muslims, a subject that has been given ample attention over the years, the literature has focused on state institutions. Guided by Sharia Law, this Islamic polity created formal frameworks that accorded legal status to non-Muslims, permitting Christians and Jews a degree of self-governance and self-monitoring—it was in the nineteenth century that these vertically organized frameworks were more formally constituted and dubbed '*millets*'. More recently interest has shifted to the state's ability to incorporate subject groups into the imperial structure, and how Ottoman non-Muslims were absorbed into, and kept within, the system for so long. Karen Barkey, Aron Rodrigue, and others have emphasized the empire's institutional versatility and its willingness to broker political agreements with corporate groups.[22]

Although the emphasis has been on vertical relationships, between the Ottoman state, on the one hand, and each interest group, on the other, it is also clear that the empire also featured numerous kinds of 'horizontal' relations that were not governed by laws or monitored by state mechanisms, especially along the base levels of society, where Muslims and non-Muslims shared villages and neighbourhoods, living cheek by jowl everywhere between the border zones and the imperial centre. Confessional communities *could not* function as exclusive communal units, and flexibility with rules and identities was required with these relationships as well.[23] Thus, although Ottoman cities were usually divided into confessional quarters, these zones were never hermetically sealed. The homes of Christians, Jews, and Muslims often backed onto each other, and males of each of these communities were known to patronize the same public spaces (e.g. coffeehouses). Laws and conventions that were meant to differentiate confessional groups, such as apparel and colour regulations, were flouted more commonly than they were observed, and in most guilds there was little evidence of segregation.[24] In workplaces and in commercial ventures, Muslims and Christians frequently operated side by side. They participated to some degree in each other's religious festivals, and often formed lasting friendships. These kinds of intercommunal relations, which existed throughout the empire, were inevitably governed by social conventions or commonly held customs that stipulated rules and boundaries in regard to everyday dealings. Such conventions made it possible for groups to retain their distinctions and yet coexist in relative peace.

The histories of great empires, the world's largest and most powerful political systems, can therefore be illuminated by what happened at the ground level on a daily basis, and by the subjectivities of ordinary people. Intercommunality refers to relationships that are ascribed with meaning, and practices that reflect moral values, which means that the popular subjectivities or mentalities are important. This study will consider the workings of society at the level where 'most of life takes place', and where people navigated through life with particular conceptions of power, status, cosmology, cultural boundaries, and the other factors that were relevant to their lives.[25] While Chapter 1 sets the historical and geographical context, the core chapters (Chapters 2, 3, and 4) focus on the words and stories that former Ottoman subjects told to convey their ideas of the nature and purpose of their intercommunal engagements. Chapter 2 deals with community as a moral environment and with everyday forms of sociability, and the degree to which Muslims and Christians manipulated cultural boundaries in order to maintain them. Intercommunality was also about keeping the neighbour at a safe distance. Chapters 3 and 4 redirect the focus to popular faith, and why religion appeared to provide the most intimate field of intercommunal engagement. Working largely with studies produced at the time by Western archaeologists and folklorists, particularly those of Frederick Hasluck, these chapters show that neither confessional community believed that it had a monopoly on sacred knowledge, while also exploring the significance of the fact that there was convergence in important areas of popular belief and practice.

The spirit of intercommunal living was suspended with the outbreak of the Balkan War in late 1912, while the First World War and the Greek–Turkish War of 1919–22 appeared to make the rupture permanent. Throughout much of that period, Christian and Muslim soldiers, paramilitaries, and bandits set out to rob, rape, and kill vast numbers of civilians in Anatolia, producing the kind of civilian carnage that anticipated Eastern Europe in the 1930s and 1940s. The history of this era, which is the subject of Chapter 5, makes for depressing reading: the ethnic cleansing of Muslims from the Balkans, the expulsions and forced marches of Greek Christians during the First World War, the Armenian Genocide, the persecutions of Muslim civilians by Greek soldiers in Anatolia after 1919, and the persecutions of Christian civilians by Muslim irregulars in that same period. The forced population exchanges that followed compounded the miseries of the survivors. For many observers, this sustained level of extreme violence would suggest that the spirit of coexistence that had obtained earlier was a sham, and that Greeks and Turks had always been ready to slit each other's throats. This kind of viewpoint, however, which circulated among politicians and lesser journalists during the wars in Yugoslavia in the 1990s, ignored the critical importance of calculated political mobilization for generating so-called ethnic conflicts, and the extent to which these conflicts were waged essentially between rival political elites, soldiers, and paramilitaries. It ignores the extent to which ethnicity was the product of the resulting violence, not the cause of it: new identities were constituted *by* the violence. Although civilians have often been mobilized against each other, 'ethnic conflicts' are wars that specifically target civilians. In other words, such conflicts are not really about cultural difference, or certainly they do not begin as such, and it is telling that the victims of the violence of the last days of the Ottoman Empire were firmly of this view.[26]

Terms and concepts

Before proceeding, it is important to define the group that is the focus of this study, if anything because it defies easy classification. To this point I have used the cumbersome but accurate 'Greek Orthodox Christians' or 'Greek Orthodox community' (*millet-i Rum* in Turkish). Until recently historians causally used the term 'Greeks' or 'Ottoman Greeks', which has also been the practice of Westerners since Late Antiquity. However, the mother tongue of many Greek Orthodox Christians in Anatolia was Turkish, and some even spoke Armenian, and at the time most Anatolians used the term 'Greeks' (*Ellines*) to describe Greek nationals. In her magisterial book *Mikra Asia*, the Greek historian Sia Anagnostopoulou, with good reason, uses the term Romioi (Ρωμιοί) (singular *Romios*) because it was the official and the familiar term of religious designation within the Ottoman realm; in Turkish the word is translated as *Rum*.[27] (For similar reasons, she avoids using the term Turks to describe Anatolia's Muslims.) The term meant 'Roman', which denoted Roman or Byzantine ancestry and recalled the empire that the Ottomans replaced, but it also meant 'Greek Orthodoxy'. The Romioi also thought of themselves as 'Christians' (*Hristiani*) and took that to be their primary identity. In this study the terms 'Romioi' and 'Rum' will be used interchangeably.

I also propose to use two concepts in the same way. The first is 'community'. Although it lends itself to a variety of definitions, I take this word to refer to the face-to-face, organic variety.[28] For most Anatolians, 'community' was the village unit and its environs, whose members subscribed to a common culture, ideals, and moral values. The Greek term for it was 'fatherland' (*patrida*), while in Turkish it was 'motherland' (*anavatan*). However, in the Ottoman Empire social identity was also defined by confession; every subject was fixed firmly within a supra-local or 'imagined community' of believers, which often meant that each locality might have two or more communities. Both senses of 'community' had local resonance, as every Ottoman had to face and negotiate the demands of each on a daily basis.

The other concept is 'nation'. Although nationalism was conceived during the late eighteenth century as a means for pursuing emancipatory and progressive political agendas, by the end of the nineteenth century it came to signify cultural homogeneity and exclusive citizenship. In the intensely mixed cities and hinterlands of the eastern Mediterranean, the creation of pure culture spaces could only be achieved through forced assimilation, ethnic cleansing, and mass killings. Therefore I use the term 'nation' to symbolize the brutal rationalizing of mixed populations. Among some sections of the Rum population, however, nationalism as a category of practice had more positive connotations. For the upwardly mobile and educated Romioi, Greek nationalism seemed to express the community's progress, and it was used to define and solidify its corporate identity within the empire.[29] Thus nationalism meant church construction, building schools, promoting Greek language teaching, and promoting theatre, musical bands, and sport.[30] Although these particular Romioi did like their flags and to give toasts to the Greek royal family, their nationalism is not to be confused with nationalist separatism, or with nationalism in the Kingdom of Greece, which was focused on irredentism and especially the goal or 'Great Idea' (*Megali Idea*) of claiming Constantinople. It was only as a consequence of the sustained persecution of Anatolia's Christian groups after 1912 that these two Greek nationalisms became more aligned.

A final qualification has to do with coexistence and 'realism'. What follows is not a disquisition on social harmony. It does not give succour to the naive notion that cultural groups cooperate because they are good-natured, or that peoples can live amicably once they recognize the humanity of the Other. After all, the most savage communal violence has often erupted among peoples who have coexisted for centuries, and where people have intimate foreknowledge of the Other's 'humanity'. As will be discussed in later sections, intercommunal accommodations should ultimately be seen as practical arrangements that serve the interests of each party. Nor does it countenance the 'realist' but equally naive idea that cultures have a natural propensity to clash, or that the fundamental divisions of humanity are cultural. Culture (including religion) has always been used to mobilize peoples against each other, but serious historians, who give no quarter to Samuel Huntington's 'Clash of Civilizations' thesis and the like, understand that culture in itself does not generate conflict.[31]

It is well worth noting that multiethnicity has been a normative feature of history's larger and more complex societies. The cultural units that Huntington used for his purposes are essentially false models of reality that have inhibited our understanding of the range of relationships and interests (not just cultural or national ones) that have accounted for historical change.[32] The doyen of world historians, William H. McNeill, makes the point that 'the ideal of ethnic homogeneity within a particular geographic territory, and of national sovereignty conformable to ethnic boundaries, was time bound and evanescent', and might be found along the world's 'barbaric' margins. The mainstream, however, has always been characterized by agglomerations of many peoples brought together through trade, migration, disease, and military conquest.[33] This study of intercommunality refers to a societal arrangement that should not seem unusual or paradoxical. If, as has been recommended, we need to return to an understanding of history

as the 'history of society' in order to restore the discipline's analytical efficacy for interpreting the world,[34] then part of that effort must come to grips
with the variety of ways in which societies have managed cultural
difference.

Note on social memory and nostalgia

In Greek, 'Anatoli' (Ἀνατολή) means 'East', and it refers to that landmass that
corresponds to what is now the Asian part of the Republic of Turkey. It was
also commonly called 'Asia Minor' (Μικρασία), although the latter has usually denoted the western regions. The Romioi were mainly found in these
regions, although significant groups also traditionally inhabited the eastern
Black Sea area (Πόντος) and pockets of central Anatolia. Many years after all
the Romioi were expelled and resettled in Greece, they began to speak of
Anatolia and the 'lost homelands' (Χαμένες Πατρίδες).[35] Anatolia became a
site of memory of enormous significance in Greek cultural life. Its reson-
ances were found in prose fiction, in new place names (e.g. Nea Michaniona in Thessaloniki, Nea Halikarnassos in Crete) where the refugees were
resettled, and in musical genres that were imported from 'the East', especially *rebetika*. This Anatolian-sounding musical tradition emerged from the
taverns and hashish dens of Smryna and has since maintained the kind of
regard in Greek society that jazz enjoys in the United States.[36] Memory also
shaped the identities of the refugees in their new national 'homeland'. Even
those whose parents and grandparents had only migrated to Anatolia just
before the expulsions identified strongly with its 'lost homelands' and found
common cause with the diverse peoples who formed the refugee population. The refugees continued to identify with their particular villages and
towns, but they also developed as a collective, and for a prolonged time they
voted uniformly.[37] As the anthropologist Renée Hirschon confirms in her
ethnography of one of these communities in Piraeus in the 1970s, the progeny of the refugees continued to find it meaningful to describe themselves
as 'refugees' (πρόσφυγες).[38]

However, the host society and certainly the state itself took no interest in
the cultures of these refugees, and certainly wished them to assimilate
quickly. Turkish and Anatolian Greek dialects were extinguished gradually
through censure and natural attrition, and with the eventual passing of the
refugees most of their local custom and folklore traditions would also be

forgotten.[39] The problem was partly remedied by the efforts of one particular woman named Melpo Logotheti-Merlier (1890–1979), who set out from
the mid-1930s to create a repository of information about Anatolia, including a collection of oral testimonies that became the centrepiece of her Centre for Asia Minor Studies. By the time the last interviews had been
completed in the early 1970s, the *Archeio Proforikis Paradosis* (Archive of Oral
Tradition) contained the oral transcripts of some 5,000 informants, who
provided first-hand information on 2,163 towns and villages, including
some obscure settlements in northern Mesopotamia. Merlier sent out teams
of researchers to locate and interview refugees, who were asked to respond
to a set of questions designed to elicit basic information, such as the name
and location of their native village, its approximate population, names of
churches and chapels, the defining features of its built environment and
natural environs, the local customs, folklore, and religious traditions. They
were also asked about relations with the local 'Turks'. Having lived in Constantinople in her formative years, Merlier had experienced intercommunality at first hand, but she also knew that the dominant line in Greece was
strictly monocultural. Greek nationalism defined 'the Greek' as the civil-
ized opposite of the irredeemably barbarous 'Turk', hence the histories of
Anatolian coexistence were not only deemed fictions but a cause for shame.
It was this threat to historical truth that Merlier's archive was designed to
counteract.[40]

The Centre's agenda was therefore political. Researchers were told to
seek out those who had come from humble villages, and people from central
Anatolia and the Black Sea regions, who were least influenced by the Greek
nationalist line.[41] The effect, however, was to build an archive of popular
memory that was a representative sample of the Anatolian Rum opinion,
since most Anatolians *were* humble rural folk or townspeople, and since
nationalism was the culture of an educated minority. More to the point, the
interviews merely confirmed what was widely known at the time: that the
refugees generally harboured deep nostalgic feelings for Anatolia and for a
pre-national, Ottoman *belle époque*. Reflecting on her experiences doing
fieldwork among elderly refugees, Renée Hirschon claimed that:

> *Generally, when talking about their relationships with others goodwill and harmony
> were emphasized; rancour, bitterness and hatred were noticeably absent. People often
> mentioned how they had lived peacefully with their Turkish neighbours. They noted for
> long periods an atmosphere of mutual respect existed in the urban centres, for people
> knew how to get on with one another.*[42]

The Centre's corpus of transcripts forms the bedrock of this study. My intention is to draw out the significance of these transcripts as sources of social or collective memory. Anthropologists have often used this archive in order to study refugee memory per se and the social lives of refugees, but rarely has it been used to study that *belle époque* history to which the archive refers.[43] That, after all, was the primary intention of Merlier's Centre and its interviewers. All historians who use oral testimonies routinely declare that for the historian's purposes, the oral source is problematic on a number of levels, and particularly in terms of establishing reliable facts without other corroborative sources. However, oral sources also have unique strengths. They are particularly useful for the reconstruction of social or group mentalities, and for gleaning collective experiences of a given period of time. Insights into this realm of consciousness are very hard to find in any other source, and yet these are insights that can recover ignored or taken-for-granted phenomena.[44]

Some words are warranted, however, about the peculiarities of this particular oral archive in order to convey something of its limitations and potential. These limitations are indeed substantial. The first problem is that the documents do not record actual dialogues or monologues. The transcripts take the form of handwritten notes taken during the interview, with supplementary notes sometimes added later. The passages that I have translated and reproduced in this book are taken from these notes, although occasionally the interviewers make it clear they are quoting the interviewees by using Greek quotation marks (<<>>). The second problem is language. The notes are in standard demotic Greek and thereby give the impression that the interviewees represented a coherent cultural unit. In not being written in Anatolian Greek or Turkish dialects, the transcripts lack the nuance that is usually inscribed poetically in the vernacular. Finally, information deemed irrelevant to the Centre's preoccupations was not recorded, which means the particular preoccupations and interests of the interviewees do not surface in the material. In other words, there is not much scope here for the kind of self-representation that can provide a great deal of insight into cultural identities.[45] Notwithstanding such limitations, these sources are extremely illuminating, and they certainly do fulfil the Centre's aims in preserving memory of lost homelands that are only recorded in song, literature, and social memory, but which seem to have no place in conventional historiography.

Their greatest contribution is that as collective representations these oral sources problematize the historiography and illuminate its blind spots. The refugees generally seemed to express very similar viewpoints regarding communality and intercommunality, about the Ottoman system, and about the reasons why it was dismembered. Together they provide a coherent anti-History that can be counterposed to 'History' with a capital 'H', in that they offer an alternative ground-level perspective on how the Ottoman system once worked and why it stopped working. At the very least, these sources help to rescue the Romioi from 'the extreme condescension' of historiography. For historians of modern Greece, the catastrophic consequences of the period 1912–22 for ordinary Romioi have been treated as peripheral to national political developments.[46] Slightly more interest can be found among the nationalistically motivated writers, whose guiding aim has been to 'prove' the Turks are criminally barbarous—nationalists and partisans on both sides continue to wage war on the internet and in print, using such tragedies as the destruction of Smyrna in September 1922 to score points against each other, to argue the case for Turkish or Greek innocence or criminality.[47]

Needless to say, the same partisans have no truck with claims of everyday coexistence in earlier times, regardless of the fact that the refugees themselves talked about it constantly. As will be demonstrated in the following pages, the oral testimonies show that the average Anatolian had an understanding of Ottoman history that was far more mature and nuanced. Although most had little education, the experiences of living in Anatolia, and having witnessed its destruction 'from below', meant that the refugees were able to offer a perspective that was largely unencumbered by the exigencies of the nation.

I

Great Curse of Babel

Late Ottoman Anatolia

Monday Dec 8ᵗʰ [Salonica]. *Lovely day. Ashore & visited the walls. Was repulsed from a tower by a soldier who refused money. Went through the bazarrs. At the landing watched for an hour or two a vast crowd & tumult. An Austrian steamer from Constantinople just in, with a great host of poor deck passengers, Turks, Greeks, Jews & c. Came ashore in boats, piled up with old dusty traps from which the Plaige seemed shaken. Great uproar of the porters & contention for luggage. – Imagine an immense accumulation of the rags of all nations, & all colors rained down on a dense mob, all strugling for huge bales & bundles of rags, gesturing with all gestures & wrangling in all tongues....*

Saturday December 13ᵗʰ [Constantinople]. *To the Bazarr. A wilderness of traffic. Furniture, arms, silks, confectionary, shoes, saddles – everything. Covered overhead with stone arches, with side openings. Immense crowds. Georgians, Armenians, Greeks, Jews & Turks are the merchants. Magnificent embroidered silks & gilt sabres & caparisons for horses. You lose yourself & are bewildered & confounded with the labyrinth, the din, the barbaric confusion of the whole time...Came home through the vast suburbs of Galata &c. Great crowds of all nations – money chargers – coins of all nations circulate – Placards in four or five languages; [(Turkish, French, Greek, Armenian) Lottery.] Advertisements of boats the same. You feel you are among nations. Sultan's ships in colors – no atmosphere like this for flags. – No wonder poor homes. Dont want them. Open air. Chairs in the streets – crowds & c. Great Curse that of Babel; not being able to talk to a fellow being, & c.*[1]

Herman Melville, Journals, 1856

To the uninitiated, the 'Orient' could have an overpowering effect on the senses. It could either alienate or enthral, and in Melville's case it was both. The wearying effects of apnoea could not affect his urge to explore as far as his legs could carry him, and to see a world that he found both repellent and enchanting. In Constantinople he braved the dog-infested maze of alleyways where the absence of open spaces or parks made it very easy to get hopelessly lost, although navigating these labyrinthine passages seems to have been part of the fun: he mused that it would be good to climb a tree and get one's orientation, and that a pocket compass would come in handy.[2] He was also intrigued by the close proximity of the beautiful and the repugnant. He was attracted by the local women: 'ugly faces are rare' and 'so exceed ours in that respect', but one could only see them when they'd peep through the narrow window shafts of their dilapidated dwellings.[3]

Melville's diary entries read like a walk through a cultural exhibition, the type where Europeans requited their insatiable curiosity for the exotic.[4] Throughout the day, at every turn, he was confronted by different civilizations at work, at prayer, and at leisure. On 14 Sunday he reports stumbling across a Greek church famous for its miraculous fish, and after making his way through sections of the great Walls of Theodosius, he came across a dervish lodge where he just missed seeing the whirling dancers, only to then get caught up in a highly elaborate Armenian funeral procession. He noted that there were effectively 'three Sundays a week in Constantinople: Friday, Turks: Sat, Jews; Sunday, Romanists, Greeks, & Armenians', and pedlars pawned their commodities in many scripts (Hebrew, Arabic, Greek, Latin, Armenian).[5] In fact, the cultural categories that Western visitors knew belied a much greater complexity, for 'Greeks' was shorthand for Greek Orthodox, which accounted for Bulgarian, Serb, Albanian, Turkish, and Greek speaking peoples, while 'Turks', meaning Muslims, could mean Yörüks, Circassians, Kurds, Pomaks, Bonsians, Dönme, and Türkmen, as well as 'ethnic' Turks.[6] Even these categories often meant little to the people in question. Western accounts often refer to Balkan peasants who seemed puzzled by the ethnic labels ascribed to them, who simply referred to themselves as 'locals', and whose 'ignorance' in regard to their ascribed ethnicity was deemed a measure of their 'barbarity'.

Needless to say, cities such as Constantinople and Salonica did manage to function, and indeed flourish, despite the seemingly infinite variety of communal interests, the many tongues, religious rituals, holidays, and cultural idiosyncrasies. There was always the potential for violent conflict, particularly during wars when the empire was pitted against powers that had ties with certain minorities. In 1821, for example, the Greek Orthodox community in the imperial capital paid dearly for the Greek revolt, and yet tensions eventually abated and the community's fortunes revived.[7] Writing more than fifty years after Melville, another American, the essayist and diplomat H. G. Dwight, published an account of a city caught between tradition and modernity, where 'living together' was a matter of fate but also routine:

> One assembly of Easter week which still is to be seen in something of its pristine glory is the fair of Balîklî. This takes place on the Friday and lasts through Sunday. The scene of it is the monastery of Balîklî, outside the land walls of Stamboul... Temporary coffee houses and eating places are established there in abundance, and the hum of festivity that arises from them may be heard afar among the cypresses of the surrounding Turkish cemetery. I must add that spirituous liquors are dispensed with some freedom; for the Greek does not share the hesitation of his Turkish brother in such matters, and he considers it well-nigh a Christian duty to imbibe at Easter. To imbibe too much at that season, as at New Year's and one or two other great feasts, is by no means held to impair a man's reputation for sobriety. It is suprising, however, how soberly the pleasures of the day are in general taken. As you sit at a table, absorbing your own modest refreshment, you are even struck by a certain solidity in those about you. Perhaps it is partly due to the fact that the crowd is not purely Greek. Armenians are there, Bulgarians, Albanians, Turks too.[8]

Dwight was born and raised in the imperial capital, hence he was surely familiar with the kind of intercommunal intimacy described in his text, but he nevertheless anticipated a discordant reception by his Western readership. There is, of course, the mere question as to whether Turks and other non-Christians should be participating in Easter celebrations at all. The violation of religious boundaries was certainly the most baffling aspect of a social world in which faith was meant to be the fundamental source of identity. There was also the received image of the Turkish Empire for persecuting Christians. Western public responses to the so-called Bulgarian Horrors of 1876, for example, which included greatly exaggerated reports of the scale of the massacres, are notable for their depictions of Turks as religious fanatics who harboured a thirst for Christian blood. William Gladstone's intemperate polemic, *The Bulgarian Horrors and the Question of the East*, which described 'the Turk' as an 'anti-human' specimen of humanity, sold thousands of copies within a few days of publication.[9] Notwithstanding the shock that these reported horrors generated, the villainous 'Turk' depicted in such material simply confirmed what were commonplace and longstanding prejudices.[10]

At a more subconscious level, however, lay Western sensibilities regarding the importance of such identity distinctions and the need to define societies in culturally precise terms. That the Ottoman Empire was particularly complex in that sense was cause for comment. The British folklorist Lucy Garnett put it thus: 'No country in the world perhaps contains a population so heterogeneous as that now comprised under the general term Ottoman.'[11] Whereas Ottomans presupposed that cultural difference within society was a given,[12] Westerners tended to proceed from a diametrically opposite position, seeing societal homogeneity as normative and the Babel-like conditions in the Near East as symptomatic of societal degeneration. Since the time of the Classical Greeks, the notion that an authentic state should be culturally coherent has remained implicit in Western political thought,[13] but it was the rise to global domination by the likes of relatively homogeneous Britain and France that made this notion axiomatic. The link between multiethnicity and decadence seemed particularly self-evident by 1900, by which time 'nation-states' like Germany, Britain, and France enjoyed a commanding ascendancy over multiethnic Russia, Habsburg Austria, and the Ottoman Empire. The prevailing attitude within Western Europe was that the latter were anachronisms that would have to be dismembered and replaced by nation-states. At the same time, St Petersburg, Vienna, and Constantinople were each consumed by their own 'national question', each seeking to turn their disparate subject populations into loyal citizens.[14]

That these multiethnic societies could function at all was regarded as paradoxical in Western thought. Babel was synonymous with cultural disorder, a dissonant state of affairs that in literature is often associated with alienation or deemed a curse. And yet there is little to suggest that these intensely multiethnic empires, many of which endured for many centuries, were necessarily more violent or less stable than more homogeneous ones. As political scientist David Laitin has pointed out, explaining the fact that groups tend to cooperate most of the time is more challenging and more critical than explaining conflict. He appears in agreement with William McNeill that world history is more accurately characterized by the 'near ubiquity of ethnic cooperation'.[15] By the same token, scholars of Hindu–Muslim relations have consistently pointed out many times over in empirical studies that communal violence is restricted to certain places, and that it has to be concocted or fomented by radical political interest groups.[16]

Far from being fragile, therefore, the fact that 'Babels' were durable meant they were also robust. A case in point is the Pale of Jewish Settlement

in Eastern Europe, an area best known for pogroms and what Timothy
Snyder has aptly described as 'The Bloodlands'.[17] As Annamaria Orla-
Bukowska points out, it was also known for its long histories of peaceful
symbiosis:

> In the wake of the trauma [of the Holocaust], scepticism is inevitably aroused when
> shtetl recall peace rather than pogroms. Yet if the mutual hatred and animosity was the
> norm, then how was it that Jews and Christians lived side by side for so many centuries
> in so many places under so many different rulers? Moreover, how was it that – instead
> of assimilating – their cultural differences remained strong, grew deeper, and even
> flourished?[18]

She goes on to say that there is a powerful logic to such nostalgia for the
days of 'living together' in multiethnic empires, since the accommodations
reached between peoples prevailed for generations. It is significant that it
'took the exported and imposed urban and modern ideology of Nazism,
executing a premeditated mission with Western technological advancement
to bring this [the world of the shtetl] to an end'.[19]

A similar point can be made of Ottoman multiethnicity. To a significant
degree, the success of the Ottoman Empire—'success' meaning that it
remained a large and powerful polity for roughly half a millennium, and for
much of that time lived up to its ideology of protecting its domains—had
to do with its extraordinary capacity for accommodating a great variety of
interest and corporate groups, particularly non-Islamic religious communities. It was, as Karen Barkey has aptly described it, an 'empire of difference'.
It is certainly the case that this capacity to manage diversity was adversely
affected by the empire's diminishing international standing from the mid-
eighteenth century, and especially because the military and economic
ascendancy of Christian European powers lifted the stocks of Christian
groups within the empire, thereby sharpening religious and ethnic differences. Barkey claims this 'was a recipe for intercommunal disaster'.[20] Even
so, her analysis shows that 'difference' was not so much a causative factor of
imperial decline but a function of it.

Multiethnic Anatolia, 1071–1774

The historian of intercommunal relations in Ottoman Anatolia is best
advised to start with the violent beginnings of Christian–Muslim relations,
when the region was indeed contested ground. It was during these early

centuries of protracted struggle, when Islam and the Turkish language inched their way across Anatolia towards Constantinople, when a great deal of bloodletting certainly did take place, but when Christians and Muslims also forged working relationships and learned how to share spaces. It is possible that Anatolia's enduring structures of coexistence were founded in this early period.

Anatolia had long been the heartland of the East Roman or Byzantine Empire, and happened to feature its richest and most heavily urbanized provinces. Caesaria (Kayseri), Ikonio (Konya), Ankyra (Ankara), Nikomedia (Izmit), Trebizond (Trabzon), and Smyrna (Izmir) had been important bishoprics, as well as centres of commerce and administration.[21] Why Roman/Byzantine civilization should have persisted in this region throughout the Middle Ages has something to do with its geography. Anatolia forms a vast plateau that is bound by the Mediterranean, Aegean, and Black seas, and is separated from the southern Caucasus region, Syria, and northern Mesopotamia by the Taurus and Pontic mountains. Despite the fact that these ranges ran along an east to west axis, invaders could only access the region via a few narrow passes that could be effectively garrisoned. Thus the Taurus range proved to be a particularly effective barrier against Arab Muslim expansion in the seventh and eighth centuries. On the European side, the Bosporus and the Dardanelles, along with Constantinople's remarkable walls, the greatest in western Eurasia, each acted as effective barriers to incursions from the Balkans. Anatolia was not only allowed to retain much of its Graeco-Roman culture but it also persisted as the bastion of Greek Christianity. It featured dense patchworks of dioceses, monasteries, and sacred sites, and boasted saints whose significance transcended the Greek-speaking world, including St Nicholas, St Basil, and St George. The historian Speros Vryonis Jnr goes so far as to claim that Anatolia had been the bedrock of Greek Christianity: 'The Greek church of history is in a sense the church of Asia Minor.'[22] Anatolia was also very Greek in another important way. Much more so than Greece proper, which had been ravaged and extensively settled by Slavic groups between the sixth and ninth centuries, Anatolia had been the heartland of Greek culture and language.[23]

When the Turks arrived for the first time as settlers in the 1070s, therefore, they found a region that by medieval standards was thickly populated and highly urbanized, and largely Greek in cultural terms. Many Turkic groups had threatened the empire in the past (Avars, Pechenegs, Bulgars) from the European side, but it was the Seljuk Turks who finally managed to invade Anatolia from the East and prized it open. The Seljuks (Saljuqs) were Oghuz Turks from the region east of the Aral Sea, in what is now northern Kazakhstan, who sometime in the late tenth century converted to Islam, and who established the first great Muslim Turkic empire.[24] In the early eleventh century the Seljuks conquered Iran and Mesopotamia, and from the 1040s threatened the frontiers of Byzantium. When the Byzantines were consumed by a civil war in 1071, following a military defeat against the Seljuks, Anatolia was left wide open to Turkmen nomads and settlers, and by 1081 they controlled territories along the Aegean coast and close to the capital. The emperor Alexios I Komnenos (1081–1118) and his immediate successors managed to drive back the Turks from the coastal regions but were unable to dislodge them from Anatolia's central plateau.

Over the next two hundred years or so, the borderlines between Christian and Muslim Anatolia shifted back and forth; towns and villages changed hands, new Muslim settlers competed for land with indigenous Christians and Muslim converts, while Turkic nomads moved across the Anatolian massif and competed for pasturage. In his important study of the 'de-Hellenization' of Anatolia, Vryonis follows the contemporary sources in emphasizing the violent nature of these encounters. The Greek sources make clear that Turkish incursions brought extensive physical destruction and mass killings,[25] but as in many other frontier zones the protagonists also settled into working relationships and found ways of living together. As the borders shifted, Muslims often found themselves under Christian rule, and Christians under Muslim authority. Warriors of both religions were in the employ of Christian and Muslim masters, and these masters often forged alliances with each other. Adding to this growing complexity was the presence of heterodox elements on both sides (Shi'ites, Sufis, Christian heretics), as well as Christian Turkmen who had converted before entering the region, and Muslim men whose beliefs were influenced by their Christian wives. In addition, historians of this period suggest that the Turkmen kept many of their animistic and shamanic beliefs, that they maintained a traditional Turkic openness to other belief systems, and that this openness allowed for much movement between identities. Thus, Elizabeth Zachariadou notes the example of Sultan Ghiyath al-Din Kaykhusraw, who as a youth took refuge in Constantinople and converted to Christianity, converted back to Islam when he ascended the Seljuk throne a few years later, and then promised King Andrew II of Hungary that he would convert again if he could marry his daughter.[26] Much later, the Ottoman sultan Bayezid I was known to have promoted the idea of creating a syncretic Christian–Muslim faith. This flexibility was to some extent influenced by the fact that the Oghuz Turks had been converted by heterodox Sufis and were not restricted in their thinking by an orthodox Islamic framework.[27] This state of affairs was exacerbated with the continuing influx of Oghuz Turks who were still migrating from Central Asia during the fourteenth and fifteenth centuries. Among Anatolia's Muslim population, therefore, one found a certain flexibility in their approach to Islam and an openness to dialogue with other faiths.

Indeed the picture that emerges of Anatolian life in this politically fluid era is that of religious orthodoxies being compromised through the mixing of peoples, and of identities that were unstable. The Ottoman state emerged from within this kind of milieu, where two cultures developed a tenuous but mutually influencing modus vivendi.[28] It began life at the very beginning of the fourteenth century, at a time when western Anatolia was dominated by a number of Muslim principalities (beyliks), and when Byzantium under Andronikos II (1282–1328) had become a minor and declining power. The Byzantines were driven out of Anatolia by a number of beyliks that waged holy war (gaza), but as Cemal Kafadar has pointed out, fanatical devotion to defeating the enemies of Islam did not mean that Turkish rulers were not open to inter-marrying with Christian counterparts or forming alliances with Christian rulers.[29] It was the Ottoman beylik that finally harried the Byzantines out of Anatolia by the 1330s, and all the while, 'tolerance and conversion, accommodation and warfare, and friendship and vassalage worked together'.[30]

By 1400 the Ottomans were the dominant power in Anatolia and the Balkans. By 1500 they dominated the Mediterranean world, and for the next two centuries theirs was the greatest military power in western Eurasia. Aside from military prowess, Ottoman success had to do with such stabilizing institutions as the timar system and the Janissaries, which helped to guarantee the absolute power of the sultan, but of greater long-term significance was a willingness to integrate large non-Muslim population into the imperial order.[31] However, as the Ottomans achieved unassailable power they could integrate all groups much more on their terms, especially as the ruling order became more religiously orthodox. After the seizure of Constantinople in 1453, and particularly by the reign of Süleyman the Magnificent (1520–66), who inherited what could be described as a 'world' empire, relations with non-Muslim subjects came to be organized rather differently. Non-Muslims were formally excluded from offices of power and influence, and were no longer seen fighting alongside Muslim soldiers and horsemen.[32]

By this stage the classical Ottoman system of rule had long since come into being. Non-Muslims *(dhimmi)* were subject to their own laws and courts, paid different taxes, and had different kinds of obligations imposed upon them. They were tolerated in accordance with Sharia Law and enjoyed state protection, but were strictly subordinate and meant to exist separately to members of the Muslim faithful. To make for easy distinction, the *dhimmi* were formally subject to different dress and colour codes, and observed a range of impositions that were clearly meant to impress upon them their inferiority and dependence on Muslim sufferance. These included the head tax *(cizye)* and the child levy *(devşirme)*, and more minor restrictions such as the prohibition of riding horses and bearing arms, and that churches and Christian homes should not exceed the height of local mosques and Muslim dwellings. In keeping with the need for communal separation, Ottoman cities were divided into religiously defined *mahalle* (neighbourhoods). In predominantly Christian regions, urban Muslims (and Jews) were often found within walled cities, from where Christians were required to leave before the gates were drawn.

Distinctions were therefore important, but when it came to matters of governance and the observation of the above-mentioned restrictions, there was also a marked difference between form and practice. Over time we find that many of the rules governing communities and their interrelations were renegotiated or simply flouted. There was little consistency in the way the empire was governed, and with regard to the laws that applied to certain cities, tribes, islands, and such ungovernable regions as Montenegro. Special obligations and privileges seem to have applied to most regions. Critically, the Ottomans understood that subjects had to move *between* communities if markets, neighbourhoods, villages, grazing areas, and other zones of social transaction were to function successfully. In other words, the Ottomans were extremely practical and versatile when it came to the observation of boundaries: one Ottomanist usefully described the empire as one governed by exceptions.[33] There was often pressure from some quarters to enforce the Islamicization of the remaining non-Muslim population through conversions and expulsions, but such pressures were resisted by a state that was more concerned about social order, and which always recognized the important skills that Christians and Jews had to offer.[34]

Throughout Ottoman history, boundaries were markers that were constantly being negotiated, which was the key reason why the empire for much of its long history was not threatened by Christian rebellion. At the state and local levels, stability was ensured through the management of diversity, and, as Barkey argues, it 'remained the *sine qua non* of imperial persistence'.[35]

Sick man of Europe, 1774–1908

The situation changed over the course of the eighteenth century. Up to that point, Ottoman Christians had little to gain from making common cause with the empire's Christian rivals, including Catholic Venice and Austria, and Orthodox Russia. The Romioi were subjects of the power that had no peer at the international level, and official tolerance of the Orthodox faith meant that they could practise their faith more freely than was possible in the Catholic West. There was much about Ottoman rule that nevertheless ensured that the Romioi would never fully commit to the empire. The main reason was the exclusions. The *dhimmi* were legally inferior, technically barred from nearly all the important offices of state, and subject to restrictions as long as they remained non-Muslims.[36] The Romioi were considered conquered peoples, whose continuing presence within the empire reflected Muslim benevolence for which gratitude was expected. For such reasons, the Romioi hoped that one day the Turkish yoke might be removed, and were known to place a great deal of faith in prophecies that foretold the return of the last emperor, Constantine XI. For the Romioi, therefore, Ottoman rule constituted domination without hegemony; the state's dominance was based on a power relation in which persuasion was outweighed by coercion.[37] There was always the potential, therefore, that the Romioi and other non-Muslims might alter their allegiances in the future, particularly as the empire's standing began to diminish at the international level, and especially during its final decades when its dismemberment seemed to many to be imminent.[38]

The second siege of Vienna in 1683, the first major military debacle suffered by the Ottomans since the fifteenth century, marked a turning point in interstate power politics. Habsburg Austria and Romanov Russia achieved military parity with the Ottomans, but by the mid-eighteenth century the former two had developed a decisive edge. The calamitous Russo-Turkish War of 1768–74 exposed a yawning gap in terms of military technology, training, and organization, all of which reflected far-reaching institutional and financial reforms. In short, Ottoman power had diminished to the

point where it was unable to resist territorial encroachments by major Western powers. If not for the divisions among the European powers, and particularly a determination among other European states to keep Russia away
from Constantinople and Anatolia, the empire might have disappeared
much earlier.

Another important factor was the growing influence in the eastern Mediterranean of Britain and France, whose combination of political and commercial power was irresistible enough to foster profound social and economic
change in the region. Although claims that the empire had become a colonial dependency have been shown to be exaggerated, it is nevertheless true
that the imperial economy was increasingly tied to a globalizing market,
and that the socio-economic changes that came with Western commercial
penetration, particularly after the Napoleonic Wars, had a profound effect
on intercommunal relations.[39] As elsewhere, the nineteenth century proved
to be an age of unprecedented social, economic, and political change for
the Ottoman Empire.[40] Western demand for raw materials fostered the
commercialization of agriculture and the expansion of urban centres, creating new social formations (i.e. working class and bourgeoisie) and hastening
the decline of the traditional professions and institutions, such as the guilds.
These immense changes inevitably caused great social dislocation *as well as*
social mobility. Critically, Muslims believed that non-Muslims were reaping
most of the benefits.[41] It is certainly true that foreign interests preferred
dealing with Christian and Jewish intermediaries, in part because of their
facility with Western languages and established expertise in commerce,
especially external trade. Western companies also preferred non-Muslims as
employees, especially for managerial roles.[42]

Recent research has shown, of course, that non-Muslims did not have a
monopoly in commercial activity (or in any occupation for that matter), and
that Muslims continued to dominate the empire's domestic trade. Yet the
fact remains that the former did capitalize disproportionately on the burgeoning commerce with the West, and the latter believed that much of that
prosperity could be attributed to unfair advantages, particularly the tax and
legal exemptions that came with foreign protection. For such reasons, Muslims sensed that they were in danger of becoming second-class citizens in
their own empire. That impression was reinforced strongly by state reform
measures of the Tanzimat Era (1839–76). Ottoman political elites believed
that for the empire to survive it had to adopt a raft of Western-style reforms
that would vastly enhance the power and efficiencies of the state, especially

through the centralization and rationalization of imperial administration. It also had to end discrimination against non-Muslims so as to secure their loyalties to the state.[43] The Ottomans were mindful of the fact that Russia and minor states like Greece, which secured independence by 1830, were dangerously well placed to compete for the loyalties of Ottoman Christians. As early as 1774, a Christian warlord in the Peloponnese had rebelled against the state with the expectation of receiving Russian support.[44]

It was deemed vital, therefore, to move towards a more inclusive state system. The period 1839–76 was known as the period of 'reordering' (tanzimat), a time in which power was exercised by a reform-minded civil elite who sought to modernize imperial institutions and see the empire function with the same kinds of efficiencies found in nation-states like France and Britain. When it came to non-Muslims, the reform process saw to the reorganization of the confessional communities as formal administrative units known as 'millets' (nations or national communities), while also moving towards the extension of imperial citizenship (Ottomanism) to non-Muslims in order to promote a new kind of state patriotism. Each of these well-intentioned reforms created new problems, however. Thus, the millets had the effect of strengthening corporate identities rather than drawing non-Muslims closer to the state, while Muslims greatly resented the diminution of their status implied in the elevation of non-Muslims. Muslim grievances on this issue and what appeared to them as the increasingly arrogant behaviour of Christian groups led to a series of pogroms in the Arab provinces in the 1850s and 1860s.[45] By 1876 a constitution had been drafted in the teeth of enormous opposition from many sections of society, including from within the imperial court. When the reformers were discredited by a major foreign policy disaster that saw the loss of territories across the Balkans and the Caucasus, the new sultan, Abdülhamid II (1876–1909), rejected constitutionalism and promoted instead an Islamic identity designed to appeal to the empire's Muslim population. However, the pace of reform during his reign could not offset the empire's fast diminishing position at the international level, and by July 1908, a new constitutionalist movement known as the Young Turks overthrew the Hamidian regime with the intention of saving the empire. The movement called for the institutionalization of an inclusive political order, one in which Muslims and non-Muslims had access to power. Throughout the empire, news of the revolution was greeted with considerable enthusiasm, since most groups were attracted to the slogan heralded at the time that Muslims and non-Muslims were now to live together 'as brothers'.[46]

At this point it might be worth considering why the Young Turk leaders, many of whom were inspired by Turkish nationalist ideas, nevertheless seemed committed to creating an inclusive political order, especially as the empire from their perspective had been greatly diminished by secessionist nationalism and sectarianism. The Greek revolt in 1821 was followed later by similarly successful uprisings by the Serbs and Bulgarians. Large-scale anti-Christian riots in major Levantine cities (Aleppo 1850, Mosul 1854, Nablus 1856, Jeddah 1858, Damascus 1860, and in Egyptian cities in 1882) exposed the depth of sectarian animosities.[47] In 1908, communal relations in some parts of the empire appeared to have broken down irretrievably. In the Macedonian countryside, pro-Greek, pro-Bulgarian, and IMRO (Internal Macedonian Revolutionary Organization) paramilitaries had been waging an armed struggle against each other, clearly anticipating the end of Ottoman rule. On Crete, Greek Orthodox and Muslim communities had long been engaged in a succession of violent confrontations. Christian notables were determined to see the island united with Greece, while Muslims feared that Greek rule would ultimately see them driven off the island. Eastern Anatolia had provided a much larger zone of sectarian strife. For decades, Kurdish tribal leaders had sought to combat the encroachments of central state power and were incensed by the refusal of local Armenian peasants to render the traditional taxes and services. These leaders destabilized the region by fanning popular Muslim antipathy for the Armenian community, whose rising economic fortunes were also cause for resentment. Violent reprisals did occur in response to the activities of Armenian nationalists, the Hnchaks and the Dashnaks, whose avowed aim of creating an Armenian homeland raised fears among local Muslims, many of whom were refugees who had been driven out of their homelands by Christian armies.

However intractable these conflicts appeared, the new political order had little choice but to press on with its inclusive political agenda if the empire was to remain an empire. The Young Turks were especially concerned about securing what was left of the European part of the empire, where Christians were thick on the ground. Macedonia in particular was considered as much a heartland as Anatolia, and it happened to be the birthplace of a disproportionate number of the Young Turks. For many loyal Ottomans the loss of Macedonia and its capital Salonica was unthinkable. Despite the strong influence among the movement's ranks of Turkish nationalists, it was evidently not of the exclusivist kind.[48] The Committee for Union and Progress (CUP), as the Young Turk movement was formally known, believed the only way that the empire could be saved was as a 'union of the peoples'.[49]

'Roman' Anatolia, *c.* 1900

Meanwhile, foreign observers throughout the nineteenth century generally believed the empire's collapse was inevitable. The distinguished archaeologist William Mitchell Ramsay (1851–1939), a leading Pauline scholar in his day, was firmly of the view that the Turks were a dying race. His extensive trekking through Anatolia told him that even 'where the Greek have not begun to settle, the Turks are diminishing in numbers owing to conscription, mis-government, and certain diseases'. Ramsay was convinced that the Turks were being overtaken by Western progress, for since they had 'no heart' they were 'unable to deal with the tide of Western ideas and thoughts' and 'the movement towards freedom'.[50] The Greeks, he believed, were thriving in the same conditions.[51] Wherever the railways could be found, 'the Greek element goes with it and even in front of it'.[52] It was also widely believed that Rum prosperity had to do with pedigree. As another traveller put it:

> *Watching them, it grows upon the observer that traditional Greek characteristics have survived strongly in the race, and that an Asia Minor Greek of to-day is probably little different from a Greek of twenty centuries ago.*[53]

Other Westerners, however, did not take to the Romioi at all:

> *The Greek… is markedly deficient in practical ethics; he is notably untrustworthy, and his word has little value. Honesty likewise is not one of his virtues; his cunning – to quote from a writer friendly to the Greeks – 'comes very near fraud, and he lies in the most impudent manner. He is noisy, blustering, familiar, obsequious, dissolute, a gamester, and a drunkard. The Greek is also charged with being quarrelsome, volatile and presumptuous, and he is genuinely disliked by Franks and Turks because of his turbulence and unreliableness'.*[54]

Who exactly were these 'Greeks'? And why were the Romioi called 'Greeks'? Part of the answer lies in the fact that Westerners could only read the Ottoman world in terms of familiar ethnic categories. For them, Ottoman Anatolia consisted of Turks, Arabs, Kurds, Armenians, Jews, and Greeks, with each group defined by its unique qualities and character flaws.[55] The 'Greeks' were effectively defined as those who belonged to the Greek Orthodox Church, used Greek script, and often spoke dialects that were recognizably Greek. For such reasons, other members of the *millet-i Rum*, such as various Orthodox Slavic and Arabic-speaking peoples, did not count as 'Greeks'. Rather, the Greeks were seen as the detritus of the ancient Greek world and the Byzantine Empire, and what was left after Turkish butchery and conversion had run out of steam.

It was also generally agreed at the time that the Romioi were the modern face of the Ottoman Empire, for they were seen as the most adept at exploiting the opportunities of the modern era. Westerners saw these Greeks everywhere: in the ports, at the railway stations, banks, restaurants, and archaeological sites. 'Greeks' were typecast as the quintessential middlemen, as merchants of great skill and cunning, but also as petty operators (guides, translators, hoteliers, shopkeepers) whose wily ways seemed to bristle the sensitivities of Westerners who were reliant on their services. Some facts did much to buttress impressions that the Romioi were in the ascendant. They did indeed dominate the empire's financial and banking sectors, as well as its external commerce.[56] Families like the Baltazzis in Smyrna were so rich and influential that they were visited by sultans and had Turkish soldiers carry candles at their funerals.[57] So prosperous were Rum merchants that they were happy to live under Ottoman rule, or at least that was the opinion of many disappointed Greek nationalists, who noted disinterest in political causes that might be disruptive to business. The noted Greek intellectual Ion Dragoumis was convinced that the Greek Orthodox elite in Constantinople were in no hurry to see the return of the prophesied Greek emperor.[58]

It was certainly the case that rich and upwardly mobile Romioi became more 'Greek' in the nineteenth century in the sense that, as discussed earlier, they associated Greek culture with upward mobility and communal progress. Wealthy Romioi generously funded Greek education and were behind the proliferation of specifically Greek clubs and voluntary organizations. At the same time, this class was notably cosmopolitan. Their lifestyle and attire was 'Frankish' (i.e. Western), their children attended schools in which they often studied and played with the children of other elites, and they could converse in French, English, Italian, Turkish, or sometimes Arabic. Unlike their Muslim counterparts, the Greek bourgeoisie moved easily between the empire and places like London, Paris, Trieste, Vienna, and St Petersburg.

Needless to say, the Romioi in social terms were a much larger and complex group, though in some ways did not constitute a 'group' as such. Only a small proportion of them were prosperous entrepreneurs, and an even smaller number were rich, cosmopolitan, and polyglott. The vast majority lived in humble circumstances, most often in village communities, and some had little interest in Greek education. In dress sense, habit and outlook, they had much more in common with local Muslims than with the Rum bourgeoisie in Smyrna, Constantinople, or Alexandria.

And if it is difficult to define the 'Romans' of late Ottoman Anatolia, it is much harder to count them. The primary sources are extremely patchy and the subject of much partisan wrangling.[59] Muslims certainly formed an overwhelming majority. During the last quarter of the nineteenth century, Christians made up just under a quarter of the entire population of the empire, but the bulk of them were to be found in European provinces.[60] In some eastern Anatolian provinces, Armenians accounted for as much as 30 to 40 per cent of the population, but in central and western Anatolia non-Muslims never constituted more than 20 per cent, and usually less than 10 per cent. According to official Ottoman statistics, Anatolia's Romioi in 1897 numbered about 820,000 out of a total population of 11.5 million. That figure had increased to 925,000 out of 13 million by 1906/7, and 1,003,283 out of 14.5 million by 1914. The Turkish population historian Servet Mutlu has adjusted the Rum figures for 1914 at closer to 1.2 million.[61] Greek scholars have more trust than their Turkish counterparts in the census of 1910–12 organized by the Patriarchate of Constantinople, which had Rum numbers at closer to 1.5 million.[62] Despite the discrepancies, the available information confirms that the Romioi were always a minority even in the Aegean coastal areas.

At the beginning of the twentieth century, Greek Orthodox Christians could be found in most parts of Anatolia, even in Kars near the current Armenian border with Turkey.[63] It appears that from the time of the Turkish conquests in the late eleventh century through to the eighteenth century, the Rum population had been steadily diminishing through conversion. That trend was reversed by the nineteenth century, as conversions became rarer, and as the Romioi began to prosper economically and enjoy high birth rates. The most significant source of growth, however, was immigration from the Greek islands and the Balkans. In Smyrna, where the Romioi represented a mere 20 per cent of the population in 1800, they had come to form a slight majority by 1900. A large proportion of the city's burgeoning Greek Orthodox community was from the islands, while others had descended from Anatolian villages, and from as far as Konya and Kayseri.[64] Immigrants from Greece and the Aegean Islands also settled in the environs of Bandırma (Panormos) and Gemlik (Kios) in the Sea of Marmara region, and around Avvalık and Edremit near the northern Aegean or 'Aeolian' coastal area, while significant numbers had also established near Aydın and in the Menderes riverine area.[65] Growth appears to have plateaued between 1900 and 1912, and was offset somewhat after 1909 by the emigration of males seeking to avoid conscription: an official Ottoman survey stated about a third of Christian males had emigrated for that reason.[66]

Other significant concentrations of Romioi were located in the eastern Black Sea region, from Sinope to Rize, as well as in central Anatolia, near Kayseri, Nevşehir, and further afield near Konya. Small communities were also to be found within most Anatolian towns, in places as far apart as Muğla, Kastamonu, Ankara, Isparta, Sivas, Adana, and Mersin. In such places they usually filled particular economic niches in retail and in the building trades, while merchants and highly skilled tradesmen were known to move between these communities. The Hatzitheodoridis brothers, for example, Petros, Antonis, and Pantelis, were Pontic Greeks who developed a strong reputation throughout the Ankara-Konya region as master builders, and were better known as 'Haciustalar' (Haji-'master builder').[67]

A marked feature of each of these communities was a strong interest in organized cultural activity and voluntary organizations, which was largely driven by the more upwardly mobile members. In Gümüşhane (Argyroupolis), for example, an inland mining town and hometown of the Hatzitheodoridis brothers, local Romioi produced a succession of voluntary organizations, such as the *Philoptohos Adelphotis* (1875), *Mettaleus* (1888), *Sokrates* (1892), *Kiriakidis* (1908), and *Philarmoniki* (1912). Each was meant to promote learning and cultural activities. Thus *Kiriakidis* was established to create a library and set up weekly folklore classes, and dedicated considerable attention to educating workers.[68] Quite typical was the Rum community of Kastamonu, which had no more than 2,000 people, but which managed to fund and organize schools for girls and boys.[69] Since the Ottoman state deemed primary school education a matter for each community, the Romioi formed voluntary organizations (*somatia*) for the promotion of Greek education.[70] It became the primary aim of village and town elders in every locality to ensure that local children were all schooled in Greek.[71] In 1909 the 3,000-strong community in Ankara launched 'I Anorthosis' ('The Restoration'), with the express aim of reintroducing Greek to its Turkish-speaking community. In the meantime, it also promoted Greek theatre and staged a number of performances in Turkish translation.[72]

The great proliferation of voluntary organizations and community-focused activities during the second half of the nineteenth century was a clear indication of a strengthening consciousness among the Romioi. While some Greek Orthodox elites in Constantinople and Anatolia had thrown in their lot with the Greek revolt in the 1820s, and some would later support the idea of restoring Greek rule in Constantinople (i.e. the *Megali Idea*), most sought to develop and express that corporate identity within the Ottoman milieu.[73] Throughout the nineteenth century and during the first decade of the twentieth, Rum identity was closely linked to the Rum *millet*, and was influenced more by local and cosmopolitan social conventions than by Greek nationalism. The case of Stephanos Vogorides (1780–1859), a Phanariot who worked at the highest levels of the Ottoman state, shows how some could be loyal to the Sultan, the Church, and the Rum community. As with many members of his class, Vogorides hoped for 'civilization to be fully realized with Turkey', but with Christians more firmly integrated into the polity.[74] Similar views were held by subsequent generations of his class, which indicates that the Greeks in Greece were different. More broadly, this distinction was seen in the commonplace designation of Greek nationals as 'Ellines' (Greeks). The Byzantinist Peter Charanis recalled as a boy a moment of cultural dissonance on Limnos in 1912, after the Greek navy seized the remaining Ottoman-controlled islands. Soldiers were perplexed when the boy referred to them as 'Greeks' and to himself as a 'Romios'.[75]

The Greeks in Greece were similarly ambivalent about their brethren in the empire. The Romioi who did not support the Greek revolt and were indeed hostile to it, like Vogorides, were branded as traitors in Greece, and there was some frustration shown towards those members of Vogorides' class in Constantinople who continued to serve the empire. More commonly, Greek nationals regarded the Romioi as unredeemed countrymen, and their presence in the empire was used as an important moral justification for irredentism. There was some fascination in Athens for the 'Greeks' who lived within the depths of Anatolia, particularly the Turkish-speakers of central Anatolia, whose very existence was deemed remarkable, given that they had suffered hundreds of years of Turkish 'slavery'. The survival of Orthodox Christianity here was seen as reflecting an undying will to remain 'Greek'. Readers in Greece learned about these Romioi and many other exotic 'Greek' brethren in the periodical *Xenophanes*, which was issued in Athens between the 1890s and 1900s, and which provided information regarding the location, population, communal organizations, and customs of these 'lost' or 'forgotten' Greeks.[76]

Historians often give the impression that ordinary people in the past were as preoccupied with the politics of identity as their literate elites, when on closer inspection it can usually be shown that the opposite was the case.

Studies on the promotion of nationalism before the First World War show that subjects at the local level were usually unresponsive to the callings of the national fatherland.[77] In dealing with the Ottoman Empire, it is also important not to exaggerate the salience of ascribed identities (Turks, Greeks) in everyday contexts. As this study will show, poor Romioi, as much as poor Muslims, did not necessarily share the political and cultural interests of their social betters. Children who attended schools in Turkish-speaking communities such as that of Nevşehir (Neapolis) often conveyed a lack of interest in Greek.[78] In many oral testimonies, subjects conceded that they were not particularly attentive in Greek classes and learned very little.[79] 'We were coerced into learning the little we managed to learn', admitted Iraklis Ioannidis, who was brought up in a village that had little practical use for Greek and whose local priest could barely read the Bible.[80]

Ottomans generally did not regard themselves as pure sectarian/ethnic subjects who operated with ethnic or sectarian identities firmly in mind and at all times.[81] Historians of the empire have generally come to the view that one cannot read Ottoman society as a collection of pre-national or (say) ethnic groups, since such identity signifiers are too easily confused as categories of practice *and* analysis. Rogers Brubaker and Frederick Cooper make the basic point that identity categories as used in everyday discourse are assumed as real and self-evident, but from an analytical perspective identities are constructed and contingent, and that the boundaries between identities are often quite permeable.[82] They also note a broader problem in the social sciences where identities have been read as reified entities that exist in relation to, or conflict with, other entities, and that this 'identitarian focus on bounded groupness limits the sociological—and the political— imagination, while alternative analytical idioms can help open up both'. More specifically, this preoccupation with seeing the world as composed of essentialized categories means that the focus has been on 'boundary formation rather than boundary crossing, the constitution of groups rather than the development of networks'.[83]

This observation is germane to the study of the Ottoman Empire, where confessional identities were certainly critical in political and social life, but where inter-confessional relations and boundary violations were also necessary.[84] Being a Romios did not preclude other identities or the salience of other relationships. To paraphrase historian Usama Makdisi, the average Ottoman subject was not a pure communal actor.[85] The same people who believed in prophecies that foretold the destruction of the Turkish empire

had close Muslim friends, helped these friends in times of need, and visited
Muslim shrines that were renowned for their miracle-working powers.

Pontians and Central Anatolians

Another problem with ethnic group labels is the impression they give of
inner uniformity. The designation Roman/Romios/Rum belied profound
internal cultural differences that might easily have formed the basis for separate ethnic identities. For the sake of simplicity, one can identify three sub-
categories of Anatolian Rum: the Central Anatolians, the Pontians, and the
Mikrasiates. (This study will occasionally refer to two other groups, namely
the people of eastern Thrace (Thrakiotes) and Constantinopolitans ('Polites'),
whose experiences of Ottoman rule and the war years were similar, but
who were not Anatolians as such.) *Mikrasiates* basically refers to the people
of Asia Minor, and in particular the western provinces of Anatolia. The
Central Anatolians were largely Turkish-speaking Romioi known as the
Karamanlides or *Karamanli* (in Turkish), while the Pontians were Greek-
speaking communities native to the eastern Black Sea region, although
large expatriate Pontic communities were also to be found in central Anatolia and further west near Kastamonu.

Perhaps the most coherent of these groups were the Pontians, or Pontic
Greeks. Their homeland was the eastern Black Sea littoral, with Trabzon
(Trapezounta) being its centre. Researchers from the Centre for Asia Minor
Studies counted 894 Pontic towns and villages in the region, with another
560 further inland near such places as Gümüşhane, Sivas, and Zile, and
another seven in the vicinity of Kastamonu and Inebolu.[86] Their most dis-
tinguishing characteristic was Pontic Greek, a dialect or set of related dialects preserved within compact communities that benefited from relative
geographical isolation. 'Pontos' literally means 'sea' (i.e. the Black Sea, *Eux-
inos Pontos*), but Pontic communities were not restricted to the shoreline
and were scattered among the inland valleys and the steeply rising ranges.
These ranges protected the region from armies moving between the southern Caucasus and western Anatolia, including those of the Seljuk Turks. For
more than two hundred years before the Ottoman conquest, Pontus was
ruled by a Byzantine-styled monarchy known as 'the Grand Komnenoi',
and prospered from the high volume of trade that moved through its ports
and inland routes. Historically, the region was part of a caravan trail that

linked Constantinople (and therefore Europe) with Persia and the Silk
Road. Its seaside towns had also served points of exchange for goods moving around the Black Sea.

Before the First World War, the Pontic Greek population was somewhere
between 260,000 and 300,000.[87] Traditionally most Pontians were to be
found inland, where they lived as farmers and shepherds among the fertile
inland valleys and lush hill areas. In terms of climate and vegetation, Pontus
is unlike the rest of Anatolia in that it enjoys heavier rainfall which makes it
more verdant and heavily wooded. The lowlands at the time were lined with
numerous villages that produced wine, oil, and nuts, and where the people
were organized into extended kin groups in which the male patriarch exercised immense moral authority.[88] The clergy also were a focus of power and
influence in the region. Orthodox Christianity and the Greek language survived largely because of the protective watch of the local monasteries, which
were awarded significant privileges and autonomy in the mid-fifteenth century. The large Christian village communities effectively were governed by
monasteries such as Panayia Soumela near Trabzon.[89] Identities were strongly
tied to such localities and, as in Crete, the local Muslims were also local
converts, and kin and family ties were retained for generations. As Anthony
Bryer has argued for Pontus, and Molly Greene for Crete, these ties were
important and comparable to ties with fellow Orthodox Christians.[90] Because
of their expertise in mining, some Pontic communities had relocated in the
mid-nineteenth century as far as Konya, central Anatolia, the Taurus mountain ranges, and to sites near Diyarbakır.[91]

The Pontic Greek community changed significantly during the nineteenth century with the reopening of trade routes that linked Anatolia to
the Caucasus, and because of the general rise in commercial activity following the liberalization of external trade from 1826. As in much of Anatolia,
the local Rum merchants played a leading role in external trade in the Black
Sea and Caucasus regions. Ordinary Pontians also began to migrate from
the villages to coastal towns like Trabzon, Giresun, and Samsun, as well as
further afield, to the central Black Sea region (Paphlagonia), the region east
of Constantinople, and to towns like Adapazarı and Iznik (Nicaea).[92] More
commonly, migration was a seasonal preoccupation with Pontic men, who
travelled annually to find work at the larger ports, especially Constantinople, where they were often employed as boatmen (*kayikçi*) on small sailing
craft.[93] A significant number of Pontic males had also migrated to Russian
port cities like Odessa, where large diaspora communities were formed.

Exile had a way of ascribing meaning to Pontic identity. It was in Russia and later in Greece that people from different parts of Pontus intermingled and could see where they stood in relation to other Greek Orthodox groups more clearly. In these situations, Pontic identity as a regional designation became more meaningful, and Pontic Greek language was revealed to be distinctive. The language sustained many of the archaic features of ancient and medieval Greek, such as η (eta) with a long 'e' sound rather than the short ι (iota), and the plural possessive 'emon' which is the Koine 'ημών'.[94] More so than any other extant Greek dialect, it retained many differences in grammar and especially in vocabulary, and was not comprehensible to other Greeks. Just as important as markers of identity were the region's distinctive dance and music traditions.

The historian Anthony Bryer argues that Pontic Greeks only really became Pontic 'when they left Pontos', suggesting that regional identity became a matter of importance only when members of this group were threatened with the loss of identity in Russia and Greece. Prior to that, Pontians were tied to their locality (patris) and to their Orthodox faith. They were also 'Romans'. The Pontians pronounced this word 'Rome-ii' and used it as a synonym for 'Christian'. Thus as one particular Turk told Bryer in 1969: 'This is (Roman) Rum country; they spoke Christian here'.[95] To complicate matters another study shows that the remaining Pontic-speaking Muslims in the region often described themselves as 'Romans'.[96]

A different group of 'Romans' in central Anatolia had not only survived many more centuries of Turkish rule, but in the nineteenth century appeared to be enjoying something of a renaissance. Whereas the Pontians could be distinguished by the patronym 'idis' (e.g. Tirekidis, Stamboulidis, Peonidis), central Anatolian names usually featured the more Turkish 'oglu'—the family name of Hollywood film director Elia Kazan, for example, was Kazantzoglu. Like most central Anatolian Romioi, the Kazantzoglu came from the area near Kayseri and Niğde, which included such towns as Sinasos (Mustafapasha), Prokopi (Ürgüp), and Neapolis (Nevşehir). Another cluster of communities was located further west in the area of Konya and Isparta. By far the largest group among these Central Anatolians were the Turkish-speaking Karamanlides, who were distinguished by the fact that they produced a written language consisting of Turkish in Greek script. These groups considered 'Karamanlidika' to be their mother tongue, but the most tangible indication of Karamanli group consciousness was the fact that this community supported a trade in books printed in Karamanlidika. As earlier as 1781, a religious book (*Apanthisma*) had been produced specifically for the Karamanli readership, and was the first of 331 books printed by 1820. Many of these were religious texts, although an increasing number were on secular themes, including French novels and works of history. Publishing in Karamanlidika was to continue in Greece and Cyprus for a few years after the population exchange.[97]

Another reason why the Karamanlides were a self-conscious grouping had to do with seasonal and permanent migration. Although Karamanli communities were prosperous, as indicated by a flurry in church building activity in the later decades of the nineteenth century, central Anatolia itself was a relative backwater, and Karamanli towns and villages were shrinking as people moved to ports on the southern (Adana, Mersin), northern (Trabzon), and western coasts. Having survived some 800 or so years, robustly Orthodox Christian centres such as Sille and Selme were now being deserted. Karamanli families were shifting to the commercial centres that lined the rail tracks, such as Konya and Niğde.[98] The parishes of Ankara and Kayseri, important ecclesiastical centres in Byzantine times but with very few Christians for most of the Ottoman era, were suddenly overflowing with worshippers and in desperate need of new church buildings. More so than the Pontic Greeks, the menfolk of central Anatolia migrated seasonally for work and there was also a long tradition of migration to and from Constantinople. Here the Karamanlides formed permanent expatriate communities, particularly in the Yedikule, Samatya, and Narlıkapı neighbourhoods. Among other Anatolians the Karamanlides had a reputation as an exceptionally enterprising and commercially minded people. The semi-arid landscapes of their homeland seemed to foster a greater resourcefulness, as did an agricultural crisis in 1874–5, which resulted in many families migrating permanently from the region.[99] Muslims could also distinguish these Turkish-speaking Christians from other Romioi, and they were even considered for exemption from the population exchange of 1923–4.[100]

As in other Greek Orthodox communities in Anatolia, the prosperous Karamanlides also began to adopt or reclaim Greek because it was deemed the language of education and social progress, and in this they received a great deal of encouragement from the Greek Church hierarchy in Constantinople and political authorities in Athens.[101] This push to teach Greek was supported largely by the prosperous merchants and professionals, who often faced resistance from more humble members of the community who sought a more practical education for their children, and for whom the merits of Greek were not altogether apparent.[102]

There were at least 80 Karamanli towns and villages in the region of Kayseri, of which 25 were mixed confessional villages. Karamanlidika was spoken exclusively in 49 of these villages. A further ten Turcophone communities were to be found near Konya, eight near Ankara, and six near Isparta.[103] Greek was spoken among the rest of the central Anatolian Rum population. The doyen of Greek language and folklore studies at the time, the archaeologist Richard MacGillivray Dawkins, argued that there were twenty Greek-speaking villages on the eve of the First World War, although in many cases he found that the language was either at an advanced stage of attrition, in that it was limited to a few elderly people, or it had been adulterated by school Greek.[104] Dawkins rated highly the villages that kept the least corrupted form of Greek, such as Delmeso, but lamented the fate of Greek in the mastic-producing village of Fertek, where close proximity to Turkish-speaking groups accounted for the importation of Turkish vowel-harmony.[105] One of the most significant Greek-speaking centres was Sinasos, where the retention of Greek had less to do with schooling and more to do with strong commercial and familial connections with Constantinople.[106] Dawkins was most impressed by an isolated group of Greek-speaking communities that were located approximately 90 km south of Kayseri, where the language was more pristine because of the 'miserable condition' of its schools. The fiercely independent community of Pharasa (Çamlica) had between 1,500 and 1,800 inhabitants, and it shared the archaic dialect with several smaller nearby villages.[107] Dawkins identified a third group of Greek-speakers in Sille, a town of 8,000 people to the north-west of Konya. These people formed less than half of the population of Sille, and Dawkins argues that the greatest threat to the language was emigration and exposure to local Turkish-speaking Muslims.[108]

Mikrasiates

The largest group that only really became recognizable as such after the population exchanges were the *Mikrasiates*. The term simply applied to the Romioi of Asia Minor or Anatolia's Aegean regions, but included areas to the south and east of the Sea of Marmara, and the Mediterranean coastal regions. At the beginning of the nineteenth century the Romioi were scattered among various towns and regions, but the larger concentrations were along the coastline, where Greek was still in use in towns like Ayvalık (Kydonies), Foça (Phokies), Urla (Vourla), Çesme (Krini), Kuşadası, Fethiye (Makri), and Finike (Phinikes).[109] Smyrna had a large Greek-speaking population and a famous School (Evangeliki Scholi), and happened to be the birthplace of the great Greek intellectual, Adamantios Koraïs. Further inland, the indigenous Romioi tended to be Turcophones. By the end of the nineteenth century there were at least 122 Christian communities in towns and villages in western and southern Anatolia in which Turkish was spoken exclusively.[110] It is difficult to know how many other inland settlements were still speaking Greek at this time, but according to Dawkins, who admittedly was not as well acquainted with these areas as he was with central Anatolia, purely indigenous Greek dialects had long since disappeared. The exception was the town of Livisi near Fethiye, where the local dialect was still thriving, while there were reportedly some elderly women in the village of Gyölde near Alaşehir who spoke a few words of Greek.[111]

From the 1830s, by which time Greece had secured its independence from the Ottoman Empire, Greeks from the kingdom began to migrate in significant numbers to Anatolia, as did Greek islanders. Labour migration was channelled towards Constantinople and Smyrna, but the rising demand for Anatolian cash crops and the availability of land also drew large numbers of seasonal agricultural workers and settlers. The Anatolian countryside appears to have been underpopulated because of declining numbers of Muslims, since Western observers were struck by the absence of people in fertile arable areas.[112] The same Westerners failed to notice, however, that the 'Greeks' encountered in these areas, particularly in western Anatolia, were often recent immigrants or the children of immigrants. This region was also receiving Muslim refugees from the Russian Empire, as well as various groups from the Balkans, and Romioi from central Anatolia and the Pontus region. The cultural complexion of Asia Minor was to change significantly over the course of the nineteenth century.

During this century, therefore, Greek enjoyed a dramatic revival in western Anatolia. According to research undertaken at the Centre for Asia Minor Studies, there were as many as 380 Greek-speaking villages in Asia Minor before the First World War: 125 villages in the region spanning Bandırma, Bursa and Adapazarı (Bithynia), 37 in the region of Çannakale (Mysia), 41 near Ayvalik and Bergama (Aeolia), 90 in the Smyrna region (Ionia), 22 in the region of Alaşehir (Lydia), 50 in region of Aydın and Muğla (Caria), and 11 near Fethiye and Kaş (Lycia).[113] The Kapıdağı

(Cyzikus) Peninsula that juts out from the southern Marmara shoreline was dotted with many villages where Greek was spoken exclusively, while many more such villages were to be found throughout the much larger peninsula of Çesme.[114] In many cases the increase in the number of Greek-speaking residents had taken place within a generation. A village like Saraîkoi, where there was only one Rum resident left in 1883–4, had upwards of 450 by 1894.[115] During the second half of the nineteenth century, settlements along the Menderes River, and particularly along the rail line from Aydın to Denizli, or the lines running south from Mudanya and from Adapazarı, were burgeoning with newcomers. Included in this mix was the traditional intake of new settlers and seasonal workers from the Aegean Islands, which always suffered from surplus labour, but now there were also migrant Romioi from Macedonia and Thrace, and from the newly independent Kingdom of Greece, which had been a relative economic backwater when part of the empire. As happened with agriculture in post-independence Bulgaria, Greek agriculture became more subsistence-oriented and its commercial sector less connected with broader eastern Mediterranean commercial networks.[116] Farming was more profitable in Anatolia for small landholders, especially for immigrants who were less burdened by kin or other traditional obligations, and because vast tracts of fertile land were being opened up to cash crop agriculture. Once-derelict or partly abandoned villages in the Menderes River basin were being resettled by Christian newcomers from across the Aegean, who blended in with the existing Muslim population with little apparent difficulty.[117]

In most cases, however, the incoming Orthodox Christians, whether they were arriving from the Balkans, central Anatolia, or the Pontus region, appeared to favour the larger villages and towns where there was demand for builders, millers, olive-pressers, and bakers, and other such skills. The region of Bursa, for example, which saw Turkish- and Greek-speaking migrants attending the same churches and schools, received silkworm farmers from Thrace and miners from the Pontus region. In the Smyrna region, Romioi were usually found in villages that were large enough to hold a weekly bazaar.[118] In these areas, farming remained largely in the hands of Muslim estateholders and smallholders, although Christians did begin to acquire land, and with the rising commercial value of farming, wealthy Romioi were also buying up estates.[119]

At the beginning of the twentieth century, the Romioi of Asia Minor had reason to look to the future with great optimism. Smyrna in particular was a source of great pride. Giles Milton writes that the city was 'domi-nated by the Greeks', and that they 'left their mark on every walk of life',[120] a judgement borne out by the city guides which confirm that Romioi were involved in every conceivable business, trade, and profession, and whose surnames betray backgrounds from every part of Greece and Anatolia. Listed were 6 Rum-operated cinemas, with names such as 'Star' (Ἀστήρ), 'Pantheon', 'Parisian', and 'Phoenix', almost 200 barbershops, 19 dental practices, 65 doctors, and 10 architects.[121] Smyrna had ten Greek printing presses as compared with three Armenian, two French, one Turkish, and one Hebrew, and some Turkish schools were even teaching children Greek because of its common currency.[122] Some commentators noted an air of arrogance about the Romioi. In *Sur les routes d'Asie*, the French archaeolo-gist and journalist Gaston Deschamps claimed the 80,000 Greeks in the city regarded Smyrna as their 'domaine'. He claimed that the typical Greek cof-feehouse proprietor showed such disregard for Turkish authority that he often swore at Turks and argued openly and passionately for Greece's annex-ation of Asia Minor.[123]

For those Orthodox Christians who migrated to Asia Minor for work and gainful endeavour, however, it was regarded as a promised land that could be compared in some ways to the United States. It certainly had its advantages. In contrast to New York, Smyrna was more accessible, famil-iar, and a far less daunting trip, and its hinterlands were more accommodat-ing to the skills of Greek peasants. That these same regions were full of 'Turks' did not seem to deter Greek settlers, and there is little evidence to suggest that the local Muslims were significantly perturbed by their influx. The newcomers came to see their Anatolian villages and towns as their homelands, and their progeny continued to strongly identify with them long after they were forced to leave.

Ethnogenesis *c.*1900

> *By turning names into things we create false models of reality. By endowing nations, societies, or cultures with qualities of internally homogeneous and externally distinc-tive and bounded objects, we create a model of the world as a global pool hall in which the entities spin off each other like so many hard and round billiard balls.*[124]

The Marxist anthropologist Eric Wolf recognized that such a conception of the world encouraged a model of relations based on conflict and antipathy, in which civilizations were always clashing. He also notes that through this model of reality the West found excuses to control the non-West and to impose its vision of authentic civilization upon the rest. When it came to the writing of history, this domination of 'false models' would not only produce a distorted sense of how the world changed in modern times, but it would make the internal histories of the more culturally complex parts of that world inexplicable. To people like Melville, Constantinople simply did not seem possible. Such a 'Babel' was not meant to function at all.

To understand how the Ottoman Empire *did* function, or indeed the rest of the world, anthropologists and an increasing number of historians and archaeologists find they can no longer think in terms of hard cultural categories.[125] To understand the history of the Greek Orthodox Christians of Asia Minor, known to outsiders as Greeks, to other Anatolians as Romioi/ Rum, but even more commonly as 'Christians', we need to understand that these peoples existed in a world in which identities, or ethnicities if you will, were nevertheless changing. The cultural complexion of Anatolia had been altered significantly during the last century of Ottoman rule. Muslims from various parts of the Caucasus, southern Russia, and the Balkans joined the indigenous Muslims, who were also a mixture of cultures, sects, and linguistic groups, including Kurds, Alevis, and Yörüks. The simple Western ethnographies of Turks, Arabs, Greek, Armenians, and Jews belied a much more complex reality that reflected a history of constant demographic movement. Identities were never stable. Of the Pontic Greeks, Anthony Bryer argues that at the beginning of the nineteenth century they identified in the first instance with locality and clan, 'and as...Roman subject[s] of the sultan second', but that by 1923 they had become 'Greeks', and only later, Pontic Greeks.[126] *Mikrasiates* similarly only saw the necessity of developing an identity as *Mikrasiates* after they had to abandon their beloved Asia Minor, and when they had to negotiate a place within a new cultural milieu.

2

Ottoman *belle époque,* c.1890–1912

Intercommunality in Practice

Sofia Delvetoglou (Kayseri region): *Before the war we lived well with the Turks. We got on like brothers. They came to us [our homes] and we went to them. The Turks would come to our religious festivals, our weddings, our funerals. They didn't come to baptisms, because it was a mystery of Christ, and we didn't want the Turks there.*[1]

Evangelia Peristeridou (Alaşehir region): *With Turks we had brotherly relations. We'd give them our land and they would pay us with half the produce. We didn't need to work. In summer we'd go to our fields and we'd give the Turkish women halva. They'd give us baklava. They looked after us.*[2]

Sofia Anastasiadi–Manousaki (Kayseri region): *After the Kaimalak-Kaugasi* [sic] [1856] *and through to the Hurriet* [1908 Revolution] *we got on well with the Turks. They loved us and we loved them. We had a word among us. The word* ekiz *(twins). That word says everything. Our houses had shared walls. We did not care if our neighbours were Christians or Turks. We played with the children of the neighbourhood. Between the walls we called each other 'ekiz'.*[3]

Sofia Lapazidou (Black Sea region): *We had no complaints about the Turks. We never heard of them harassing our women, or to say a bad word to us. These things we never experienced... We worked and celebrated events together... We invited them into our churches, where they would light a candle. They were blessed, the Turks. They were people of God.*[4]

Yannis Hatzidoulis (south-western Anatolia). *We got on well. Everything was good. We toiled together with the Turks. At Giougekouma the Turks were like our people, the Greeks. And to Master Osman our boss, for whom we worked during the war, he never did us any harm. They were good people and we got on well. But with the wars and the foreign powers...*[5]

Alexandros Kontos (Izmit region): *We were more atsali [unruly] than them [the Turks]. We got on well with them. We didn't really think about such things much.*[6]

The most striking characteristic of Anatolian refugee memory was not the nostalgia for lost homelands but the extremely charitable depiction of former neighbours. When asked about the quality of intercommunal relations in Anatolia, the refugees usually responded with the definitive but simple claim 'we got on well with the Turks' (kala pernousame me tous Tourkous), or used very similar wording. Other commonly used phrases included 'we lived well' (zousame kala) or 'we lived like brothers' (zousame san aderfia). The key is the plural personal 'we', for the word 'lived' in these claims signified community. In each case the interviewees were speaking on behalf of their community, and what emerges with indelible clarity from the rest of the transcripts is that well-being was tied to community. What they valued particularly was neighbourliness and mutual assistance. And in localities where the daily life of one community was entangled with that of another, then both communities came to see cooperation as a cardinal virtue. In such situations subjects usually ascribed to mixed communities the moral solidity of a single community. To underscore the 'we lived well' claim the refugees usually followed up with other stock images of sociability that had the effect of projecting an image of intercommunal harmony: 'we went to their homes, they come to ours', '[there were] "comings and goings"' (πήγαινε-έλα), 'they'd invite us to their weddings, we'd invite them to ours'.[7]

Read literally, such imagery offers an implausibly idyllic past, one without conflict or antagonism, but the purpose of refugee memory was not to give a definitive portrait of a particular historical phase. Its purpose, rather, was rhetorical. The function of the 'we lived well' phrase was to impart meanings that listeners could be expected to decipher and understand, suggesting in this case that a better quality of life had obtained in the past, and that life would later take a wrong turn.[8] The chief intention of the refugees, rather, was to depict the prevailing tenor of that life during a distinct temporal phase, namely the period before 1912, when Anatolia's Christians recalled having lived a relatively contented existence, and that, critically, that contented existence was predicated on a constructive relationship with the Muslim majority.

Social memories of that epoch came to symbolize normalcy, a paradigm of how life ought to be—when routine aspects of daily experience (family, work, community, faith) were seen to have functioned in accordance with an acceptable set of standards, and when people lived a reasonably secure and dignified existence. Given that Muslims, Christians, and Jews had to deal with each other on a daily basis, any conception of normalcy presupposed a cooperative relationship. All groups shared similar challenges in life, and these challenges were best handled in an environment that was orderly, convivial, and mutually supportive. Thus, Muslims and non-Muslims were in agreement that to 'live well' they had to 'live well *together*'. Despite the confessional distinctions that defined Ottoman society, Muslims and non-Muslims often made a point of ignoring such distinctions in their everyday affairs.

This chapter deals directly with the nature of intercommunality and everyday life in Anatolia before the violent and fatal intrusion of modern identity politics. It approaches the topic without the excessive scepticism that (mainly Western) historians have had regarding the efficacy of multiethnic societies, but seeks to explain why the Anatolian regions where the Romioi were located (central Anatolia, Pontus, and western Anatolia) were also remarkably stable until 1912.[9] The focus will be on western Anatolia, where optimal economic conditions in the late nineteenth century and the years leading to the Balkan Wars saw the formation of many new mixed communities, yet where religious groups learned within a relatively short time to develop and maintain forms of accommodation.

The oral sources allow an ethnographic investigation into the role of social values and notions of community in the construction of intercommunal bonds. These sources confirm that cultural boundaries were essential in Ottoman life, yet they also tell us that boundary transgressions were routine. As historians of the Ottoman Empire and the Mediterranean at large are showing through their research, cultural or religious identities did not always determine the conduct of social relations, in part because too exclusive an identification with one's culture makes it impossible to function with other cultures.[10] Jews, Christians, and Muslims certainly did see themselves as belonging to fundamentally different faith-based communities, but most of the time these identities were flexible enough to permit a range of trans-communal links.

Making mixed communities

Ypsili (Doğanbey, near Seferhisar) was the typical kind of village where it was said that Muslims and Christians 'lived well together'. The cultural mix varied in western Anatolia owing to the steady influx of peoples from all directions, and while the newer settlements mentioned by the interviewees tended to be exclusively Christian, the more established ones usually featured an indigenous Muslim majority. Located in the environs of Smyrna, within a prosperous agricultural zone, Ypsili had an established Muslim community that accounted for 300 of its 450 families.[11] The Christian residents were the Greek-speaking progeny of settlers who had arrived a generation or two earlier, mostly from Samos. Kostas Kipreos, whose name suggests Cypriot provenance, noted that the Romioi of Ypsili were not natives:

> In the village there was a [man known as]Psiliotis the Tsopanos [the shepherd], gero-Trakmakos [old-man Trakmakos], Karamanolis, and Giorgos Liapis, my grandfather. The first three were from Samos, while my grandfather was a Vlach. I do not know from where he originated. There were foreigners from other places too ... but mostly we were from Samos. My father was from Imbros. He came to work and my [maternal] grandfather noticed he was resourceful [prokomenos], and so he gave him his daughter's hand.[12]

Kipreos' account points to the fact that communities, like villages, might only hold together for a few generations. Whereas Anatolia's cities were ancient—a listing of modern cities in central and western Turkey can also be found in the Notitiae Episcopatuum, documents compiled during the early Middle Ages—villages were viable only as long as economic activity might allow. Disease and drought could deal a mortal blow, particularly cholera, and once abandoned a village would be pilfered for building materials, thus giving it the appearance of an archaeological site—for such reasons Anatolian refugees who visited their patrides decades later very often could not find a trace of their old homes.[13] From the middle decades of the nineteenth century, however, depopulated agricultural zones were being reclaimed under the direction of the Ottoman state. Refugees and immigrants were resettled in half-empty, dying, or deserted villages, where new accommodations had to be reached between communities that often spoke different languages and practised different religions.

Ypsili was one of countless Anatolian villages that had been rejuvenated in late Ottoman times. The roads of Ypsili were narrow and therefore typically Ottoman: 'There was no urban plan. You could build a house wherever you wanted. It was a Turkish village [after all].'[14] The village consisted of stone dwellings that spilled over a hillside, forming upper and lower mahalle (neighbourhoods). The Romioi were concentrated in the upper mahalle, where communal life centred on its tiny square and the parish church, and where a large maple tree provided ample cover from the sun. As with many of the churches found in western Anatolia, St George's Church was built to service the earliest Rum immigrants and could only accommodate 100 standing parishioners. Kipreos recalled that most people were forced to follow the liturgy from outside on special occasions. He also recalls renovations in 1910 that opened a section that was reserved for women (*το γυναικείον*). A flourishing community also had to cope with a burgeoning death rate. The small churchyard cemetery was full of simple wooden crosses and could only cope with the number of burials by having bones interred in a communal vault after three years. The elders (*demogerontes*) were also forced to create another graveyard about a five-minute walk outside the village.

There were, of course, less morbid measures of prosperity. While emigration was usually a signifier of poverty, the people of Ypsili, known to all as *Psiliotes*, were proud of the fact that theirs was a village that actually received immigrants and seasonal workers from Greece and the Aegean Islands. In Kiperos' time the village was prosperous enough to have a purpose-built primary school and residence for the teacher. Since there were many other local Rum communities that were also building schools, teachers were in high demand—Kipreos recalled that due to a shortge the local priest was forced to cover three grades for three years. He also remembers that the Rum neighbourhood of Ypsili supported three coffeehouses. Someone named Roumeliotis owned the main coffeehouse, where the men played cards and backgammon late into the evenings. Roumeliotis also served as a butcher and cobbler and dispensed pharmaceuticals. His rival was one Sotirakis, who also sold textiles. Kipreos himself had a barbershop that also doubled up as a coffeehouse. It was in the square that the Christians held their weddings and festivals, since there was enough room for dancing, and this was also where farmers and fishermen set up their stalls. The village bazaar, however, was always held in the much larger square in the lower *mahalle*, around which the Muslim community was concentrated. The mosque nearby had an annex large enough to function as the local school, and it was here that the Christian children were sent to learn Turkish. The larger square was where most shops (*bakal*) were to be found and where the Muslims conducted their own celebrations.

Thus Ypsili was a combination of two communities, and as with every mixed village in the Ottoman Empire, Muslims and non-Muslims were administered as separate corporate entities. Every Rum community in the

Ottoman Empire had its own council (*kinotis*) and council of elders (*demogerontes*), who abided by written conventions and followed standard procedures, and whose responsibilities included the management of local schools and church property.[15] Ypsili also had a representative, a *muhtar*, who acted as the state's point of access to the community. 'Anything that happened in the village,' claimed Kipreos, 'he was responsible. The authorities had to speak to him first. For a gendarme to step inside a Greek house, a *muhtar* had to be present.'[16] The *millet* system ensured that many aspects of communal life were dealt with internally, including religious matters and legal disputes between co-religionists. It ought to be emphasized that subjects also deemed these distinctions to be important. The system did not merely signify imperial Ottoman determination to maintain the integrity of the Muslim community, and by extension the integrity of each *dhimmi*, but it also acknowledged what every Ottoman subject wanted, namely that Muslims, Jews, and Christians should remain separate.[17] For ordinary people throughout the Ottoman Empire, religious identity distinctions were fundamental, and these boundaries were to be retained at all costs.

And yet everyday life also required the manipulation and permeation of these boundaries. In western Anatolia in particular, where commercial opportunities fostered a great deal of cooperation and exchanges between Muslims and non-Muslims, legal restrictions were routinely flouted. For example, despite an imperial decree restricting the sale of property to Christians, the British consul of Bursa noted in 1861 that Muslim vendors were 'constantly' evading ordinances.[18] Even when it came to matters of faith, particularly when people sought miracle cures, the boundaries could often seem to be of no consequence. In some aspects of popular religious ritual (see Chapters 3 and 4), everyday social interactions, and annual social events, Muslims and non-Muslims usually did things together.

Mixed communities proliferated across western Anatolia during the nineteenth century, particularly in the environs of Smyrna, in the Menderes riverine region, along the Marmara littoral and to the east of Constantinople, and along the expanding railway lines. The immigrants and refugees who inundated the region brought much needed skills and labour. In Köprü to the east of Nikomedia (Izmit), for example, Muslim farmers received Greek Orthodox migrants who brought with them a range of trade services, while Armenians came as retailers.[19] In nearby Geyve, the Romioi were the merchants, bakers, carpenters, builders, shoemakers, and butchers, while the Muslims continued with more traditional roles such as boatmen, fishermen, charcoal burners, woodsmen, and lime-makers.[20] In such localities, where there was a division of labour along confessional lines, one has to assume occupational complementarity and hence a great deal of daily contact. At Ypsili, however, Muslims and non-Muslims alike were farmers, and hence cooperation was needed for such things as water access, pasturage, seasonal fruit picking, and other matters requiring mutual assistance. Even in localities where Muslims and Christians were distributed in separate villages, communities still found reasons to develop friendships and various kinds of economic partnerships. Cooperation between regional villages was necessary for negotiating grazing areas, sharing spaces in the bazaars, and ensuring orderly behaviour at festivals. And as in the towns, those who operated stalls had to be mindful of religious holidays and dietary proscriptions.

Ultimately, the necessity of mutuality gave Muslims and non-Muslims reasons to develop intercommunal bonds, although these relations worked best if expressed as genuinely intimate friendships. That much was suggested in refugee discourse when idioms of kinship or communal intimacy were applied to the Muslim neighbour, such as claiming that they lived 'like brothers', or said 'there were no differences between us'. The kinds of affective bonds that allowed these confessional communities to *feel* like single communities inevitably took time to develop. The original Orthodox Christian families that came to settle in places like Ypsili often faced hostility as newcomers. Iordanes Mavromatis complained that the locals of Tzaitzouma (Çaycuma) were very unfriendly to his immigrant grandfather, who recalled being pushed into a ditch because he was *giavour* (infidel). Even where mutual bigotry persisted, however, cooperation was necessary for the sake of social stability and prosperity. The mill owner of Ypsili, a Muslim named Haj Ali, who happened to be the richest and most powerful man in the village, made the point that the Christians and Muslims had become interdependent: 'if the Greeks were evicted, as some appeared to want, he claimed the village might fall apart'.[21]

Overall, the refugee testimonies present a picture of stability underscored by a spirit of cooperation. In some cases these kinds of relationships were of long standing, as in Pontus and Cappadocia, while in much of western Anatolia they could be relatively new. Iordanes Mavromalis noted that the Romioi of Tzaitzouma were originally from the much larger inland town of Safranbolu (Safranopolis), from where they brought skills such as shoemaking, carpentry, building, rendering, and trading. They bought houses or built new ones, and not long after Iordanes Mavromalis' grandfather had been pushed into a ditch, the local Turks had come to embrace the immigrants. He proudly proclaimed that by his time 'we had "great loves" with the Turks' (εἴχαμε μεγάλες αγάπες με τους Τούρκους). He conceded that the local Greeks sometimes attended mosque because it was a 'house of God', although it was essentially as a reciprocal gesture of respect, since the Muslims came on occasion to their church.[22]

'Blessed Land': between myth and history

Why were the 'loves' (*agapes*) for the Turks described as 'great loves' (*megales agapes*)? Why such grandiloquent descriptions of Anatolia as a land of 'milk and honey'? Can we seriously countenance such nostalgic hyperbole? What was the purpose of caricaturing intercommunal life in terms of perfect conviviality and contentment?

Fiction offers a useful comparative reference to the oral sources because it also grapples with a similar problem regarding nostalgia. I refer specifically to the works of such seminal novelists as Giorgos Theotokas, Stratis Myrivilis, Ilias Venezis, Kosmas Politis, Stratis Doukas, and Dido Sotiriou, all of whom were born and raised in the Ottoman Empire, and most of whom had experienced life in the pre-war Ottoman *belle époque*. Those who hailed from Anatolia were later to become refugees and lose their homelands: Venezis was from Ayvalık, Sotiriou from Şirince near Kuşadası, while Politis was from Smyrna. Having lived in an Ottoman milieu and among Muslims, these authors depict that culturally complex world with a great sense of familiarity and empathy. Although most of these writers are preoccupied with the traumas of wartime, expulsion, and resettlement, ample attention is accorded to the pre-war *belle époque*, where Anatolia is mythicized to the extent that it seems an implausible paradise. Peter Mackridge has described the 'Anatolia' depicted by these authors as a 'dreamworld', one that is 'nearer to the Heart's Desire'.[23] In Myrivilis' *Panagia i Gorgona* (*The Mermaid Madonna*), which is actually about refugees who have been resettled in the author's homeland Mytilene (Lesbos), locals can see the Anatolian mainland and speak of her as 'mother of the poor' (*ftochomana*), where nature could provide enough for people to work and eat.[24] Anatolia is blessed because it is a place where poverty can be averted and where a normal life is possible.

'If paradise really exists', claims Manolis Axiotis, the protagonist and narrator of Dido Sotiriou's *Matomena Chomata* (*Bloodstained Earth*), 'Kirkınca, our village, was a little corner of it.' As the title suggests, the novel depicts a world ravaged by war, but it begins when that world functioned in its pristine form. Manolis' beloved Kirkınca (Şirince) was located near the ancient city of Ephesus, and near the mouth of the Menderes River, one of the more fertile regions of western Anatolia. His was a contented community where 'each villager owned the land he tilled', and 'each had his own two-storey house, not to mention a country place with a water melon patch, walnut and almond groves, apple, pear and cherry orchards, and bright blooming flower gardens'. Manolis goes on to describe the yearly routine, the feast days, the dancing and singing. 'Could it have been the natural warmth of Anatolia, or perhaps the soil? ... Whatever the reasons, we were always singing.' Not a great deal is said of the local Muslims, but enough to make the point that the relationship was warm and civil. Kirkınca was an all-Greek village, but among the nearby Turkish villages there were friends they would occasionally host and put up for the night, and these courtesies were reciprocated. More is said of the itinerant Muslim labourers, who were described as 'Kirli' because of their sun-scorched skin. The Kirli came from afar to work, in search of better pay than that offered on their local pasha's estate. The Kirli particularly loved Greek feast days, since on such days they could eat well. On St George's Day, when the Kirli departed for home to spend the summer with their own families, they routinely sought blessings from their Greek employers: 'Give me your blessing, little *effendi*, for the bread we ate together.'[25]

Seen through the rose-coloured lenses of his youth, Manolis' village is as good as paradise, but the itinerant paupers who do not eat well normally remind him that Anatolia of course is *not* paradise, which means that his idyllic description of Kirkınca, and therefore Anatolia, is relative rather than definitive.

Indeed, the Kirli were more representative of peasants in nineteenth-century Europe and the Mediterranean, most of whom had struggled to scratch a living, and who had occupied a space somewhere just above destitution. To stave off such a predicament, the Rum of Pontus, central Anatolia, and the Greek islands had long recognized the critical importance of *xenitia*, of living and working in a foreign place.[26] Once the tilling and sowing had been done, islanders spent the warmer months as labourers on the Anatolian mainland: European consular staff noted their regular presence all along the western coastal regions as far inland as Kasaba (Turgutlu).[27] During the second half of the nineteenth century, however, we find more and more islanders moving permanently to western Anatolia to escape poverty and debt collectors.[28] In general terms, the 'long' nineteenth century, the most revolutionary age in world history in terms of global economic transformation, was catastrophic for peasantries in much of the 'Old World', as population growth, land scarcity, enclosures, indebtedness, rising taxation, volatile agricultural commodity prices, and underemployment led to unprecedented levels of pauperization and mass emigration. In Greece, inequitable land redistribution, tax burdens, and burgeoning numbers since independence made it very difficult for the average peasant family to make ends meet, hence a vast proportion of the population emigrated to avoid destitution. Anatolia appeared to offer land and a future. In his assorted notes about life in Kios (Gemlik), a minor port of the east Marmara area that received vast numbers of Greek immigrants in the late nineteenth century, Basili Gouligkas explains why they came: ' "This place is underdeveloped" they used to say. "There are many opportunities here for which one can progress". The region was much more beautiful and fertile than poor Greece.'[29] Vangelis Kokkolinos, who lived on the island of Naxos, the Cycladic island with the most arable land, wrote in his journal that the average person struggled to eke out an existence, and that the people of his village, Galanado, flocked to the east regularly to 'find their solutions':

> for many Galandiotes the only source of some money was the temporary emigration to the City and the East. The women tended to migrate for a few years (two to five years) to the City, while the men went to Smyrna and the surrounding region.[30]

Implicit in Anatolian nostalgia, therefore, is an understanding of the wretchedness and humiliation of poverty. Manolis' village is paradise because the economic and environmental conditions allow for a future within the *patrida* and without resorting to *xenitia*. The 'dream worlds' of Ypsili and Kirkınca and hundreds of other communities in Anatolia offered at the very least the modest prospect of a dignified life, in which average families could hope to do more than simply feed themselves, find shelter, and pay their taxes. These Anatolians could also expect to meet certain social obligations, such as providing for their children's primary education and for their dowries. Far from being fatalistic, peasants never accepted poverty as a legitimate condition. To these peasants, Anatolia promised a kind of life that *ought* to be a normal one.

For most Anatolians, therefore, 'living well' referred to a humble but dignified existence. Well-being also had to do with social success, and how communities functioned as social and moral units. Relations with the local Muslims were particularly significant in this regard. Manolis' description of his happy and well-functioning village is dependent on how the Romioi get along with the Turks, who live in the villages nearby, and who are just as interested in maintaining an atmosphere of conviviality. The interviews with the refugees also revealed intercommunality as a vital aspect of well-being. In places like Kirkınca and Ypsili, as indeed in every Greek Christian community in Anatolia, the prospects of 'living well' were predicated on how good their relationship was with the Muslims.

The necessity of nostalgia

The argument thus far is that while the 'myth of Asia Minor' cannot be accepted as a literal description of objective historical reality, it nevertheless says something substantial and compelling about that reality. Nostalgia identifies the distinctive nature of a given time period by the aspirations and desires that it satisfied, and which have not been met since. It puts forward a characterization that privileges these particular qualities, thereby defining the times as 'good' times. These depictions of the nature of a given past can be plausible. Thus, nostalgia can draw attention to a time within living memory when incomes fulfilled expectations and needs, when social tensions were contained or managed, and when food quality and quantity was satisfactory. Memories of such computable and plausible attainments become useful references for measuring declining or diminished standards.[31] However, nostalgia also has to do with coveting desires or aspirations that take precedence over veracity, which involves distorting the past to meet desired ends.[32] Nostalgia of this kind is purposive misrepresentation and is a form of deception.

In our case, nostalgia is seen more as an irrational response that reflects a lack of education. In *Panagia i Gorgona*, the refugees concoct an implausible past because the real past is too traumatic to contemplate. Once the refugees realize that they will never be able to return to their homelands, their descriptions of Anatolia become more and more embellished. They see the need to exaggerate their personal wealth as a way of dealing with their immense losses, but also to impress the humble locals with bogus claims of high social status. The poor indigenous fishermen listened patiently to the refugees as 'they spoke of estates that were never theirs, and they kept their haggard eyes fixed on Anatolia as if they could still see luxury and magnificence'. The locals had reason to think that the refugees were delusional:

> The islanders listened patiently to all these silly fabrications. They nodded their heads and exchanged glances with each other, for they knew that the really wealthy landowners over there had vanished into the work battalions and had perished in the flames or by the sword. Those who escaped were the rabble, the nondescript spawn of beggarly fishermen who lived from hand to mouth.[33]

This nostalgia, as Myrivilis' narrator concedes, evokes a deep-seated anguish, but one that is meant to deflect from their poverty and the humiliation of being refugees.

Truth, suggests Myrivilis, was one of the many casualties of the Asia Minor Catastrophe. Although they are eyewitnesses to history, the refugees are dismissed as unreliable witnesses because their nostalgia results in them conjuring up fantasies. It is this kind of nostalgia that inspires visceral hostility from historians, who can often show through their research how certain nostalgic traditions are demonstratively absurd. In his searching critique of the modern heritage fetish and the highly profitable industries that fashion pasts that attract 'a very healthy tourist trade', David Lowenthal, who states that 'a past nostalgically enjoyed does not need to be taken seriously', can point to a long list of absurd 'sites' of nostalgia, such as Stalin's Gulag or the London Blitz.[34] Although the nostalgia for the Blitz had to do with inter-class solidarity and society's indomitable 'business as usual' spirit, nostalgic sentiment did not provide an appropriate basis for characterizing a period of well-attested and unspeakable horrors.

Lowenthal's powerful critique, however, unnecessarily dismisses nostalgia as a mere symptom of malaise. After all, 'the good old days' are sometimes demonstrably good, while decline presupposes a better past. And people often do develop a distinct sense about a time experienced. Often the problems with nostalgia lie with the premises of its critics. With a topic like intercommunal relations, commentators often hold deeply problematic working concepts of ethnicity and ethnic conflict, and often think histories of 'ethnic' conflict were simply about identity politics and intolerance. When dealing with nostalgia for intercommunality, it is worthwhile considering the premises on which the usual misgivings are based, and seeing whether social memory can expose the problematic assumptions behind these misgivings. As Luisa Passerini says of historiography, collective memory can provide for a comparative reference against which historiography's preoccupations and distortions can be brought into sharp relief.[35]

The point is illustrated by a well-meaning study on the problems of reconciliation after ethnic cleansing. In *My Neighbor, My Enemy: Justice and Community in the Aftermath of Mass Atrocity*, a collaborative work on post-war Yugoslavia and Rwanda, the participating scholars, mainly human rights experts and psychologists, observed that all the traumatized victims who served as informants said that before ethnic cleansing they had enjoyed a 'good quality of life':

> *Most participants said that relations among the different ethnic groups were harmonious during the pre-war years. It was irrelevant whether their neighbors, co-workers, and friends belonged to a different ethnic group. 'We lived normally', an informant said. 'We did not even know who was who (meaning who was from which ethnic group). We visited each other at our homes and celebrated each other's religious holidays together.' Both Vukovar and Mostar residents proudly noted their cities' long and celebrated history of multi-culturalism and tolerance.*

The authors, however, feel that these claims were dubious. Their understanding is that pre-war relations were only 'harmonious on the surface', and that the participants had 'failed to acknowledge that ethnic divisions had begun to occur in the years and months before the war'.[36] The refugees are thought to have muddled their memories, perhaps because of the effects of trauma, or the need to rehabilitate the past so that it can set a positive contrast to an unhappy present, or simple because memory can be defective.

The critical point here is that the authors are guided by the dubious, albeit commonplace, premise that communal tensions were brewing and ultimately led to the destruction of Yugoslavia. Based on this assumption, the refugees could be accused of conveniently or unwittingly forgetting political 'realities'. In *Panagia i Gorgona*, the nostalgia is also assumed to be a coping mechanism since the refugees have developed a means for avoiding their traumas. They might wax lyrical about the good times in Anatolia, but when questioned about Turkish atrocities they become evasive: 'their eyes became veiled and their tongues twisted into knots'. The narrator implies that the nostalgia creates pasts that these sufferers of trauma can live with, but which are nevertheless delusional.[37]

It is certainly the case that historians of the empire's Romioi and the Asia Minor Catastrophe have always assumed the nostalgia for an Ottoman *belle époque* to be absurd. They have never dealt with the nostalgia of the refugees, even though its existence is well known. This palpable silence might have to do with a traditional aversion to oral testimony per se, or because the very idea that Greeks and Turks 'got on well' in the late Ottoman times seems too ridiculous even to be broached. Intercommunality certainly cannot be related to the dominant academic questions, which have been Greek irredentism, Ottoman state degeneration, and the rise of national self-consciousness. To date, the only serious attention to these nostalgic traditions has come from outside the historical profession.[38]

For many reasons, therefore, refugee nostalgia is nearly always subjected to perfunctory dismissal, and as a consequence, so too is the competence of the subjects. To effectively claim that the social memories of such large groups as the Bosnians and Anatolia's Romioi are pure fancy, that they are unreliable witnesses to their own experiences, is enormously condescending, especially when no attempt has been made to explicate the historical factors that produced the nostalgia.

Intercommunality, truth, and values

Furthermore, as every anthropologist knows, it is *always* a mistake to ignore the meanings of people's words, and to assume that any group, whether peasants, 'pre-modern' societies, or pre-literate communities, lacks a rational sense about the economic and power realities on which their welfare and survival is based. Anthropologists know it is critical to consider what is being said, to try and decipher the rationale of the message, and consider the world that is reflected in the message. The 'problem' under discussion is epistemological rather than historical, for the kind of challenges presented by Anatolian nostalgia are elementary for anthropologists and historians of pre-literate societies (e.g. pre-literate Africa), for whom the social, cultural, and historical contexts of orality are critical for understanding what is actually being said about the past.[39]

An important consideration here is motive. Why did the Anatolian refugees wish to preserve their memories in the teeth of a hardline nationalist discourse and a disapproving official culture? Why risk being tainted as unpatriotic? Were the refugees simply expressing their present-day bitterness over the humiliations and poverty by creating a fanciful Ottoman *belle époque*? Or were they concerned that their histories would be misrepresented by the dominant culture, which has an interest in pre-

senting their Ottoman homelands and the Turks with extremely dispar-
aging characterizations?

Looked at closely, the oral transcripts convey a conscious need among the
refugees to hold on to memories that were more true to lived experience, and
especially because their own truths were under threat. The *belle époque* of
refugee memory not only had no place in national Greek memory but was
anathema to it, given that a national culture based on the Turk as the barbarous Other could not accommodate a concept of 'good Turks'. And yet for the
refugees, to expunge that *belle époque* from memory, as Greek national culture
demanded, effectively entailed the denial of truth. It would also mean forgetting the values associated with that past. As will be made clear in the following sections that deal with community, moral worth, and joint social activities,
the refugees drew inspiration from their memories of intercommunality. The
refugees were determined to integrate into Greek society, but not completely
in accordance with the terms set by the host society, which insisted on the
vilification of Turks as the eternal enemy and depictions of the Ottoman
Empire as a relentlessly oppressive, anti-Greek environment.[40]

Aside from an elementary need to tell truths, the refugees were motivated by a need to salvage a past worth recovering, for intercommunal living was thought to provide a fair measure of their moral worth. The
practices associated with living with Muslims were important precisely
because the relationship was seen as exemplifying the values embedded in
these practices. As studies of Bosnian memory have shown, refugees often
identified with their former multiethnic society because these relationships
epitomized values that would be subverted by the onslaught of exclusivist
nationalist values.[41] These values, namely compassion, friendship, reciprocity, and honour, could be found in their purest form when extended to
people outside one's moral community. This kind of sensibility can be
found in existing mixed communities in the Levant.[42] Anthropologist Glenn
Bowman shows in his ethnography of a Palestinian town (Beit Sahour),
which is populated by Muslims, Catholics, and Orthodox Christians, that
all members insist to outsiders that they are 'one' community:

> It is you outside who try to make a difference between the Christians and the Muslims.
> We are a people, we all go to each other's feasts, we visit with each other, we live the
> same life. We are one people.[43]

In Beit Sahour, as in other mixed communities past and present, behaving
'as brothers' while at the same time observing each other's boundaries was

the most effective means of preventing conflict. A romantic or sexual liaison between Muslim and non-Muslim would certainly threaten the intercommunal order, and all were wary of what would happen to the locality if it began to focus too closely on communal identities to the exclusion of extra-communal bonds. The principles of mutuality that were observed within multicultural societies in the Habsburg, Russian, and Ottoman empires presupposed that the alternative to coexistence was catastrophe.[44] The Greek-speaking Muslims of Crete realized that catastrophe beckoned once Christian Cretans began listening to Greek nationalists and began to see their Muslim neighbours as enemies.[45] Far from being naive, therefore, Anatolian nostalgia sought to counter the nationalist perspective that presented Greek–Turkish relations in terms of theodicy; of a perennial struggle between good and evil. Nationalism did ultimately succeed in destroying intercommunality, but by preserving memories of intercommunality the refugees showed a determination to deny nationalism a complete victory.

Morphosis and *amathia*

A final ground-clearing exercise relates to authority and who can speak about Anatolia and its history. For neither historians nor the non-refugee population in Greece ever heeded the nostalgic reminiscences of the refugees. It was not merely the fact that claims for an Ottoman *belle époque* were unacceptable, but that the refugees had no business talking about such things. In Greek society, only the educated were deemed qualified to recount history; that is, people who were well read and therefore knowledgeable about the world and its politics. The Greek term for this social category is *morphomeni* (lettered ones or enlightened ones), which applied to the relatively few who could claim a secondary education. Of critical importance was the fact that these *morphomeni* had been imbibed in Greek history with a Greece-centred view of the world. This history essentially focused on Classical Greece, the enslavement of the Greek *laos* (people) under the Turkish yoke, and the sacred mission since 1821 to reclaim lost glories.[46] As such, *morphosis* was almost synonymous with 'nationalism', and it carried with it nationalist values and an unremitting hostility for all things Turkish.

Of the Anatolians who were resettled in Greece during the exchange period, only a small proportion could be described as *morphomeni*, but

among the exceptions were Philipos Tsenoglu of Isparta, a lawyer who also
went by the patronym Nikolaidis (Philipos Nikolaidis).[47] His case is useful
for present purposes in that his views on Anatolia, which are in line with
those of ordinary Anatolians, inverted the nationalist logic regarding who
had standing when it comes to recounting history. Tsenoglu was born in
1888 and therefore had spent his entire youth in Anatolia. As a *morphomenos*
(educated man) Tsenoglu could be expected to know what it meant to be
Greek. As was common among lawyers, he wrote about his locality and its
history, but Tsenoglu was an unusual *morphomenos* in that he did not regard
Turkish rule as oppressive, at least not in his homeland of Isparta. Rather,
he accepted the more positive views of his parents and grandparents, and
those held by most Ispartans. Like Melpo Merlier, Tsenoglu held to a counter-narrative of Greek history that rejected the Greek/Turk theodicy, essentially because local and personal experience told him otherwise:

> *In Isparta the relationship between the Greeks and the Turks until the last years were
> very friendly, and we never heard our parents say anything to the contrary. Since the
> beginning of the 19th century there was not even one act of aggression, one assault, one
> act of plunder, a murder or forced exile committed by the Turks against the Greeks. By
> about 1870–1880 some bandits appeared, like Kefinsix, Kotanak, Tavaslis and others,
> who robbed the state postal service, but they happened to be in league with the post-
> man, who also connived to rob and extort merchants. But these things had always
> occurred under the Turkish occupation as far back as the Seljuks, the Turkmens, Tartars,
> Venetians, Byzantines, Romans and the successors of Alexander... We never heard of
> any merchants being robbed or killed by Turks from the surrounding villages, where
> there weren't even any police stationed. There was much solidarity and mutual trust
> between the two ethnic groups...*[48]

The above passage from Tsenoglu's work appears in an anthology of 'Pisid-
ian' writings—Pisidia refers to the old Roman/Byzantine province and
Orthodox diocese based in Isparta. The comments are strikingly seditious.
If the naive utterances of the humble Anatolian could be ignored because
they were the product of ignorance or *amathia* (uneducatedness), then Tsenoglu showed that *morphosis* (learnedness) and Greek nationalism did not
necessarily go together.

This apparent dissonance troubled the editor of the anthology, Charis
Sapountzakis, who explains that Tsenoglu was once associated with a movement that sought an accommodation with the Turkish Republic by seeking
to exclude the Karamanlides from the population exchange, and thus allow

them to remain in their Anatolian *patrides*. What was deemed anathema in Greek minds was the fact that these Turkish-speaking Christians were prepared to accept a new 'Turkish' identity. Sapountzakis presents these facts to show that Tsenoglu had 'suspect' views: 'We cannot agree with Philipos' philosophy.' However, Sapountzakis concedes that his 'philosophy' is worth considering. After all, Tsenoglu could claim that his homeland Isparta could never be part of Greece, that it was too remote for the Greek army to liberate and occupy, and therefore it was perfectly reasonable that the Romioi of central Anatolia should seek to come to terms with the Turkish Republic.[49]

Significantly, no excuses are made for the positive descriptions of Ottoman rule offered by ordinary refugees, precisely because no reasonable position could be expected of the 'unlettered' (*agrammati, amorphoti*). The ignorant masses could have little or no understanding of their Greekness, and that they had to be spoken for by their social betters. From a typical *morphomenos* perspective, the words of the *amorphoti* (uneducated people) on such heady matters as history and politics were worthless, even where history and politics had a relevance to their lives. As *amorphoti,* the Anatolian refugees were not expected to understand the historical and political reasons that led to the war that turned them into refugees, much as they *could* be expected to utter such shameful nonsense as 'we lived well with Turks'.

The Anatolian refugees, in turn, were conscious of this 'symbolic violence', and that they were being manoeuvered into seeing their pasts in a manner that accorded with official national history. Such symbolic violence involved subjecting the refugees and refugee cultures to ridicule. Throughout their lives, the refugees suffered official condescension on a regular basis, in schools and in routine encounters with officialdom, through which they were made acutely aware of their low status as *agrammati,* as people deemed so backward that they could not be accepted as authorities on their local histories. As typical subalterns, however, the refugees could use that imposed caricature to their advantage, and use their lack of *morphosis* to *excuse* their potentially seditious nostalgic reminiscences as the musings of ignorant *agrammati.* As the rest of this chapter will show, the ill-educated chose to resist this symbolic violence and the imposed discourses of the *morphomeni* by holding firmly to their memories of their beloved lost homelands and their good neighbours. The refugees knew that the *morphomeni* controlled the writing of history and dominated national/official memory, but they could at least pose a counter-narrative in oral form.

'We lived well with the Turks'

The history of coexistence as experienced at the grass-roots level, how-ever, immediately raises a problem of historical description, for inter-communality is a mode of living that does not lend itself easily to standard narration. After all, it refers to accommodations that were spe-cifically arranged to avoid 'events'—in everyday Greek usage the term *istories* (histories) denotes troubles, experiences, or quarrels over differ-ences.[50] The interviewees had a great deal to say about the later years, in that they provide, in very fine detail, personal *istories* of trauma and near escapes. In the first volume of *I Exodos*, in which the Centre for Asia Minor Studies published lengthy excerpts from its oral history archive, there are numerous such accounts that focus on the month of Septem-ber 1922. Interviewees had a great deal to say about the moment they received news of the collapse of the Greek military front, the desperate measures that people took to escape the approaching Turkish army, and about their travails once caught behind enemy lines.[51] The editors of *I Exodos* surmised that it was these particular parts of the oral history archive that the general public could be expected to find interesting because they contain ample drama and also because such material was more recognizable as 'history'.

As for the decades of relative normalcy before 1912, the interviewees had relatively little to say precisely because they were remembered as une-ventful, good times. There were not many stories to tell. Rather, the interviewees resorted to depicting this Ottoman *belle époque* and its rou-tines with stock phrases and stock images that sounded like throwaway lines, but which in fact were pregnant with meaning. Phrases like 'we lived like brothers' and 'we got on well with the Turks' (περνούσαμε καλά με τους Τούρκους) were used for their symbolic efficiency, or their cap-acity to express meanings that could be instantly recognized and under-stood by the listener. Such phrases were a means by which the refugees could convey concepts and abstract meanings that were otherwise hard to illustrate through anecdotes. The most commonly used phrase, 'we got on well with the Turks', which was used by refugees from every part of Anatolia and eastern Thrace, by town and country folk, was used precisely because all these groups were in agreement; that in general the Romioi enjoyed a more acceptable standard of material and communal life in Anatolia.[52]

The key term is 'pernousame' (περνύοαμε), the first person plural in Modern Greek for 'I pass' or 'to move through' (περνώ). The claim was that the Romioi had passed or lived 'through' a given period, and the 'we' could be understood as the local Rum community. Sometimes it included the local Muslims. Either way, the refugees were referring to a lifetime or a period covering generations that was experienced *with* the Turks. 'We lived well with the Turks' (*persnousame kala me tous Tourkous*) referred to an era when Greek Orthodox and Muslim lives were entangled, and that this entanglement not only brought social stability but made for a relatively convivial coexistence. It was certainly the case that many interviewees had nothing to say about relations with the Muslims, and that some were prepared to dispute the 'we got on well' line. However, even in such cases the interviewees were forced to engage with the dominant Anatolian refugee discourse. Such was the case of Yannis Mavroudis of Vori, who tried to present a more critical perspective by claiming: 'we did *not* get on well'. His particular portrait of intercommunal engagement suggested a relationship that was less socially genial than the norm:

> They'd invite us to weddings, but we would not invite them to ours because they could not drink or dance. No kefi. They respected our religion, and when we went into exile they respected our churches.[53]

Thus, according to Mavroudis, the Muslim and Christian communities of Vori tended not to mix socially, and hence did not live 'together' or share much in common, although the interviewee did note that the two communities still found ways to recognize their coexistence. In his interview, Mavroudis conceded that the local Romioi occasionally attended the local mosque during prayers as a sign of respect for their Muslim neighbours, and we can assume that the Muslims did the same by attending church, since that was known to happen among mixed settlements elsewhere. Such reciprocal gestures of mutual respect appeared to make other forms of intercommunal engagement unnecessary. However, as will be discussed below, for most Anatolian Romioi, 'living together well' involved a range of social practices that gave substance to the claim, ranging from daily greetings in the street and conversations in coffeehouses, to home visits and invitations to weddings celebrations.

While these practices were meant to make for a more pleasant and some-times pleasurable existence, their primary role was to preserve social order. Muslims and non-Muslims were agreed that peace and stability depended upon adherence to a common set of values, and in the more detailed testi-monies that allow for a searching appraisal of these values, we find that 'liv-ing together well' presupposed a shared moral environment in which subjects could find ethical fulfilment as Muslims or as Christians. Put another way, Muslims found they could live exemplary lives as Muslims by practising such values as charity and compassion with their non-Muslim neighbours. In her ethnographic study of a Bosnian village which covered the years before and after the Yugoslav wars, the anthropologist Tone Bringa shows how good Muslims identified strongly with the days of mixed living, when they paid scant regard to difference, because they lived in full accord-ance with their moral beliefs. They therefore could claim greater moral worth than those who succumbed to the ethno-nationalist politics that ruined Yugoslavia.[54]

The Anatolia of refugee memory depicted very similar moral environ-ments, in that Christians and Muslims alike appeared to abide by the same social norms and values, a fact that was recalled with pride by both sides many years later. In their joint testimony, Maria and Stefanos Hatzistefanos depicted Muğla, a large town in south-western Anatolia, as a place where Christians lived well because they lived a shared existence. Muğla had a population of 12,000 before the war, and while the Romioi accounted for only about 10 per cent, they seemed to play an integral part in local social life:[55]

> It was a good life, and it never came back. We were dispersed like the 'Children of the Nation'. Every Sunday [in Anatolia] we'd put on our best, go to the big Church of Panagia, or the Three Ierarchon. We'd go to school, to the Arrena, and there'd be a big festival. On the Friday on Easter, early morning we'd prepare to go to Asari, to our [chapel] Panagia Asariani. The mountain would become one big 'Turkomania'. They'd come to see our celebrations. They'd also eat with us, the lamb that we'd take up there with us... O Muğla, Muğla, to remember and never forget![56]

For Maria and Stefanos Hatzistefanos, it was the pastimes and annual festi-vals involving communal interaction that epitomized the 'good life'. The term 'Turkomania' (Τουρκομανία) was meant here as a boast: the presence of multitudes of Muslims at a Greek Orthodox festival was not deemed an intrusion but presented as testimony of a properly functioning intercom-munal order.

Many other testimonies also sought to make the same point that Turks were not barbarous Christian-haters. To counter that impression, interviewees tried to recall situations in their lives where cultural difference was an irrelevance or of very minor importance. The following story, which presents itself as a parable on compassion, shows that even a notorious Turkish bandit was capable of acts of kindness towards the Romioi:

> Once a Turkish boy grabbed a pita bread and ran. The baker caught the child and beat him. My father, who witnessed the scene, said: 'Why hit the child. The child is hungry. Give him more bread instead of hitting him'. That is what happened.
>
> Five years later, this child, named Kurt, had become a bandit. One day he found me in the fields and said he wanted to speak to my father. My father was frightened, but the robber said to him: 'Tzopartzi, I won't ever forget your kindness. I have some money with me; if you ever need it it's yours. I'll give you more if need be'…He never attacked us. He'd rob the rich regardless of whether they were Turks or Greeks. He wandered widely, as far as Adramitti [Edremit].[57]

This anecdote from the testimony of Patroklos Komenoglou effectively disavows communal boundaries by asserting the indiscriminate observance of ethical standards. Patroklos claims the child must be fed because he is a child; that the child is Turkish is immaterial. In later life, when the child grew to become a notorious bandit leader, when he robbed 'Greek' or 'Turk' indiscriminately, he made a point of repaying the kindness of Patroklos' father, his cultural identity again being of no consequence.

In other anecdotes we find interviewees delighting in recalling stories of social intimacy that provided comforting proof of common humanity:

> We had a Turkish midwife. She even served as midwife for our women. Orguz we called her. She was great: she loved Greeks even more than she did Turks. If she was not midwifing for Turks she'd be midwifing for us. Even when she was not working, she'd come and see us; to see the children she helped deliver. She helped with four of my children. She loved them like they were her own. If a day passed, she would not forget to call in. You'd find her most often in our homes. We'd invite her to stay and feed her. She'd often sleep over.
>
> Generally speaking we got on well. And with religious matters we left them alone and they left us alone. I don't recall our people going to a hodja, but their people did seek the help of our priests. But they did not work on St George's Day. They regarded that to be a sin. They prepared food a day before and ate on the day; they'd make prearrangements for feeding their livestock.[58]

Kleodimos Landos' story treats the outsider as if she were an insider. The home was an intimate space that was sometimes opened to strangers, but as a rule it was restricted to kin. Kleodimos takes the ultimate step of treating the Turkish midwife as a family member who was often invited to stay the night. Oghuz loved Kleodimos' children as her own, even preferring them to children in her own community. Kleodimos' intention in telling this story is to show that difference was ultimately meaningless. That such love could be extended across communal boundaries was a measure of the strength of that love and the irrelevance of the boundaries.

Of course, culture *was* essential in Ottoman life, and as will be discussed below, many of these acts of social intimacy were meant to preserve the integrity of the boundaries. Ottoman mixed communities did not meld into one organic unit. However, such local stories confirmed that where such distinct units lived cheek by jowl that it was also essential that boundaries shifted whenever dictated by necessity and social norms, and in order to promote an atmosphere of civility and cordiality.

Friendship and empathy

Needless to say, all multiethnic societies were rife with cultural prejudices. Talk of brotherhood and friendship belied the fact that each Ottoman community harboured deep-seated prejudices towards other groups, and that these prejudices were expressed through ethnic or cultural stereotypes. In places like Smyrna, to take an extreme case, where aside from the major 'ethnic' groups one could also find Tatars, Circassians, Bulgarians, Gypsies, 'Franco-Levantines', and Albanians, among others, it was useful for the purposes of navigating such dense cultural terrain to have some a priori knowledge of each group, however bigoted and distorted. The most likely scenario of ethnic violence, for example, was between the Romioi and Jewish communities. The Romioi were notorious for harassing Jews during pre-Lenten celebrations (*apokries*) or in response to rumours of blood libels.[59] Jews are rarely mentioned in the oral transcripts, but where they are discussed Jews are usually assumed to be of sinister character. Thus when Yannis Hatziprodromos recalled the financial troubles experienced by a Turkish family friend, Halil Salih Bey, the severity of his situation was indicated with mere mention of the fact that the moneylender was a Jew: the implication was that the Jew expected Halil to default so he could then seize his properties. Yannis' grandfather is said to have saved Halil Salih Bey from ruin by paying his debts.[60] Another interviewee, whilst reflecting on life in the Pontus region, began with the usual 'we lived well' line, but then added the following qualification:

> Only in the large cities, in Trabzon, say, you heard of things going askew . . . and only when the Turk-Jews from Salonica and the Cretans arrived. They were fanatical Greek haters. They had some reason to be that way, as they were driven out by the Greeks, who forced them from their villages to our villages.[61]

Thus, as people who had been harried from their homelands by Christians, the Cretan and Salonican Muslims at least have cause to hate Anatolian Christians, although the claim that the latter were 'Turk-Jews' indicates that sectarian spite was also a factor.[62] The specific group referred to were the Dönme, a particular Muslim sect formed by the descendants of Jewish converts, although the Anatolian Christians suspected most Salonican Muslims were converts from Judaism. Given that Dönme were also prominent in Turkish nationalist circles, the Romioi often claimed that Turkish nationalism was something of a Jewish conspiracy.[63]

The relationships that mattered to interviewees was that with the majority Muslim Turks, largely because Rum welfare, and that of all non-Muslims, depended essentially on the goodwill of this dominant group. Unlike Jews, the behaviour of Turks is presented in the oral sources as contingent. For example:

> We got on well with the Turks . . . During the Greek occupation [1919–22] I took in and fed the farm animals of my Turkish neighbour and I looked after them. 14 head of cattle and horses. He was an officer in the Armenian Genocide. And he became wealthy. He later saw me in Smyrna [after it was reclaimed by the Kemalists] and told me: 'don't leave, nothing bad will happen to you'. He hid us in a stable and looked after us.[64]

The same officer who persecuted Armenians and profited by doing so was nevertheless kind to his Greek friends and was even prepared to risk his own life to protect them. This friend showed compassion despite general Muslim hostility towards the Romioi during the Greek–Turkish War. Although all Ottoman communities held to unflattering stereotypes of each other, there was also recognition of the logical inconsistencies of the knowledge contained in stereotypes. The refugees occasionally conceded that Greeks too committed barbarous acts against ordinary Muslims, and that the Turkish reprisals could not be explained just by Turkish barbarity. Unlike the *morphomeni*, the interviewees sought to emphasize their belief that barbarity is not specific to any culture.

This truism is certainly a feature of Asia Minor fiction, in which Turks and Greeks have no claims to greater humanity or barbarism. And while the focus in these novels is on Greek sufferings, Turks are also shown to suffer. Individual Turks do not figure prominently in the works of Myrivilis, Sotiriou, Venezis, and Politis, but where they are encountered they are no less human than the Greeks.[65]

The theme of common humanity is best explored in friendships, where cultural difference is not permitted to preclude intimate social engagement. This disregard of boundaries is evoked most effectively in everyday scenes where prejudices are suspended, and where Muslim and non-Muslim converse as friends. In the second chapter of Kosmas Politis' *Stou Hatzifrangkou*, a novel set in an urban neighbourhood at the turn of the twentieth century, and one reminiscent of the Smyrna of his youth, a priest named Nikolas has coffee with a Muslim official named Hafuz effendi Beyoglu. They are not of similar age, but they happen to be natives of Thessaly, a region that had been ceded to Greece as recently as 1881. They are thus *patriotes*, that is, men of the same homeland. As such, and because they are on familiar terms, they smoke a *nargile* (Arabic *hookah*) and even talk politics:

> *When he chatted with the priest, he often threw in some Turkish words . . . since Papa Nicholas, despite having been in Turkey for more than 25 years, hadn't learned more than 25 Turkish words. The Commissar spoke Greek perfectly – not only Romaïka* [Anatolian Greek] *but also national Greek* [kalamaradika—meaning standard bureaucratic Greek[66]]. *He was born in Larisa, and the priest from a village near there, at Tapuklar. In 81* [1881], *with the* [Greek] *annexation in Thessaly, Hafuz effendi Beyoglu was a 13-year-old child. He would have got used to the new situation, but his father Tahir Bey could not cope watching the cross replacing the crescent over the following three years. In fact he couldn't cope even for one year, because he spent the following two having closed himself off on his estate, refusing to enter into the polity. It was akin to closing his eyes so he would not have to see, clasping his ears so as not to hear the bells, so that memory can make him hear the calls of the muezzin, who from the top of the minaret, with his hands over his ears, called the faithful to prayer and spoke to the grandeur of Islam. The Turks left one by one, so too did the muezzin. The old man did not know much geography, but he knew that Islam covered a world that could be traversed over six moons on a camel – go, go! And what was Yunanistan* [Greece]? *But a handful of dirt. Kismet!*[67]

The move from the homeland was heartbreaking for Hafuz's father, since it also meant leaving behind the tomb of his beloved first wife, although he hoped to return one day: 'God is great' after all. Hafuz did return to the *patrida* following the Greek–Turkish War of 1897, when the Ottomans temporarily reoccupied Thessaly, but he found little trace of the tombs, the shrines, and the minarets. Most traces of his homeland had been physically erased. In the meantime, Smyrna was inundated by a new wave of Muslims from Greece, 'more uprooted brothers', only this time from Crete: 'The same went for them. How can one forget? How? *Romiospori* [seed of Romioi] to be sure, they knew not a word of Turkish, but they had the faith of Islam.'[68]

In recapturing the kind of atmosphere of his old neighbourhood, Politis presents us with Greek characters who are deeply aware of cultural differences and cherish all things Greek, and yet who have the additional capacity to feel empathy and compassion for Turks, as witnessed by the nonchalant familiarity of the scene.[69] This is not the place to consider the politics of nationalism and ethnicity in the Asia Minor literature, but one ought to note that these works did speak to such ambivalences in Greek society at large, and not just within the refugee communities. Such literature appeared in the decade or so before the Second World War and in the post-war years, when hostility towards Turkey rarely abated.[70] *Stou Hatzifrangkou* was first published in 1963, when memories of the Turkish riots against the Rum community in Istanbul (1955) were still fresh, and when the political crisis over the post-colonial future of British-occupied Cyprus could easily have led to war. In the teeth of hegemonic nationalist culture that had been framed by a Greek/civilized and Turk/barbarian binary, the writings of well-educated and cosmopolitan writers like Politis nevertheless enjoyed a mass audience. *Stou Hatzifrangkou* was serialized and therefore one assumes was very widely read. More striking still was the landmark and extremely popular music album of George Dalaras, 'Mikra Asia' (1972), which marked the fiftieth anniversary of the torching of Smyrna, and yet where the lyrics by Apostolis Kaldaras were unambiguously ecumenical. This disjuncture between universal and national values, between indiscriminate compassion and ardent exceptionalism, has nevertheless been a critical feature of Greek public culture.[71] Despite its hegemonic position in Greek society, nationalism has been consistently problematized by universal ideas espoused by very popular writers and musicians. Most explicit in this regard was Stratis Doukas, author of an important novella about Greek soldiers in captivity, *Istoria enos Echmalotou* (*A Prisoner of War's Story*), who dedicated the first edition of his 1929 publication 'to the common ordeals of the Greek and Turkish peoples'. These inclusive sentiments were broadened by the fifth edition in 1969, in which the wording was altered to the 'common ordeals of peoples'.[72]

For the refugees, however, the need to rehabilitate the image of Turks
had little to do with defending universal truths, and a great deal to do with
describing the Turks as remembered. The demeaning nationalist caricatures
that confronted them in Greece bore little resemblance to the real Anatolian
Muslims, particularly friends or 'our Turks' (*i diki mas i Tourkoi*) but also the
average Anatolian Muslim. To combat the nationalist caricature of Turks,
the refugees created their own. Thus, male interviewees often presented the
Turks as 'brothers':

> *At the time of the Hamid (Abdülhamit) we and the Turks were like brothers. We kept
> company with them, we shared company in the coffeehouses.*[73]

> *Relations with the Turks were first rate. There was no animosity between us, we only
> remember friendship, goodness* [kalosini]*and love from them…I will never forget the
> innocence* [agathotita]*and moral integrity* [timiotia] *of the Turks. We knew a Turk
> who was educated in Greek. Another, an officer in our villages, would bring a lamb for
> Easter celebrations and we'd celebrate together.*[74]

> *Things were very good with the Turks, and the most Christian-friendly were the Tsem-
> kezi* [Circassians]. *They were our friends until the very end. Once, we took refuge in
> Gotzali, and we saw some water in a hole. I bent down to drink. I was spotted by a
> Tzemkezos who knew me, and he said to me, 'I ate bread from your father's hand',
> and so he brought me a clean jug of water to drink'.*[75]

When he discussed his friendship with debt-ridden Halil Salih Bey, Yannis
Hatziprodromos began by claiming implausibly that he 'never heard of
quarrels between Greeks and Turks', but that (plausibly) 'there were far
more quarrels between Romioi than with Turks':

> *We had friendships with other estate owners. When it came to the Turks we
> treated each other like brothers. We knew Halil Salih Bey, owner of* chiflik *at
> Agasilikoy, and I still have his letters. He got himself into debt with Jews and my
> grandfather gave him a large loan and saved his estate. We also paid for his son's
> studies in Paris and he managed to finish his studies. We introduced him to our
> relatives in Paris, the Serafidis family, who helped him during his studies . . . This
> boy later became a member of parliament and he helped us with our legal
> problems . . .*[76]

The Hatziprodromos family and that of Halil Salih Bey not only regarded
each other as social peers but also as families intimately linked through a
history of mutual assistance. All such intercommunal bonds were tested by
politics and war. The refugees understood the need to account for how the
Turks behaved towards them during the troubles, and here Hatziprodromos
makes the usual distinction between the true character of Turks and the

inordinate pressures that make all people, not just Turks, forget their true selves. Alexandros Iosifidis, who described the Turks as people that were 'good and loving', also noted that despite the war, their friends continued to treat them as friends:

> We were good with the Turks. These were friends that were good and loving. They never harassed us. Kemal ruined everything, but we remained friends to the end. They helped us. They took people into their homes, and they'd use their own institutions to speak on our behalf so we weren't harmed by the Kemalists or chettes.[77]

Ion Nikolaidis said as much for his native village near Nikomedia/Izmit, noting that there were bad Turks, who were always strangers, and Turks whose values with regard to friendship were exemplary:

> We always had Turkish friends, and even as we were leaving the quality of friendship was not lacking. Things did become frightening, however. About a year before we left the village, it must have been in 1919, a traumatic event took place. Some Turks found some locals that had been carrying corn along the roadside. The Turks took their corn and killed them. Some of the dead they threw in a ditch, and others they tied to bulls and dragged them to Nicaea [Iznik].
>
> The Turks, our friends, would learn of such things and would counsel us to get up and leave and go to Nikomedia for security.[78]

Ion Nikolaidis, Alexandros Iosifidis, and indeed most of the interviewees formed a chorus that sought to set the historical record straight about the Turks, particularly as wartime experiences seemed to give credence to the nationalist perspective. Friendships and intercommunality are usually forgotten in wartime, yet many Turks were described as having the strength of character to uphold their values. As Yannis Hatziprodromos put it:

> These bad memories about the Turks did not reflect on the Turkish people but on the powers of government and the military who had on their heads the fanatical Young Turks. The Turkish people are naturally light hearted and good hearted, and for the Romios they always showed respect and honour.[79]

Women and men

The clearest measures of moral worth had to do with questions of gender. For individual males in this deeply patriarchal world, personal honour rested squarely on the integrity of wives and daughters, and the same logic extended to the community. The integrity of the collective was predicated on the good name of its womenfolk: a slight against a local female by a stranger was an insult to the whole community. For the sake of intercommunal concord, therefore, special care was taken not to ruffle sensibilities in this particular area. Indeed, the most important function served by intercommunal engagement was the rigid supervision of gender boundaries.

After all, encroachments over sexual boundaries offered the surest way of inciting violence. In the following story, one Kleodimos Landos sought to emphasize that his community was inflexible when it came to questions of honour, although the consequences could be tragic:

> *When I was 10 we had a festival in the village. We were celebrating St Haralambos' Day. We were dancing near our houses. A Turkish Cretan came with his goats. He had come from Constantinople. He went to one of the houses and 'pulled' at a girl to dance. 'What is this!' Chairs were smashed and candles broken, and he was killed. The man who killed him escaped to Greece, but another Greek paid for it, a young shepherd. Another Turkish Cretan killed him in revenge. This incident hurt us all. What did HE do?*[80]

Tellingly, it is a stranger who violates the sacred boundary. In the oral testimonies, the Cretan Muslim often plays the role of the hostile interloper who has no regard for intercommunality, given that he is a victim of Christian ethnic cleansing and has no liking for Christians. By seeking to engage with women on the other side of the communal divide, the (possibly drunk) Cretan was only interested in his self-regard and committed an act of ultimate manliness (*palikaria*) by blatantly ignoring the perilous consequences of his act. He knowingly made a mockery of the community's hospitality and violated the most sacred of taboos. That he 'pulled at a girl' (τράβηξε μια κοπέλα) to dance, in full view of the community, was an open incitement to violence. The violence was contained since he was an outsider, although the event started a vendetta and, as it happened, everyone was 'hurt'.

The interviewees wished to give the impression that there was no room for negotiation where women's bodies were concerned. However, liaisons across religious boundaries did take place, and young Christian women were known to seek conversion in order to marry Muslims. Thomas Milkoglou of Kayseri admitted that women did become 'Turks' ("*Tourkepsan* Hristianes sta teleftea hronia"), but insisted the women of his local community kept their virtue intact:

*The Kesariotisses [the Christian women of Kayseri] were not 'turkified' because
they were intelligent women and were not easily charmed by the Turks. But in the
farming villages where the women were more naïve, the Christian women were
vulnerable.*[81]

Milkoglou also recalled that the officials who were sent to supervise the
populations exchange in Kayseri in 1923 approached these women to see if
they wished to follow the Rum community to Greece or stay with their
Turkish husbands.

The interviewees rarely broached the subject of sexuality in intercommunal relations, just as there was little in their comments that referred to
the oppression of women. It did seem important to male interviewees to
note that Turkish men respected the integrity of Rum womenfolk, the
implication being that Rum male honour remained intact:

*The Turks respected our women. Sometimes a Turk might swear at you but never at
your religion. You could take them to court...*[82]

*Their stance regarding Greek women was beyond reproach. They respected our women,
they never harassed them.*[83]

*Ohhh, we got on very well with the Turks! They were gentlemen. They never harassed
our women; they respected them. Of course we respected their hanoumises [Turkish
ladies].*[84]

These interviewees wished to confirm that there was a very clear understanding of each community's gender sensibilities. Rum males were deemed
to be so trustworthy that, according to one Giorgos Makris, Turkish women
in his locality were known to venture out freely in public. 'Such was their
confidence', he claimed, 'that Turkish women walked about the village
without concealing their faces.'[85] This remarkable claim was also meant to
convey the deep level of familiarity. Another interviewee claimed it had to
do with the great faith that the Turks placed in trust. Pavlos Aslanidis, a
Turkophone from the Pontic coast, described a particular Turkish notable
and patron named Küldüglü, who was prepared to leave his womenfolk
under the supervision of Pavlos' father:

*'Lefteri, hey Lefteri, let my Fatima go and sleep beside your wife.' And my mother
would often be seen in his company, because, as they say, there were the bad Turks and
the Turk that had clean blood.*[86]

Küldüglü was held in such reverence by the Aslanidis family that they carried his photograph with them to Greece.

Gender and intercommunality were also significant in terms of the meanings and proper use of physical space. The necessity and desirability of intercommunal engagement inevitably raised questions regarding the timing and location of such interactions, and propriety in such matters was always influenced by the fact that time and space were symbolically organized. More to the point, the meanings ascribed to particular spaces were indelibly influenced by gender imperatives. Every region and village varied in this regard, much as each had its own folklore, idioms, and rituals, but there were elementary rules observed by all cultures in the empire. Thus, townspeople, villagers and nomads, Muslims and non-Muslims, migrants, and even Western visitors, understood the coffeehouse to be an exclusively male space, and that homes were 'female' spaces that were not freely accessible to males from outside the household. Beyond the village precincts women could gather in groups at religious sites and work together in the fields, otherwise the only females who could be expected to loiter in inappropriate spaces were promiscuous women and water nymphs or *neraides* (Nereids). Any Ottoman subject would have understood such basic gendered geographies, much as the 'girl-pulling' Cretan undoubtedly knew that his actions were brazen and deeply insulting to his hosts.

Coffeehouses were a feature of every village worthy of the name, and where men could legitimately idle away their time when not engaged with work or family responsibilities. For Muslims and non-Muslims the coffeehouse was designated as an exclusively male space where men were untrammelled by family constraints and 'free' to reaffirm their masculinity. 'A woman would never set foot in a coffeehouse', claimed Kostas Kaiserlis, who then feigned nostalgia for those days when women 'knew their place': 'There, in Petroumi [Halikarnassos/Bodrum], women were like *hanoumakia* [young Turkish girls]. There would be beatings if a woman didn't listen to her man.'[87] Ethnographers dealing with more recent subject matter have noted how the traditional Greek coffeehouse is an everyday space where males pursue such forms of sociability as sharing small dishes of food (*mezedes*), playing games (cards, backgammon), arguing about politics, treating each other to drinks and, on occasion, singing and dancing.[88] Muslims and Romioi usually had their own coffeehouses, although it is clear that these were not exclusive communal spaces. According to Kostas Halkias of Halikarnassos/Bodrum, the local Turks found an escape in Rum coffeehouses: 'In their coffeehouses there was a strict official prohibition and penalties for alcohol and [musical] instruments. In our coffeehouses you could drink to your heart's desire and listen to musical instruments as much as we liked.'[89] During Bayram, claimed another local Romios, 'the Turks would flock to our coffeehouses to find ouzo and to celebrate. Generally, we'd only go to their coffeehouses for work reasons, and they would do the same.'[90] The coffeehouse was the primary space where Muslim and non-Muslim men could develop and sustain a sense of familiarity and friendship:

> At the time of the Hamid (Abdulhamit) we and the Turks were like brothers. We kept company with them, we shared company in the coffeehouses.[91]

> Our men sat in the coffeehouses together and played cards and talked politics as if they were of the same nation.[92]

Anthropologists describe the coffeehouse as a place where relationships and boundaries are negotiated and regulated. Traditionally, social bonds are created or affirmed through reciprocal hospitality (coffee, food, alcohol) but also through competitive actions (card games). Basic etiquette is also very important. The ritual greetings and toasting formalities that were strictly observed by all patrons constituted, as Michael Herzfeld has put it, 'a formal expression of manhood'.[93] Although there is not enough detail in the refugee transcripts to reconstruct the life of any particular Anatolian coffeehouse, let alone one that catered to a mixed clientele, we can assume that whenever Anatolian Muslims and non-Muslims met, whether regularly or occasionally, they could find a common understanding based on mutually recognizable codes of honour. As such, the coffeehouse played a levelling role, where 'one regarded the Romios exactly as one regarded the Turk': where males could meet, chat, make deals, establish a partnership, and forge lasting friendships.

Festivals and weddings

Annual festivals and life cycle ritual celebrations (weddings, circumcisions, baptisms, and funerals) served as the more publicly visible venues for affirming intercommunal ties. The key features of these occasions were shared activities such as singing, dancing, and feasting. Participation in such activities signified open declarations or confirmations of solidarity. The shared exuberance and high spirits of the participants was also communal in nature and signified a suitably vigorous celebration of kindred solidarity. The interviewees did claim that they often celebrated together, although it was never quite clear how much active participation was permitted. In the following case, for example, the Muslims of a particular village called Fountouklia near Adapazarı are said to have concealed their womenfolk from their Christian friends: 'Our Turkish friends, our *gnostoi* [people with whom we are familiar], we'd invite to our weddings and they'd invite us. But we never saw their wives.'[94] Another interviewee fondly recalled that in his Pontic *patrida*, the village of Kökse, the men at least participated in activities 'all mixed up' (*olo anakatomeni*):

> Something great went on there. They'd organize a feast. There was eating and revelry. There was glendi [merriment]. What instruments! What contests took place! Wrestling contests! Greeks, Turks and Armenians all mixed up.[95]

Another Pontic informant recalled that both Muslim and Christian women in his village (Zana) wore veils and were certainly segregated from menfolk during festivities: 'You ought to know that our women and the Turkish women chatted amongst themselves. They danced and laughed behind closed doors, inside private homes.'[96]

The oral testimonies do not provide enough ethnographic information to permit a nuanced investigation of the ritual practices of weddings and festivals. We cannot know whether the gender segregation referred to in the above-mentioned Pontic cases was exceptional or the norm within that culture. What can be said with some confidence is that Muslims and non-Muslims throughout Anatolia routinely attended the same festive gatherings, and that these gatherings served as a more formalized expression of social identities and relations. In her ethnographic study of a wedding celebration on the island of Karpathos, Anna Caraveli noted that during the heightened emotional state of the occasion, kinfolk and community guests could challenge and renegotiate the terms of their relationships, and while participants sometimes spoke too frankly and opened old wounds, the intention of such occasions was to confirm and strengthen solidarities.[97] Although scanty and formulaic, the information divulged by the Anatolian interviewees does confirm that Muslims and Christians did not wish to test their relationships but to strengthen them. If anything, interviewees presented these celebrations as an indication of the solidity of intercommunal relations.

It was accepted practice throughout the Balkans and Anatolia for Muslims and non-Muslims to participate in each other's religious festivals. The

Romioi had fond recollections of Şeker or Ramazan Bayramı, the feast that signalled the end of Ramadan, and of Muslim enthusiasm for Easter festivities. Regarding the mixed village of Kioski in the Smyrna region, our informants recall that the Romioi entered fully into the spirit of Ramazan Bayramı: 'We'd celebrated Bayram with them and enjoyed the revelry through to morning.'[98] One Kiriakos Kilitzis of Ankara recalled how both Easter and Bayram called for ritual visits between friends: 'My father had a friend called Hussein. He'd come to our house for Easter, and for Bayram we'd go to his place.'[99] Many interviewees saw the exchange of gifts during Easter and Bayram as gestures of mutual respect:

> They would come during Easter and bring gifts. They gave gifts to their friends, to the people that they knew well, to their gardiako ['friends of the heart'], a lamb, and would say: 'Bayramı mubarek olsun', 'may your Bayram be blessed'.[100]

Interviewees recalled looking forward to the sheer enjoyment of these celebrations and to the exchanging of gifts. For the most part, gifting involved the exchange of prepared foods. Fotini Tzamtzi of Kios explained that Bayram and Easter were associated with particular kinds of foods: 'On Şeker Bayramı, they would give me sweets. These things we ate very happily! And we would give them red eggs at Easter as well as tsourekia [a sweetened twisted bread]. They were thrilled to receive these gifts.'[101] The Turks reportedly loved Easter eggs, which in the Greek Orthodox tradition are hard-boiled, dyed red, and blessed during the midnight liturgy. 'At Easter we'd send red eggs to their homes. They expected them. If they didn't receive these eggs, they'd feel affronted.'[102] Muslims believed the eggs brought good fortune and afforded protection from evil powers. One Eleni Kolasidou recalled a Turkish proverb in which red eggs were said to protect the recently deceased from becoming monsters: 'Give to us some of that holy bread too, and give us some of those red eggs lest we become vampires.'[103]

All faiths seemed to look forward to St George's Day festivals. Muslims understood St George to be Hıdırellez, a saint revered throughout the Ottoman world. More will be said about the link between St George and Hıdırellez in Chapter 3, suffice it say here that Muslims and Romioi identified strongly with this saint, and while one group claimed to understand him better than the other, this common interest did not appear to give rise to competing claims over shrines and rituals. Rather, common devotion to Hıdırellez / St George was a practice that both communities took for granted:

The Turks celebrated St George [festival] *with us. Even the Turkish women took their place in the festivities. And we did the same at Turkish festivities, including Ramadan, as we went and ate beautiful sweets.*[104]

On the eve of St George's Day you would see the Turks coming, loaded with food.[105]

We enjoyed good relations with the Turks of Karioslan. It took three hours to get there. Initially there was nothing that separated the Greeks and Turks. They treated us well for that reason. To help hold the festival of St George they would contribute 20 kuruş.[106]

When springtime came the Turkish hanoumises [ladies] *would ask us when to celebrate Hıdırellez, which was their name for St George.*[107]

Much-anticipated features of a St George's Day festival were the wrestling contests and pony races, each of which was heavily ritualized. Significantly, these particular contests were organized and controlled by the Muslim community, and were seen by the Romioi as that community's routine contribution to St George's Day celebrations. Another interviewee named Anatasios Alexiades explained that Muslims did attend other celebrations out of respect rather than to express devotion:

On St George's Day, which we celebrated at the churches at Leventeköy and Kantaköy, they came from the neighbouring region because of their love for St George. They called him Hıdırellez. The Church had about 400–500 plates, forks, spoons, and they set up a table for all the strangers that came to the festival. They [the Turks] *slaughtered a calf and cooked a variety of dishes, including pilaf...*

During the Virgin Mary feast, very few Turks came, only our [Turkish] *friends came along, but a very large Christian crowd did gather, this time Armenians who came from Ferizli ... The Turks that came to our feasts liked to have wrestling matches. We'd gather our people, and brought gifts and textiles to give as prizes. The first prize was 15 metres of textile, second received 10, third 5. Sometimes we even offered a calf as first prize.*[108]

If the Muslims of Fountouklia did not revere the Virgin Mary, she appeared to mean something to the Muslims of Lefke, probably because her feast usually coincided with Ramazan Bayramı:

Our wives would bake 40 tsourekia *to pass on to Turks, and they'd return the compliment during Bayram. They honoured the Panagia* [Virgin Mary]. *Merchiem-Ana they called her. They would come for* Dekapentaugousto [Assumption of Mary]. *They came with their dishes.*[109]

Throughout Anatolia, communal celebrations always involved the sharing of food. In his studies on the anthropology of food, David E. Sutton points out that as a pre-eminently social activity, the consumption of food encodes a range of powerful meanings and promotes communality.[110] Refugees often recalled the ritual exchange of food as an affirmation of social bonds, as Muslims accepted that Christians could play a role in their most sacred holidays, and vice versa:

> At Easter you'd send things to friends, and during Bayram they'd send us meat and şeker locum [sugared Turkish delights].[111]

> Before the Asia Minor War we got on well with the Turks. Placid people, humble farmers just like us. They came to our homes on feast days, and we gave them [red] eggs during Easter. During Bayram, when we visited them to wish them well, they would give us sweets and fresh meat.[112]

Intercommunality was therefore sustained by common customs that centred on the preparation, gifting, and consumption of food. During Easter, Christian women prepared particular foods for consumption in Muslim households, and Muslim women did the same for Christian friends for Bayram. In such ways the communities tried to behave as one community, although the complementarity of roles and practices also affirmed the Muslim–Christian distinction:

> We got on well before the wars. And with the Turks we were good. We'd go to their homes, they'd invite us to their happy occasions, and in those days we'd send them large plates of kourabiedes and baklava [types of sweets]. To the brides we gave tzeberia. They did the same. They came to our religious festivals, to our joyous occasions, and they ate and danced with us, as if they were our people.[113]

The final few words here are key. Behaving 'as if ' they were one community was fundamental to intercommunality. Being like a community without being a community promoted solidarity for the purposes of social order and security, while at the same time ensuring that the distinctions remained intact. The purpose of loving one's neighbour was to keep that neighbour firmly at bay.[114]

Home visits

Interviewees also mentioned more intimate types of relationships between families and individuals from across the religious divide. Friendships were prized because they were emotionally based and entered into freely and without any moral duty. To give that bond a more structured semblance, however, friendship was managed through structured obligations or even transformed into something akin to a blood bond. In the Greek tradition, for example, a *koumbaros*, could either be a wedding sponsor or godfather to one's child, and it was not unknown to have a Muslim friend as a *koumbaros*.

The significance of home visits is best understood within the moral frame of friendship. The interviewees mentioned reciprocal home visits almost as often as they invoked the 'We got on well' line, and as such the practice merits special consideration. House visits were usually practised within kin groups, between blood relatives and relatives through marriage, since this ritual served to reaffirm the relationship, but also because the mere presence of a male in another male's home, a space normally occupied by females, always posed a threat to boundaries.[115] To exchange visits with non-kinfolk, therefore, was to honour friends as if they were family. Maria and Stefanos Hatzistefanos came from a propertied family in Muğla who mixed with Turkish families of the same social class:

> We were invited to Turkish homes all the time. In summer we'd be taken . . . to a country retreat for ten to fifteen days and there we were received with great hospitality and were treated to wonderful food. Our men went hunting. We were very friendly. They'd treat our menfolk with great respect.[116]

The impression given in the oral testimonies was that home visits were routine, and as such they only merited a passing mention. Some interviewees were content to say that there were 'comings and goings', but the more common stock phrase was 'we went to their homes, they came to ours':

> We'd exchange visits. We were very friendly. They'd invite us to their weddings and we'd bring gifts, and they brought gifts to our weddings.[117]

> We had good relations with the Turks in our village and especially right up until 1912. We were very friendly. We went to their homes, they came to ours. They came to our festivals, but they usually just watched.[118]

> We had very good relations with the Turkish families. We exchanged visits. We went to their houses and they came to ours . . . When they visited us before the onset of Easter we always set a table, and they gave us spinach pies, olives and honey, to show us that they were sensitive to our fasting rules.[119]

Interviewees further noted that casual visiting was normal between women of both faiths.[120] Visiting each other's homes, chatting on doorsteps, and exchanging gifts—these practices indicate that intercommunality had a female dimension:

> Gnorimies [acquaintanceships], friendships, coming and going between houses, they sending offerings to our church. For Christians your best friend was a Turk.[121]

They'd 'come and go' [μπηγαινωβγαίνανε]*, much as we did with other Greeks. We gave gifts, they gave gifts…*[122]

We had friendships. We'd come and go.[123]

We were good neighbours. There was strong friendships between us. We'd go to their houses, they'd come to ours…[124]

Inevitably, some intercommunal arrangements worked better than others, and in many places religious communities had little to do with each other. Tassos Giannaris of Nea Phokies felt the need to qualify what most refugees were saying: 'We lived well, but we had no relations with them, we did *not* go to their homes.'[125] Kiriakos Deligiannidis also insisted that the Romioi of his village *did not* have very close relations with the local Muslims: 'We'd just say hello. We *did not* visit their homes.' It was nevertheless important that Muslims and non-Muslims should maintain some form of mutual recognition. Thus, Tassos and Kiriakos noted that the lack of warmth was offset by mutual respect. Kiriakos claimed that there was common respect: 'If you gave a Turk a glass of water, he cherished it. I'll never forget that';[126] while Giannaris noted that if respect was lacking, there was justice: 'And if a Turk insulted you with swear words, under Hamid [the reign of Abdülhamid] you could obtain justice.'[127]

The uses of stereotypes

Community was the primary focus of Anatolian nostalgia. In claiming '*we lived well*' interviewees were speaking for the community rather than as individuals. The refugees yearned for these vanished communities, which they held up as exemplary moral environments that continued to inform their conception of community and sense of self in Greece. For the refugees the very act of nostalgic recollection was a reconstitutive process, allowing reclamation of a sense of their true original selves.[128] The idea of being the product of a well-functioning moral environment was particularly useful in Greece, where the prevailing social attitude towards refugees was uncharitable and humiliating. The Anatolians were not only despised on cultural grounds, such as for their 'Oriental' customs, food, music, language, accents, but also (predictably) for their 'base' character traits. Anatolians were lumbered with a range of ignoble attributes that included laziness, idiocy, sexual licentiousness, and criminality. Being from 'Turkey' and therefore of 'the seed of Turks' (*Tourkospori, Yaourtospori* [seed of yoghurt-eaters]), the refugees were also given racially offensive traits normally ascribed to Turks, such as pigheadedness and having backward attitudes to women.

The humiliations of displacement (poverty, underemployment) made it all the more important for the refugees to hold on to reassuring memories of a better and morally decent environment. And if memories of communality were important to the refugees, then so, too, were memories of intercommunality. Living amongst a Muslim majority meant that communal life required cooperation with the Muslim majority, who had an interest in promoting the same moral environments. The image of the Turk was therefore very important to the refugees, since Muslims essentially constituted an important feature of their lost homelands.

In this last section I deal with depictions of Turks 'as a people' (*san anthropi*) that were framed through character typologies. Unlike the simple Greek nationalist stereotype of the irredeemable barbarous Turk, the refugee versions provide us with complex human beings who could be great friends and models of social propriety on the one hand, but who in the last years of the empire were to become hostile and violent. When accounting for the Turks 'as a people', some interviewees held to the contradictory view that Turks were innately barbarous *and* humane, although the focus was mostly on the latter quality. Images of the average Turk ranged from sympathetic to glowing, and what made these Turks 'good' (*kali*) was that they extolled values conducive to intercommunality, such as trust, honesty, and fairness. Some went as far as to present Turks as paragons of virtue, as people who subscribed to custom and values with unwavering dedication. In effect, what the refugees were trying to say when invoking their own stereotypes was that the Turks were equally responsible for the 'dream worlds' of Anatolia; that the lost homelands were ideal moral environments because of, rather than in spite of, the Turks.

When seeking to describe Turkish character, the refugees often tried to do so with simple anecdotes that were meant to divulge profound truths about 'the Turk'. The following childhood incident, for example, was given as a comment on justice, and to invert the commonplace Greek view that life under the Turks was unremittingly unjust. One Dimitrios Kavoukas recalled hitting a Turkish boy who allegedly had blasphemed against the Holy Cross. He was brought to account before a Muslim cleric:

Once I struck a Turkish boy and I was brought before a hodja
  'Why did you hit the boy?'
  'He said "to Stavro sou" [I fuck your Cross] , *my hodja', but I lied, he never said that..*
  Ah siktir [fuck off] *he tells him, and then he says to me:* Aferin, ei ettin [iyi ettiniz], *'Good on you, you did the right thing.'*[129]

The subtext of this innocuous incident was that the Anatolian homeland was an ethical domain because the Muslims valued justice. As a Christian child Kavoukas felt he was at a disadvantage when hauled before the *hodja* because his protagonist was a Muslim, so he manipulated the situation by telling a lie that might work in his favour. His instincts were proven right because the *hodja*, being a good Muslim, did not play favourites but stood on principle.

More routinely, the refugees liked to convey their understanding of Turks through simple character stereotypes. For example, the Romioi generally believed that Anatolian Turks were obstinate observers of principle. One Ilias Papadopoulos claimed that despite the heightened sense of sectarian animosity during the wartime years, the Turks that he knew and had grown up with gave invaluable assistance to his family during the expulsions. For him, Turks were much more steadfast in the observation of social norms: 'The friendship of a Turk was on a higher level than that of a Greek. They were people of faith and honourable.'[130] Because they were more studious observers of principle, Turks were preferred as trading partners and for partnership ventures. For peasants especially, trust was an abiding issue in an economic sector that was becoming increasingly commercialized, where greater care and attention was required when bartering and brokering commercial agreements, and where shrewdness and cunning could bring great advantages. A superior reputation for honest dealings usually meant that Muslims profited little or were vulnerable to less scrupulous operators. The following transcript excerpts extol Turkish honesty at a time when guile and opportunism were thought to be rampant:

We were friends. We went to their homes; they came to ours. They were our guests, we were theirs, that is, the Turks of the other village. At Kougiouveli I was the only Greek. In trade they were honourable. I don't recall a Turk ever 'eating' my money.
  Ah, all in all, things were honourable, it must be said![131]

Trust and honour were limitless in those days. We lived aponierefta [without guile]. *Without intermediaries or secretaries. When a Turk gave you his hand and said 'sozum vieroum', the trust was never broken: he regarded trust as holy. The innocence and trust of the Turk towards the Greek merchant was limitless. From the villages around here they'd bring produce and they'd let you weigh it up without watching. In our homeland, of course, for various reasons, a Turkish bey took the side of a Greek and on other occasions Greeks supported Turks. We helped each other.*[132]

These nostalgic reminiscences more clearly resemble those of a more structural kind that juxtapose a perfectly functioning past, when everyone behaved honourably, with an imperfect present.[133] In effect, the moral Turk is compared favourably with the unscrupulous autochthonous Greek, a comparison that was intended to be doubly insulting. That does not mean, however, that the refugees invented the stereotype for instrumental reasons. Back in the fast changing world of late nineteenth-century Anatolia, where commonplace traditional ethics appeared to be eclipsed by the values of the market, the trusting Turk was regarded as a moral anchor:

They took oaths seriously. They believed you if you crossed yourself.[134]

The Turk honoured and kept his friendships. You did them any kindness they'd never forget it, they'd repay two-fold.[135]

We did things ethically. We traded animals; they trusted us with debts.[136]

The Turk showed respect and never forgot a kind deed, however small. Treat him a coffee and he'll remember it for forty years. When we were leaving for Greece we could not take our last trunk. We left it behind so my cousin Anargyros would pick it up over the next few days . . . The trunk lay around unsecured, but we had a Turkish helper. All day and all night he sat with the trunk, until my cousin arrived, by which time the Turk looked ragged, like a trusted dog.[137]

It follows, therefore, that Anatolian intercommunality was deemed a functional reality because the average Muslim was thought to be especially assiduous in the observation of norms of sociability. Indeed, it was this 'Turk' that provided the Romioi with a moral compass, setting standards that they would never forget as refugees. After uttering the usual line, 'we lived well with the Turks', Savvas Kavestos suggested that peaceful coexistence reigned between Muslims and Christians because they held to communal values rather than the logic of the market:

We lived well . . . We had a Turkish muhtar called Haji Kimerli, who was our neighbour and he loved all the people in the village. My father was an overseer on his estates. The muhtar trusted him completely.[138]

As with most anecdotes found in the transcripts, this passing reference to the *muhtar* is infused with ideology. In Haji Kimerli we are presented with a character who embodies that 'dream world' of refugee memory, a world of perfectly functioning communities just before it was overtaken by nationalism, and before being remade by modernity.

Stereotypes and disemia

However, the stereotypes also reveal great ambivalence about modernity, and more specifically, about the benefits that came with the commercialization of agriculture. After all, the expanding trade with the West, the building of railways, and the exposure to Western ideas brought great prosperity to Anatolian society, and it was widely perceived that the Romioi profited most from these developments. Although it threatened traditional values that were cherished by Muslims and non-Muslims alike, modernity also gave to the Romioi (and other non-Muslims) great material advantages. By the same token, the general perception was that the 'Turks' had failed to meet these challenges because of their stolid devotion to traditions and moral conventions. Haji Kimerli is a comforting figure who symbolized a world besieged by modernity, where trust and social solidarity mattered, and yet this refusal to change was also the cause of backwardness. The Ottoman Empire was weak because the Turks seemed unable to innovate quickly enough and maintain parity with the world's leading powers.[139] The qualities that made the Turk so admirable, which made for optimally functioning communities, were also regarded as serious liabilities in a world in the throes of dramatic change.

Refugee nostalgia therefore contained a moral dilemma. For while there was deep yearning for an age defined by the organic, moral community, there was also an appreciation for the dynamic changes that allowed most Romioi to 'live well', and which made many other Romioi prosperous. In order to seize the economic opportunities presented by the age, the Romioi could see the virtue of cleverness, guile, and the ability to manipulate competitors. Frequently, the interviewees seemed unapologetic about Rum opportunism:

> *We Greeks of the Adramitti [Edremit] Gulf held the entire economy of the region captive, both its trade and manufacturing. My father, Dadiotis, had an olive press, a flourmill; the same went for other Greeks of the region. We did trade. My husband had business links in Smyrna, in the City [Constantinople], in Lesbos, Alexandria and*

Marseille . . . The Turks were envious, but they could do nothing about it. Otherwise,
they benefited also from our riches. Everything went well, we filled sacks with lira. We
bought farms and chifliks.

In the days of Hamid, until 1909, we were 'honey and milk' with the Turks.[140]

The times called for more resourceful and risk-taking qualities, and thereby
revealed the Turks to be inexcusably naive. Quite often the refugees accused
the same morally upright people of being languid and lacking initiative, and
therefore found an alternative set of values to measure moral worth:

We had friendships, we had comings and goings between our homes. They were poor,
and we had plenty. We were the working types and the tradesmen. The merchants.
They were lazy and that is why they had no enterprise.[141]

Anatolia could therefore be a site of memory that appealed to two critical
but conflicting ideals: those of the organic community and of the dynamic
and competitive Romios. Depictions of Turks (and Romioi) were therefore
disemic, meaning that the stereotype evoked contradictory values that, as
anthropologist Michael Herzfeld has explained, were balanced against each
other in 'the day-to-day rhetoric of morality'.[142] Thus it was often the case
that the same interviewees who valued the communal ideals of the Turks
would also criticize them for lack of astuteness and competitiveness. Interviewees often slipped between praise and deprecation of the Turks, and used
words that could have a double meaning. Thus compliments about the trusting nature of the Turk could *at the same time* be implying a childlike naivety
that the more clever Greeks were apt to exploit. The term 'innocent' (*agathos*/αγαθός or *athoos*/αθώος) was utilized precisely because of its potential
double meaning: it could denote moral purity or 'gullible dullards'.[143] The
occasional reference to 'placid folk' (ήσυχοι άνθροποι) could mean 'the nicest
people' as well as the backhander 'docile folk'. Turks might have been ideal
community actors but they were destined to remain backward.

The 'Turk' of the refugee imagination therefore served as a frame for reading the refugee self. The rhetorical play of the communally minded but
pedestrian Turk, a figure who could be reassuring and troubling, revered or
pitied, was used in interviews as a means of self-promotion and/or critical
self-reflection. For example, in the following rumination on Turkish integrity
and Greek cunning, the latter, on balance, was thought to deserve more
respect:

Everyone respected a man's word. They [the Turks] *believed that a man's word was as*
holy as the Bible. Now and then, the Greeks played the role of the fox. The Turks

would say 'this is yours', and it was. Greeks were one point higher. Turks were illiterate.
They accepted that we were smarter.[144]

Even so, the refugee transcripts tended to evoke greater sympathy for the 'Turk' than for the foxy Anatolian 'Greek'. It was the tradition observing Muslims that bespoke the lost Anatolian homelands. For Evangelia Peristeridou, even Turkish robbers had their standards:

> *We had an estate and a house on it, and we grew cotton there. One evening bandits came. 'Your money or your life.' My husband wanted to hand the money over and save the family. One of them, however, remembered that my husband had once helped his family. When the bandit became a deserter [from the army] his wife needed help and sought a loan, offering her jewellery as security. My husband offered the loan without taking the jewels. This Ottoman remembered this good deed and just asked for a token amount. He only took 20 lira.*
>
> *The Turks never forget an act of kindness. They will not even forget a treated coffee. That's why they say: 'bir kahve bin yil hatir': 'One coffee, a thousand years of favours'.*[145]

One coffee, a thousand favours

In drawing attention to Anatolian prejudices and ethnic caricatures, the intention of the previous section was to offer a glimpse of how the Anatolians perceived the world and each other, while at the same time giving no credence to the veracity of the stereotypes as ethnographic descriptions. Along with such phrases as 'we got on well' and 'they came to our homes, we went to theirs', these stereotypes represented the means by which the refugees tried to convey ideas about Anatolian life that could not easily be related as stories, or in narrative form.

The general aim of the refugees was also to deliver their histories in ways that resonated effectively or which 'cut through' with the intended audiences. Efficacy was needed primarily because the dominant representations of the Ottoman past, those which were produced by historians and the *morphomeni*, made no reference to these moral environments of intercommunality. Indeed, the national narrative on the Greek past, which was based on a Greek/Turkish theodicy, could not accommodate these local histories. As such, the efforts of refugees to be heard resemble the 'radical' nostalgia discussed by the social geographer Alastair Bonnett in relation to British radicalism, whereby the sentimental visions of idyllic, well-fed, custom-bound, moral communities of the pre-industrial world became vital ammunition for effective critiques of modern capitalism. E. P. Thompson's imperative to rescue for history England's working poor, who had been marginalized by the onslaught of capitalist modernity, required that he recover their lost worlds 'from the extreme condescension of posterity'.[146] Although nostalgic visions could be mawkishly romantic, these visions were born of experience and had about them 'a hard headed quality'.[147] Anatolian nostalgia for intercommunality also constituted a form of resistance, an attempt to defend a cherished and familiar space, although the overblown nature and instrumental purpose of nostalgia provided the very grounds for refuting its status as accurate and objective history. To rescue the intercommunal Anatolian, it is necessary to consider refugee nostalgia, with its hyperbole, caricatures, and prejudices, so as to glean the stark historical realities on which it is based.

3

'People of God' Part I

The Logics of Popular Orthodoxy

What greatly struck me was to see with what freedom the Christians and Jews enter the mosque of Adrianople without meeting the least opposition, so contrary to the Custom of the other Turkish places where if a Christian or Jew enters a mosque he must either become a Turk or lose his head. You are even allowed here to go up the minarets and what is still more extraordinary, the Greeks are permitted to pray in the mosque of Sultan Selim on their Ascension Day. Tradition says that where that mosque stands there was formerly a Greek church called the Ascension Church. Mr Vasilaki tells me that it is a curious sight to see the Greeks with their small lighted candles, praying and crossing themselves on the one side of the mosque and the Turks and their accustomed prostrations on the other. After finishing their devotions the Greeks fill small vials from a spring which is in the centre of the mosque, pretending that the water becomes holy on Ascension Day.

Benjamin Barker (1823)[1]

There is only one Christian ruin which can be recognised with any degree of certainty [in Alaşehir/Philadelphia].It is called the Church of St. John. The Turk who showed us over it observed that it was as old as 'Husrut Esau' or 'The prophet Jesus:'...it was doubtless one of the earliest Christian churches of Philadelphia. Part of the wall, said to have been that of the choir, and four principal pillars are yet standing:...A few of the original frescoes may be clearly discerned, and among them some large crosses painted within large circles. The Turk gravely informed us, attesting the fact by his own experience, that every Saturday night the spirits of the martyrs who died for the sake of Jesus are seen going to and fro among the ruins; and sounds are heard as though they were reading! A superstitious opinion prevails among the Moslims that the sacred edifice possesses a charm for those afflicted with tooth-ache, and patients thus suffering, who affix lighted candles to the walls, derive immediate relief!

C. B. Elliott (1838)[2]

Outside the humble turbe *of the Imam Baghevi in the station suburb at Konia are two stones, popularly supposed to represent the horses of the Imam turned to stone: the idea is easily explained by their rough resemblance to pack-saddles. Cures are worked in two ways. If the patient is a child who cannot walk or a woman who cannot conceive, he or she sits astride the stones as if they were a horse. Persons afflicted with pains in the belly prostrate themselves over the stones so as to touch*

them with the afflicted part. The cure is used by Christian and Turkish women
indifferently.

F. W. Hasluck[3]

We'd go to their mosque where we'd follow their prayers. What? Is not a mosque
also a house of God? They would also come to our churches.

Iordanis Mavromatis, KMS[4]

R eligion is fundamental to our understanding of how the Ottoman imperial order was constituted. It served as the state's organizing principle of society, determining legal and political status. Ordinary people also believed it to be essential in terms of defining their personal and communal identities. Hybrid communities did exist, such as the Crypto-Christians in the Pontus region, and Linobambaki in Cyprus, but the overwhelming majority of Ottomans consciously belonged to distinct religious communities. 'To convert', as historian Selim Deringil put it, 'was to change worlds.'[5] Religious orthodoxy was as important to the average Christian, Jew, or Muslim as it was to the leading clerics. Each religious community believed its members enjoyed the special favour of God by virtue of the claim that they observed the true religion.

At the same time, being the 'Chosen' presupposed the fact that the temporal domain was to be shared with other religious communities who were captive to dangerous falsehoods. Knowing the boundaries between the true and false religions was vital in determining one's fate when it came to personal salvation. What, then, do we make of the transgressions that were so striking to the foreign observer? Why is it, queried the Protestant missionary Benjamin Barker, that Christian prayer and candles could be permitted at all within the great Selimiye Mosque of Edirne? How indeed does one explain this very unlikely intimate form of interfaith cohabitation? Did religious boundaries really matter, or could they be manipulated in ways that did not question their integrity?

The closer one looked at the local religious practices, the more it seemed that here, too, one found a world governed by exemptions; where heterodoxies seemed to be orthodox, and where religious communities appeared to bend, flout, or ignore the firm doctrines of formal Islam, Christianity, and Judaism.

In fact, local religion can be seen as covering vital areas of faith that could not be dealt with adequately by the doctrinal religions. Questions relating to the supernatural, the role played by supernatural entities in the temporal realm, and humanity's fate in the afterlife, were those for which ordinary Ottomans sought very clear and detailed answers, but for which theology and the clergy could only provide abstruse parables and aphorisms. It certainly mattered to every Ottoman subject that he or she belonged to the 'true religion', that they could identify with being Muslim, Greek Orthodox, Armenian Orthodox, or Jewish, but the same devotees of each of the great monotheistic faiths were also captive to heterodox ideas and practices that dealt directly with the supernatural. Critically, these heterodoxies also offered practical benefits such as protection from misfortune and miracle cures. For Muslims, Christians, and Jews alike, there was an entire realm of belief that mattered deeply, which required regular recourse to ritual practice, and which was believed to be as genuine and efficacious as the rituals performed in mosques, churches, and synagogues.

Because of the practical benefits of local or popular religion, Ottoman subjects were prepared to stray well beyond the boundaries allowed by high clerical authority in order to access the sacred powers of objects and sites venerated by other religious communities. Each locality in Anatolia had its repository of tried and tested methods by which supernatural powers could be tapped, and it is through such informal 'folk' routes to accessing sacred power that Muslims and non-Muslims often crossed paths. At such junctures, they took note of each other's practices and even sought access to the supernatural in joint rituals. Given the efficacy ascribed to these practices, it was generally understood that no specific religious community had exclusive access to the supernatural, and that there was virtue in sharing related knowledge. We have ample documentation, most particularly in the works of the early twentieth-century British archaeologist and folklorist, Frederick William Hasluck, that shows Ottoman Muslims and non-Muslims appealing to the same saints for favours and paying homage to the same sacred shrines.[6] They also shared beliefs that belonged to neither of the great Abrahamic faiths, including in the 'evil eye'.[7]

Historians have long been aware of this environment of intense religious transculturation, but its significance in regard to social order and communal coexistence has never properly been appraised. The general 'Orientalist' impression among foreign observers at the time, that Ottoman popular religion was essentially anarchic, a confusion of superstitions and corruptions of standard religion, is a view that remains largely unchallenged.[8] This chapter continues the investigation of intercommunal accommodation by analysing the paradox of interfaith intimacy. Its aim is to show how communities found through religion a common source of social capital, despite it also being the very source of mutual distinction. Religion provided the moral framework for intercommunal cooperation, while at the same time facilitating greater access to the sacred. For while each religious community claimed all other religions to be essentially false, ordinary Ottomans nevertheless believed that even the false religions contained some knowledge about the divine and the evil. Moreover, the fact that the religious boundaries were very familiar meant they knew *how* to manipulate them in order to access that which was deemed valuable in the other religions.[9]

Ultimately, the ability to navigate the paths between orthodoxy and heterodoxy, while at the same time remaining true to one's established faith, allowed ordinary Ottomans to access supernatural power more effectively, for what they sought essentially was greater control over their temporal lives. In other words, they were more interested in the efficacy of beliefs and practices, regardless of whether these were officially prescribed or not, and even if such beliefs and practices were associated with another religious community.

It is through this particular kind of 'popular' ecumenism that one can find the most intimate forms of Ottoman intercommunal engagement, where Muslims and non-Muslims could recognize most clearly each other's humanity without consciously crossing the line of apostasy. They could also see and be moved by the charisma of other faiths, as was the case of Iordanis Mavromatis, who sat in the mosque while observing his Muslim neighbours at prayer. He claimed to have witnessed another avenue to the sacred, and yet he did not feel that he was betraying his own faith.[10] Indeed, so impressive were these Muslim demonstrations of faith that Orthodox Christians were prepared to disregard their 'infidelity' and to see their Muslim neighbours also as children of God.

To begin to appreciate this latitudinarianism from a Christian Orthodox perspective, however, it is important to delve into the logics of popular Orthodoxy, and particularly how the Romioi approached matters of faith, their understanding of the relationship between the temporal and the metaphysical, the meanings ascribed to religious forms and practices, and the creative ways in which they fostered engagement with the supernatural. This chapter sets out the reasons why a community steadfastly committed to 'Orthodoxy' could at the same time be so flexible with its boundaries. When it came to engagement with the supernatural the Orthodox laity enjoyed a limited licence to 'make' Orthodoxy. They managed to graft their personal or collective religious experiences (dreams, visions, and miracles witnessed) onto the cumulative tradition of Orthodox religious knowledge, and stories of these experiences could be as inspiring and poignantly didactic as the lives of saints or readings from the Gospels. It was normal that each community should possess a corpus of local religious experiences that had been passed down in oral form, and which formed a constitutive part of each locality's religious traditions.

That proclivity for *making* Orthodoxy, to see the divine in their subjective experiences and read those experiences into Orthodox tradition, indicated a certain measure of creative latitude. Their capacity for 'making' Orthodoxy also allowed Greek Orthodox Christians to cross boundaries.

The limits of official Orthodoxy

> *One woman that was paralysed came wrapped up in wool and stayed in the church so she could be cured. St Dimitrios told her to get up and walk. That morning she got up and walked.*[11]

The refugees spoke of Anatolia as a land where miracles were witnessed more frequently, because people back then were pure (*agni*) and innocent (*agathi*), and had a deeper sense of faith. The relationship between the temporal and the divine was thought to be much closer. The Romioi believed that they were God's chosen people, but that Turkish rule was a form of divine punishment for the sins of ancestors. In the village of Hazambeili, St Dimitrios was the patron saint and celebrated as a miracle-worker (*thavmatourgos*). He was also a great warrior saint, although there were limits to what even he could do for believers:

> *On the eve of the catastrophe, St Dimitrios would come to our school teacher and bang on his door and say: 'The Turks are coming. Tell everyone.' Some believed, while others did not.*[12]

The fact that he was encouraging the people of Hazambeili to flee before the arrival of Ataturk's nationalist forces suggested the calamity that beckoned was fated from a higher level. St Dimitrios was only able to forewarn his people and, as the interviewee suggests, only those who had strong faith could be expected to heed the warning.

To make sense of how ordinary Ottoman Christians rationalized the world, it is imperative to begin with how they understood that relationship between the divine and the temporal; to consider the ways in which the former was meant to affect lives and shape events in the latter.[13] For Greek Orthodox subjects, as much as for other Anatolians, everything of consequence that occurred in the world, at a personal and more general level, was a function of the machinations of the supernatural. It was through spiritual interventions that the faithful often had their moral precepts as Christians confirmed. Hasluck's studies in Ottoman folk religion showed that both Muslims and Christians were preoccupied with gauging the temper and powers of the supernatural; in other words the supernatural was appreciated chiefly for its utility. However, the refugee interviews also convey that miracles, apparitions, and other heavenly signs were meant to inject meaning into temporal affairs, to give clues regarding God's expectations of humanity. The critical factor for any engagement between the two realms, moreover, was faith, which was deemed to be the fundamental criterion for salvation. Miracles and other interventions were expected to strengthen faith, to reduce the uncertainty that faith by definition presupposed. However, the greater one's faith, the further one could bear witness to God and to see into the metaphysical realm. It was the people of deepest faith in Hazambeili who had the capacity to recognize the signs and fathom their meanings. In such situations, signs served as a test of individual faith. In Anatolia, monks, Sufi mystics, and other charismatic religious figures were revered precisely because their exceptionally deep faith gave them special insights into the divine.

To attain an insight into how Orthodox Anatolians might have understood the spiritual realm, it is worthwhile beginning with standard Orthodox Church theology, since elite and folk Orthodoxy had each been essentially the product of mutual acculturation. Ordinary Christians regarded their folk beliefs and practices not as separate but as complementary to the teachings of the canonical Church.[14] As historians of religion have come to recognize, official and popular variants of a given religion are not mutually exclusive, and this is particularly the case with the Eastern Orthodox Churches, where parishioners regarded the canonical clergy as the custodians of legitimate Christianity, and who claimed to be faithful to 'Orthodox' or the 'correct' theological tenets and traditions.[15] At the same time, the institutional Church, whilst jealously guarding its prerogatives and always wary of what it often regarded as the credulous heterodoxical aspects of popular faith, generally accepted the principle that 'church' (*ekklesia*) means 'community', and that the laity could be a legitimate source of religious insight. The history of Eastern Orthodoxy has shown that it has been quite adept at absorbing or appropriating religious influences 'from below', the most obvious example being the veneration of icons, but also a succession of lay holy figures who were accorded official recognition as saints. As Hasluck has pointed out regarding the cult of saints, the hetero-doxies produced by Muslims remained strictly 'independent of central authority', whereas all Christian saints tended to find their way into the 'official church calendar'.[16] There was much 'folk' religion, however, that the Church would not countenance, but as the anthropologist Charles Stewart has noted in his important study of evil spirits in Greek popular imagination, such beliefs and practices could be ignored provided they did not challenge the authority and teachings of the institutional Church.[17]

What, then, do we know of the cosmological outlook of Anatolia's Christians? What was thought to exist beyond the temporal world? Which transcendental figures were most prominent and what were their roles?

Ecclesial and popular conceptions of the cosmos both proceeded from the idea that everything comes from God the Creator, or God the Father, and that he is all-powerful. Orthodox Christians deemed him to be the source of all that is good, and yet evil also had to exist in the cosmos for the purposes of testing faith in God. Humanity was seen to subsist within a universe in which good is pitted against evil, and yet all outcomes are also a reflection of God's will. To be sure, none of the interviewees dis-cussed God (or the Holy Spirit) in any detail: he was never the subject of stories in recorded folklore or in the oral transcripts. As with the Arme-nians, Jews, and Muslims, the Greek Orthodox invoked the name of God habitually to give thanks, to seek his favour, or to express the fatalistic notion that outcomes are a function of his will, but God was never meant to be questioned or gainsaid. Rather, speculation regarding the nature of God was a matter conceded to religious authorities, for to venture an opinion that diverged from the official Orthodox line, which was settled by the Council of Chalcedon back in AD 451, was tantamount to apos-tasy. It was a seemingly arcane point of Christology that essentially separated the Romioi and the Armenians, who never referred to one another as 'Christians', and which is why Armenian-speaking Ottomans who subscribed to the Greek Orthodox position were considered 'Romioi' and not Armenians.[18]

In the popular mind, therefore, God the Creator was a distant patriarch whom they could access through the familiar and indeed warmer figure of Christ, who, being both God *and* man, could be depicted in icons and frescoes, and appear in dreams or as an apparition. As such, popular notions of God as a distant father figure accorded with the official theological view of God as 'mystery' (*mysterion*), that he is almost beyond human comprehension, and that the near impossible challenge of comprehending his mystery through Christ is the challenge of salvation. Church theology has seen the process of navigating the path towards God, the *raison d'être* of every good Christian, as one of demystification and illumination. Thus, saints were mortals who in comprehending God had in turn become holy, and as such were living testimonies of God.[19] The principal vehicle of demystification is the Eucharist, which is conducted weekly during the church liturgy. God is meant to disclose his presence through the miracle of the Eucharist—*mysterion* also means revelation.[20] Anatolian Christians were deeply familiar with the Eucharist as a weekly miracle that witnessed the meeting of heaven and earth, and the making of the bread and wine into the body and blood of Christ.[21] One of the essential roles of the clergy was to perform the Eucharist and the other sacraments, known in Greek as 'The Mysteries' *(Ta Mysteria)*, and to ensure that the 'church' *(ekklesia)* as the community of the faithful is brought into communion *(koinonia)* with God, who gives life in Christ and through the Holy Spirit.

The average Romios did not need to have grounding in theology to understand the Eucharist as the meeting of heaven and earth. Even Anatolia's illiterate clergy, preaching their sermons in Turkish, Pontic Greek, and any other locally understood vernacular, would have discussed the Eucharist in sermons and reaffirmed the idea to parishioners as they received communion. The heady importance of the Eucharist was affirmed by the strict fasting and sexual abstention demanded before taking Holy Communion, and the requirement that the bread or wine administered from the chalice must not fall to the ground. Given that the liturgy was a weekly ritual, its meaning, as anthropologist Janet Du Boulay puts it, surely 'penetrated the culture',[22] and despite the fact that it was conducted in a language that only the learned few could understand, parishioners were nevertheless familiar with the particular lines of biblical Greek that were chanted each week.

For Orthodox Christianity to be deemed a 'Church', a single religion, it was as vital to Orthodox clerical elites as much it was to ordinary parishioners, that there be a close propinquity between official doctrine and theology on the one hand, which provided for the doctrinal uniformity that was essential to Orthodoxy's claims to being *the* authentic Christian faith, and popular beliefs and conceptions of the holy on the other, which were inevitably diverse and reflected the practical exigencies of the everyday. It was also inevitable, however, that given these practical exigencies the gap between the official and the popular on many issues would not only be distinct but could also be sometimes incompatible. The question of the nature of God is a case in point. The mystical conception of God as beyond comprehension, that he is not a being as such but the evocation of reality, ran contrary to the view of most Orthodox parishioners, for whom God was assumed to be a literal being, a patriarchal figure with emotions such as love and anger—the reason why Orthodox Christians did not speculate about the nature of God the Creator had more to do with fear that he might wreak terrible vengeance. Orthodoxy's mystical traditions certainly resonated beyond theological circles, particularly the idea that the divine could be experienced through ritual, prayer, music, and other media that could engage the senses, and yet there was also a popular need to know that their rituals were receptive to a divinity that was tangible, and a need to see the transcendental as existing in form and in a location.

Real life and the supernatural

As is made clear in the personal testimonies of Anatolian refugees, and as can be verified by many other studies of popular faith in the Eastern Orthodox world, the average believer required insight into spiritual entities that actively shaped destinies in the temporal world and in the afterlife.[23] For such matters, the Church could only provide limited assistance. Certainly, the Church offered parishioners immediate access to the divine via the miracle of the Eucharist, but the mere fact that its performance was routine and did not normally produce miracles meant that parishioners actually regarded the 'encounter' as symbolic. Rather, the Romioi usually experienced 'actual' encounters with the supernatural outside the parish church and without the supervision of priests. As the interviewees would often tell, an encounter could happen in moments of personal crisis and when one least expected it, and with transcendental figures other than God himself. Anatolian Christians understood that life's travails were ultimately a function of God's will, that moments of fortune and misfortune served as an explicit revelation, but that these moments were carried out by ancillary transcendental entities such as demons and angels, or malign spirits and saints, which were pitted in the great cosmic battle of good and evil. God was assumed to be somewhere above the fray, but performing all good works were Christ, the Holy Virgin, and a vast host of saints whose very existence was proof that mortals could triumph over death, and whose influence among the living was pervasive and profound. That St Dimitrios did not defend Hazambeili from the marauding infidel had to do with God's determination that the village and the whole of Asia Minor should be delivered to the Kemalists, but it was St Dimitrios who intervened directly to warn the faithful. When Anatolians prayed to God for rain, they did so through the agency of much more familiar figures. Thus, for Stamatis Karakosta and his fellow villagers, that intermediary was the Prophet Elijah, who was associated with hills and mountains:

> We'd go to the [chapel of] Prophet Elijah to beg for rain. We would go up there in a procession, with the priest in front, and we'd kneel down around the chapel. We'd go up with the sun, and come down with the rain. God would listen to us in those days.[24]

Anatolians assumed that the likes of St Dimitrios and the Prophet Elijah resided in another dimension, somewhere between God and humanity, where many other spiritual entities also resided and could influence the fortunes of the living.[25] This dimension was imagined to be a space, or a set of spaces, that could not be seen by the living, but from where spiritual entities emanated at will. The books of Daniel and Revelations provided insight into its 'ethnography', which included the Devil and a hierarchy of angels, while also offering some clues as to the fate of dead souls as they journeyed through it towards God or hell. For the average Christian, claims the medievalist Jacques Le Goff, 'the geography of the other world is of no small moment', especially as the journey into and through that space had implications for the fate of souls.[26] Anthropological studies of death rituals in traditional Greek villages have noted that access into, and the passage through, the other world was of critical importance. There were many local traditions, for example, on how to deal with a 'Grim Reaper' figure named 'Charos'. A central Anatolian tradition held that Charos had to be kept at bay while the dying were still breathing, which was done by keeping doors and windows firmly shut. It was then important to open all access to the house once death was confirmed, since failure to do so would inhibit the soul's departure and lead to tragic consequences. Other traditions believed Charos to be the Archangel Michael, claiming that he seized other loved ones and cut off their heads if obstructed.[27] Orthodox Christians understood the recently deceased to be in a disorientated state, and that prayer and ritual could provide aid and comfort, especially as souls were meant to linger among the living for forty days. Apostolos and Maria Stamatiadis explained in their interview that:

> It required 40 days for the souls of the dead to depart. The souls emerge from the ground and live among the living. After all, the soul is made of air, don't you see, and its all around you. This is a gift from Christ, who did the same thing.

Greek Orthodox tradition required that the dead be ritually commemorated with incense, mourning chants, and with the distribution of sweetened boiled wheat known as *koliva*. Loved ones also performed additional ritual acts of hospitality: 'We had a custom among our villages, where we would leave a glass of water at the door at midday, so that the souls might drink it.' [28] The living had further duties towards the dead once the forty days had elapsed. All deceased members of a parish were memorialized during services celebrating the Resurrection and the Ascension, and it was commonly believed that the dead actually returned to the locality.[29] The account given by Maria Birbili of Giatzilari shows that parishioners had to deal with each of their departed loved ones:

> Our ancestors would say that during Lent with the Virgin's blessing, the souls of the dead roamed freely for 50 days, and then, one by one they returned to their places. During these days a candle was lit in the room in which each had died. At the tomb, a candle remained alight all year, day and night. When a person is dying, they'd say, he would be 'startled by an angel' [αγγελοσκιάζετε]. For three days we did the bitter kolivo with barley, pomegranate, parsley and currants.[30]

Given the role ascribed to kinfolk in death and post-mortem rituals, there was some concern for itinerant merchants and migrant workers who ran the risk of dying among strangers. Pontic Greeks believed that a soul could be in jeopardy if blood relatives were not present at the death, although an article of clothing belonging to a relative of the dying person was deemed an adequate substitute.[31]

Anthropologists have long noted that danger lurks on the margins of space and time, and that death was the most significant margin.[32] It was commonly believed among Anatolian Christians and Balkan villagers until very recently that without proper observance of funeral rites an 'unchristian' counter-process could be unleashed, and that the dead might stay behind to haunt the living. At worst the corpse might mutate into a *vrikolakas*, a creature that resembled a vampire.[33] To Christians and Muslims alike, ghosts were usually regarded as malign presences, particularly if there was a violent death involved—throwing stones at the graves of murderers was thought to be one way of keeping their troubled ghosts at bay.[34] Ghosts that haunted the Greek households of Ottoman Macedonia were thought to belong to those who had not been given a proper Christian burial, or who had suffered a violent death,[35] while the ghosts that haunted the ruined church at Alaşehir (Philadelphia) were those of the massacred inhabitants who had resisted the Ottoman siege of 1390.[36] According to local tradition in the region of Fethiye in south-western Turkey, Muslims refused to repopulate the nearby town of Livisi (Kayaköy) after it was abandoned by its Rum inhabitants because it was infested with the ghosts of Livisians massacred in 1915.[37] In fact, the sectarian troubles that followed the Balkan Wars, and which continued into the early 1920s, during which communities were slaughtered en masse, or evicted and resettled, meant that ghosts had become a widespread problem. Exorcists were reportedly kept very busy.[38]

From the early nineteenth century, folklorists managed to document a vast amount of information on many other 'superstitions', and more broadly on the supernatural realm and the popular religious imagination. These beliefs had the effect of complementing the teachings of the Church and provided for a much more abundant vision of the supernatural. The purpose of this extra-ecclesial knowledge was to satisfy the insistent curiosities of the living, who needed more knowledge about the divine than could be provided by the Eucharist and Church theology. Aside from the need for more 'concrete' answers to questions about the spiritual domain, the Romioi also sought direct divine assistance for strictly temporal matters. Life itself was so difficult and precarious that one could not hope to meet its challenges without the moral guidance and (on occasion) the direct intervention of the supernatural. Since so much in life hinged on fortune, divine help was mandatory and had to be solicited through prayer, ritual, and faith.

Given that the supernatural realm was essentially mysterious, however, ordinary Romioi found it useful to engage with human beings who had already crossed into that realm. Saints were transcendental figures with whom ordinary people could identify because they had once been mere humans, and yet whose example and occasional apparitions were meant to chart a path to the divine. More so than the Bible, the clergy, or doctrine, it was the exemplary example of the saint that dominated local belief and devotion.

Local beliefs: holy men and women

S. John 'the Russian', whose body is preserved at Urgub [Urgüp], is a little known Greek neo-saint of great local repute. According to the local tradition, the saint was made a prisoner in Russia at the age of fifteen by the Turks during the wars with Peter the Great, and served the local bey *at Urgub for many years as a stable boy, retaining his faith, whereas his fellow captives became Turks, thereby, of course, bettering their condition considerably. S. John died in 1738 and on 27 May, the anniversary of his death, his sainthood was duly established by the appearance on his grave of a supernatural light. Miracles by him began to be recorded as early as 1837, when his body was preserved intact in a fire. In the sixties [1860s] S. John is said to have appeared to a woman who lost her child and to have revealed to her that it had been murdered and by whom.*[39]

It was only after the population exchange that St John the Russian (*Agios Ioannis o Rossos*) became one of the most revered and popular saints in Greece. His preserved body was transferred by the Romioi of Urgüp (Prokopi) in central Turkey to their new home on the Aegean island of Euboea, and since then pilgrims, many being the progeny of Anatolian refugees, have come each year on 27 May to pay homage, some still seeking cures for cancer or treatments for sick children.[40] As with the most celebrated of 'neo-saints', St Nektarios (1846–1920), St John is approached with the kind of devotional passion befitting such 'Olympian' saints as St George and St Dimitrios, even if his life story was somewhat staid and uneventful. Other than being a prisoner of war who stolidly resisted inducements from his initial captors to convert to Islam, St John the Russian's story is one that exemplifies meekness, self-denial, and ritual devotion. As Frederick Hasluck noted of St John, his fame as a miracle-worker only began sometime after his death. Rather, much like the more active St Nektarios, who was a teacher, theologian, seminary dean, and church hierarch, this particular St John was essentially admired for his asceticism and humility, and it is these attributes that gave him his saintly luminosity. The miracles that were attributed to him showed he had already become one with God.

Hasluck took special interest in saints within Islamic communities, in part because saint cults were deemed heterodoxical, if indeed anathema, in orthodox Islam, but also because such cults were the focus of intense religious passion, a trait that Muslims shared with their Christian neighbours.[41] As will be discussed later, Muslims appear to have revered saints for the same reasons and sought the same kinds of benefits from them. Recalling life on a chiflik (private farming estate) in the extreme south of Asia Minor near Fethiye, Nicholas Pisas noted that the local Muslims loved St George and St Dimitrios, and that when the Romioi left the chiflik Turkish women would continue to light candles day and night for the Virgin Mary. Pisas' testimony also gave a sense of how saints and other supernatural figures taught or reinforced the kind of moral values befitting of the faithful. The Romioi of this chiflik built a chapel on the spot where an icon of the Virgin Mary was first discovered, and which was to earn a reputation for its miracle-working powers:

> A woman was suffering a dangerous pregnancy. Her [the Virgin Mary's] icon was at once taken to Nazilli [some 200 km north-west], and the woman had her child, but her husband did not bother to return the icon, so the Holy Virgin became uneasy. The table where the icon was placed started to shake, the oil spilled and the candle went out. The next day they discovered that the icon had disappeared. It was found again in the chapel.[42]

Such stories regarding the activities of the Virgin Mary and of various saints circulated widely and left lasting impressions on listeners. For it was through hagiographies and such later stories of miracles that the average Christian learned most about their faith. Accounts of supernatural encounters, especially those concerning miraculous cures, resonated more deeply than did sermons or readings from the Gospels, where much depended on the priest's ability to convey the power and significance of a given passage. Stories like that of *Panagia Tsiflikiotissa* (Holy Mary of the Chiflik) would have been told and retold throughout the local region and beyond, reminding listeners of their moral duties, about what sacrifices were required to be a good Christian, and the perils that faced those who transgressed Christian norms. The miracles are certainly what made such stories noteworthy, but just as useful were the human weaknesses and short comings that were frequently depicted in such stories. In the case of Pisas' story, it was the failure to observe customary hospitality and the disrespect shown towards the divine that antagonized the Holy Virgin.

At the same time, ordinary Christians could relate to the Virgin Mary and the saints because unlike God, the Holy Ghost, the Archangels, and even Christ, they too had once been ordinary humans and had suffered life's privations. As former mortals they could be expected to empathize more readily with the humble and downtrodden, while the everyday familiarity of the saints also made them more effective exemplars of values and repositories of truth. The fact that the lives of saints were grounded in the familiar and touched on matters that related directly to everyday life meant that, much more so than theology, saint traditions had didactic efficacy. Anthropologists such as Laurie Kain Hart have found that they could access many aspects of Greek social thought at the local level by studying local engagement with saints. Hart's ethnography of a traditional village in the eastern Peloponnese in the early 1980s confirmed that saints served as 'models of personal behaviour, emblems of social groups', and indeed of most other aspects of social life, and that stories attributed to them 'were revealing of discourses of ideas of intimacy and justice and, importantly, of certain tensions in life'.[43]

In seeing saints as repositories of values and knowledge, and as 'the concrete representations of Christianity', Hart follows the path-breaking work of the Late Antique historian Peter Brown, who discerned that in Late Antiquity exemplary or numinous qualities were deemed to emanate from mortal individuals rather than from abstractly divined principles.[44] Indeed, 'the human person not only draws encouragement and validation from the moral exemplars of the past, but is actually able to make himself transparent to the values summed up in these exemplars'. In other words, a particular person can *of himself or herself* produce the norms by which a society can find guidance, although in a Christian milieu saints (as indeed every other holy personage since Abraham) were considered conduits of norms that were ultimately derived from God.[45] Thus in Ottoman Anatolia, much as in other parts of the empire, saints were not revered simply because of their capacity to work miracles, but because they offered direct access to the divine. Saints were therefore important for our understanding of popular notions of soteriology. If God and man could merge as one, and thereby defeat death, then it was clearly possible that people could become saints or follow their lead. It is *through* saints like St John the Russian or living holy men and women that the Anatolian Orthodox believed they could more readily find salvation.

This extraordinary significance ascribed to saints accounted for their ubiquity in social life. The Romioi were particularly attached to saints who afforded patronage, guidance, and protection. The refugees frequently cited stories about them, sometimes from first-hand encounters, but more often from the repository of communal memory, and each time they revealed any number of insights into the collective imagination. The most significant protection that was afforded by saints was against sicknesses, and the most valued saints were the miracle-workers. A typical story was given by Fotini Tzamtzi of Kios, where locals had built a chapel dedicated to St John the Baptist somewhere to the east of the town, whose powers were often found in springs that were believed to produce holy water: 'anyone suffering sicknesses would bath in the water and they'd tie cloth on branches, rags from their own clothing. Turks did the same because they believed in the power of holy water [*agiasma*].'[46] Holy waters with healing powers were linked to saints. Persephone Tsotridou claimed that beyond her village of Kouvouklia, there were many such holy springs (*agiasmata*) that conveyed the blessings of saints:

> All around our village there was agiasmata. There was St Vardatou. Once you went there and washed, things got better, great miracles happened. Another was St Galatinos, about 20 minutes out. Women went there every Easter, the second day following St Thomas. They took a cup of milk, threw it in, and then threw water on themselves, and then went home.[47]

The blessings of saints could also be attained through holy relics. In Izmit or Nikomedia, the locals believed that they were in possession of the hand of St Basil in one of their more venerated churches. According to Zizis Antoniadis, St Basil had finished his mission there and then tried to cross the sea (Sea of Marmara), but after finding the ship would not move he decided to cut off his own hand. The action brought on the miracle, and the sacrificed hand became an enduring source of miracle cures:

> That is what was told to us. Whenever anyone became sick, they sought out his hand. They paid a sum, and people would bring it home for three days...so the malady would go away.[48]

As with the Olympian gods, saints each had particular abilities. Especially prized were saints who combated outbreaks of cholera, which was common in the nineteenth century. In the region of Smyrna, the great protector against the disease was St Haralambos. Kleodimos Landos of nearby

Tsiflikaki told a story of when the saint appeared in disguise, which saints usually did to test the faithful:

> *There was once a cholera epidemic in Smyrna, so the women of Smyrna came here to stay in tents. They said that St Haralambos had guided them. They saw his face, claiming he looked like a village grandfather. Thinking he was the local priest, they asked the priest why he was always seen at night, walking about at night, but the priest said he could hardly walk. So the women realized the old man was St Haralambos, walking about at night and getting rid of the cholera.*[49]

Further inland towards Alaşehir, the Romioi looked to the miracle-working St Dimitrios, whose powers were such that interviewee Leonidas Davoularis claimed that 'even the Turks believed in him'. His account confirms that saints perform their miracles provided that locals have strong faith. It also shows that they are sometimes prepared to use violence where necessary:

> *In the days of cholera people were afraid and slept in tents near the edge of the village. They saw St Dimitrios, in person, hitting an old woman... because he thought she had the disease and stopped her from entering the village. My grandmother saw from her window how St Dimitrios entered the church with his red horse. The next day one could see the horse's hooves imprinted in the ground. The people back then were very pure and innocent, and had faith.*[50]

As a warrior saint and defender of the faith, St Dimitrios could use his aggression against infidels. When Muslim refugees encountered difficulties in constructing a new mosque in the village of Gambei near Muğla, the local Christians believed that St Dimitrios was performing his work:

> *Circassians tried to build a mosque in the village, but St Dimitrios would not allow it. They'd try to start building, but by the next day they'd find that the structure had fallen down and the soil was flat, as if they had done no digging...*[51]

The sword-wielding St George and the Archangel Gabriel were also occasionally deployed against Muslim attackers. Sofia Spanou recalled that the Archangel walked the streets of Bursa at night when the Romioi were being deported, and he would cut off the heads of Muslim paramilitaries.

> *They [the Turks] believed that Greeks were hidden in the church but they couldn't find them. Some of them sent for an officer and he came and saw the saint and started trembling. He lost his head. Only one of them survived to tell the story. We learned of this later from the wife of an Italian...*[52]

However, saints in Anatolia did more to foster closer links between Christians and Muslims. As will be discussed in the next chapter, even anti-infidel saints like St George and St Dimitrios were more likely to bring communities together, since Muslims also believed saints to be exemplars of their faith, that they were the embodiment of holiness, and that they were intermediaries between God and humanity. The two communities were of a mind on these matters, and being of a mind meant that they could inspire each other.

Exotika

Whereas saint veneration reflected the intimate relationship between the official and local traditions in Greek Orthodoxy, there were also aspects of local belief and practice that remained strictly outside the delimitations of official Orthodox teaching. Fortune telling, spells, and other forms of sorcery were popular but proscribed by Church authorities. As with anything conventionally described as 'superstition', these manifestations of 'credulous' and 'dangerous' belief also dealt with particular needs that doctrinal religion and the clergy could not address. Some insights about the Devil were provided by the Church, but it was reluctant to address the subject of evil except in a cursory sense, especially as knowledge about evil was dangerous, and too much curiosity might see the faithful succumb to its temptations. However, even Christians with strong faith needed to know something about evil. They had to know what roles demons and the Devil could play in temporal life, and how to combat their harmful influences.

As anthropologist Charles Stewart has shown in his ethnography of popular religious ideas and practices on the island of Naxos, until relatively recently in Greek society there existed an entire realm of belief that envisaged a cosmos in which the forces of good were in perpetual battle with the forces of evil.[53] Stewart shows that Orthodox Naxiotes inherited a number of pre-Christian beliefs that had been melded with more standard Christian understandings of evil, the Devil, demons, and Hell, the result of which was a detailed cosmology that accounted for good *and* evil. Far from representing any form of demonology, these additional ideas about 'exotika' were seen as reinforcing the teachings of the official Orthodox religion.[54]

According to most popular traditions on evil, the Devil had his own supporting cast of followers. Thus throughout the southern Balkans and Ana-

tolia, Orthodox Christians awaited the annual arrival of the 'kallikantzari'.
These goblin-like creatures were known to harass those who ventured outdoors at night during the period between Christmas and the Epiphany,
which was celebrated seven to eight days after the New Year. As Vasiliki
Vardasi of Sibrisari noted in her testimony, dealing with the *kallikantzari* (or
kallikantzouria) counted among the many ritual duties that good Christians
undertook during that holy period:

> *Christmas eve, the house was ready. We'd prepare the Christopsoma* [Christmas
> breads] . . . *We'd combine the fatty meat with crumbs of wheat called* keskeki. *We
> boiled it overnight. We'd put lots of wood in the fireplace so it kept going all night. It
> [the fire] was meant to ward off the* kallikantzari.[55]

The activities of the *kallikantzari* ranged from minor acts of mischief, such
as damaging personal property, to inflicting serious physical harm. Their
presence during the holy period was cause for vigilance, as Vasilia Kompourakou recalled:

> *From Christmas eve to the Epihpany the* kallikantzouria *would come to the village and
> do a lot of damage, that is why we kept our doors closed. Our grandmothers would tell
> us that when the washing was hung out to dry they'd urinate on our whites and left
> yellow stains, and no matter how much scrubbing was done the stains could not be
> removed.*

She noted that many of the domestic tensions that arise during that period
had to do with the *kallikantzari*, and that these wily creatures rendered their
greatest harm by luring people outdoors:

> *In those days we wouldn't bath until the Epiphany, we couldn't go out because some-
> thing would always go wrong. Our speech would be affected, or we'd have fights . . . We
> had an old lady in our village called Georgitsa. One night when the* kallikantzari *were
> at large, she heard a knocking on the door and someone called out 'Geogitsa, Geogitsa.'
> She went outside and she felt a smack on her face. From that moment her chin
> remained crooked.*[56]

Aside from the evil eye, the most commonly attested supernatural beliefs in
the Balkans and Anatolia had to do with water nymphs or *neraides*. These
were beautiful female spirits usually found near streams or waterholes, and
who were often held responsible for driving men insane. Unlike the *kallikantzari*, the *neraides* were a chronic threat. 'It is said that when there was
a wedding they would come and take the bride's clothes', claimed Lazaros
Hisekidis, 'That is why a bride had a wooden cross and placed it on her
apparel.' Hisekidis depicted the *neraides* as witches that set out to perform

malicious deeds (*poniries*): 'They were evil women, demonic. They did *poniries*. We wanted to keep them away.'[57] Most traditions, however, appear to depict *neraides* in more ambiguous terms. As the following story from the testimony of Loukas Loukidis shows, they were located on the margins between good and evil, and usually rendered harm only when approached or held captive. As beautiful females, their presence also tested the moral fortitude of men:

> *My mother told us stories she heard during the reign of Mahmud II* [1808–39]. *One man, Bouskoglou, was near a waterhole and saw a naked girl bathing with a golden cup. He seized the cup. The* neraida *could not get away without the cup.*
> '*Aman, give me the cup, I'll do whatever you want.*'
> '*I want you to be my wife.*'
> '*I accept, just give me my golden cup.*'
> *He married her and had children, but he didn't give her the cup. He hid it, and would bring it out secretly for his own pleasure. She once saw where he hid it, and when she found it she vanished and never returned. Another man had a very deep cellar, about forty steps deep, and at the bottom he found cold water. One day he dug deeper and found silver. The next day he woke up and found himself in the cellar, along with his family. The same thing happened the next day. He was traumatized, and realized that the cellar belonged to* neraides. *He sold the house and moved away* ...[58]

Most stories warn that only misfortune would follow if men allowed themselves to be beguiled by *neraides*. More commonly, men encountered *neraides* at night, and in such symbolically marginal zones as forests or near streams:[59]

> *In the homeland we believed that at midnight* neraides *emerged from the waters and danced, and that is why we avoided going to the well at night or anywhere where there might be lots of water. One day a local named Nikolas told some girls that he needed them for some work in his fields. As it happened, the girls found that this work extended into the evening. They didn't have a watch. As they returned at night through the Nif waters, the mule stopped. Nikolas then asked: 'Girls, don't you hear singing and music?' The girls were angry with him and did not respond. From that moment he became ill, and he remained that way until he passed away.*[60]

As with the *kallikantzari* and other *exotika* that occupied the popular religious imagination, the *neraides* figured as part of a cosmology that drew from extra ecclesial influences, but which helped the faithful to navigate their life journeys by addressing questions on evil and its many manifestations. As Charles Stewart has argued with regard to the exotika and their role in local Orthodox Christian life, such beliefs provided for a more comprehensive cognitive map of the cosmos than that offered by the official Orthodoxy. As a consequence, ordinary Christians gave themselves more cognitive tools for dealing with life's ambiguities and sufferings.[61]

In this chapter I have discussed the phenomenon of local 'Orthodoxy' and the capacity for the humble faithful to 'make' Orthodoxy or supplement the official Orthodoxy with additional traditions. As will be discussed in the next chapter, ordinary Anatolian Muslims also added further traditions to their faith and subscribed to beliefs and practices that were not in accordance with orthodox Islamic teachings. Their motivations for doing so were similar to those of Christians, for Muslims also needed a religion that was practical and which answered questions about the supernatural, death, evil, and other important matters for which theology and doctrine could not provide concrete responses.

The fact that both communities could be 'creative' is significant. For in the mixed local worlds of the Ottoman Empire, there was a tendency for local Muslim and Christian cosmologies to influence each other, and for their respective cosmological maps to overlap. This potential for liminality, and for traffic between religions, also saw the most intimate forms of inter-communal engagement.

4

'People of God' Part II

Accommodation, Faith, and the Supernatural

*An American missionary told me the story of a poor Moslem who went to him in
great distress. His one possession of value was a cow which had fallen ill. He stated
that the mollah had given him a verse of the Koran on a paper which he had made
the cow swallow, but without avail. He had then paid, first the Greek, and then the
Armenian priest to read prayers over it, but the cow was no better. 'If only you with
your foreign knowledge would read a verse over it,' he was convinced, a cure would
be made. It was in vain that the missionary endeavoured to explain that such a
practice was not in accordance with American religion. The only result was that the
poor fellow left, convinced that the missionary did know a charm which would cure
the cow, but that for some reason he was unwilling to use it. The missionary, however, who had some knowledge of medicine, subsequently treated the cow and thus
saved both it and his reputation.*

Sir Edwin Pears[1]

'The Orient,' according to Ziauddin Sardar, 'the land to the East of
the West, is a realm of stories' that always said something about that
Western desire to intervene and control.[2] With this particular anecdote
told to Sir Edwin Pears, a leading Western barrister in Constantinople,
the medicine-dispensing American missionary affirmed Protestantism as
authentic Christianity because it was in step with the march of progress.
The story juxtaposes the poor Turkish farmer and himself in terms of past
and present, backwardness and progress, superstition and reason, magic
and science. It is the missionary who can see the peasant's backward condition, identify his pastness, and thereby justify the necessity of the Protestant mission in Anatolia.[3]

Edward Said made the point that Orientalist literature was essentially about Western self-affirmation, and that it had little of objective value to say about the ostensible subject.[4] And yet without the writings of Pears and numerous others, which reported stories or observations in order to amuse, fascinate, and even shock the Western reader, much of the everyday history of the 'Orient' might have been lost. Ottoman popular religion is a case in point. The power ascribed to holy texts and scripts by the 'poor Moslem' was the kind of phenomenon that was taken for granted locally, but considered too embarrassing by educated Ottomans to record in writing. It was the Western observer's enthusiasm for survivals, curiosities, the bizarre, and the exotic that meant that such aspects of ground-level culture were documented for posterity. And what the story of the poor Turk and his sick cow confirms for the purposes of this study is that Ottoman Muslims manipulated religious boundaries routinely, and that local religion was practical.

Much of what follows in this chapter relies on the works of Western contemporaries who, while not immune from the standard conceits of the West, nevertheless approached their subject matter as something for serious scholarly investigation. To grasp the heterogeneity of Ottoman religion and the intensity of interfaith transactions at the grass roots level, one should consult the essential texts of Frederick W. Hasluck, whose articles and unpublished book drafts appeared within a two-volume tome that was published posthumously in 1929 as *Christianity and Islam under the Sultans*. This vital study on Anatolia and the Balkans provides a portrait of a world in which heterodoxies appeared to be the norm, where the higher clergy of the Abrahamic faiths could never enforce the official strictures, and where the desire to tap supernatural powers and find miracle cures prompted people of all faiths to venture well beyond their religious precincts. The value of Hasluck's works and those of Lucy Garnett, a folklorist who also examined local practices at close quarters, was in outlining the logics of these boundary transgressions.[5] Whereas most accounts present local religions as the kind of naive nonsense that made Western intervention all the more necessary, these observers showed that even the most bizarre of practices had a rationale.

Religion in refugee memory

Just as important for present purposes are the refugee transcripts housed at the Centre for Asia Minor Studies, which corroborate much of what is documented by Hasluck, Garnett, and others. A great deal of 'insider' information is provided here on intercommunal religious practices, including popular Muslim interest in St George and St Dimitrios, for Rum religious festivities, miracle-working icons, and other Greek Orthodox sacra. The corroboration of the oral testimonies is only partial, however, for the refugees were rarely prepared to admit any reciprocal interest in Islam, even though Western accounts provide ample eyewitness evidence to the contrary. There is plenty of evidence of Christians seeking miracle cures from Muslim sacra, for example. Comparison here exposes a weakness in the oral sources that suggests the interviewees found the subject too compromising. If anything, they often talked about Muslim interest in Orthodox Christianity in order to demonstrate the latter's superiority – Renée Hirschon's refugee subjects even claimed that the Muslims were jealous of its greater power.[6]

However, most refugees discussed Muslim engagement with local Christian religion in order to reinforce the idea of the 'lost homelands' as shared moral environments. In other words, intercommunal religious practice was yet another object of refugee nostalgia. The affectionate tone of Fotini-Tzamtzi's description of Easter was typical: 'They showed great respect for our religion. They followed the epitaph [procession] on Good Friday. And during the Second Easter, they heard the Bible reading in Turkish.'[7] Also typical was Anna Hatzisotiriou of Kasaba, whose description of Easter confirmed that Muslim interest was welcomed by the Romioi, in part because it seemed to endorse the power of their faith, but also because it served as an affirmation of intercommunal solidarity:

> We gave them eggs on (Holy) Thursday. They took them enthusiastically and ate them and threw the shells over their fields. It brought good luck. With those with whom we had friendships we would send tsoureki [twisted bread pastry] and eggs. And to thank us they'd give us kaimaki [cream], milk and butter.[8]

The oral sources also present these intercommunal activities as *habitus*, as behaviour that was routine. What seemed most striking to outsiders like Sir Edwin Pears was how such boundary crossings seemed second nature; how the Turk who tried to save his cow knew instinctively what to do: he sought out the 'magic' of other faiths until the desired outcome was achieved. Heterodoxies of that kind appear to have been an intrinsic feature of everyday life. Western accounts and the oral transcripts confirm that ordinary Muslims recognized sacred power in a selection of

Christian symbols and sites, and incorporated these selections into their own regimen of religious traditions. They also believed that certain Christian saints transcended faiths, much as did Abraham, Elijah, and Jesus. At an annual festival at a chapel near a local waterhole, Apostolos and Maria Stamatiadis of Gambei recalled of the Turks who always came along, that 'the poorest would not enter [the chapel], but the rich came in without hesitation and would light a candle and listen to prayers'. The observation of particular practices and taboos that were meant to reaffirm communal differences, also suggested that these routines were deeply ingrained: 'they [the rich Turks] would not kiss an icon or cross themselves!'[9]

The refugee testimonies refer to many kinds of religious interactions, many of which were on display during saints' day festivities, particularly those celebrating St George and St Dimitrios. One interviewee sought to emphasize local Muslim devotion to these cults by claiming that Turkish piety surpassed even that of the Romioi:

> They were more respectful towards our religion than we were. They particularly loved St Dimitrios and St George. We often worked during these holidays, but they never did.[10]

Local Muslims were also known to partake in certain Easter rituals and were very keen to receive their annual gifts of red eggs, which were thought to bring good fortune. The recollections of another villager show how Easter was incorporated into local Turkish tradition of ritual gift exchange:

> Turks were seen holding candles at Easter. We'd send tsourekia and red eggs to noble Turkish houses at Easter time. To show their appreciation, they'd fill a hanky with silver coins.[11]

Christians and Muslims alike believed strongly in the power of 'readings' from holy texts, whether it happened to be from the Bible or the Koran. A priest or mufti was normally required to perform this role, but even a literate person, or a church chanter, was sometimes deemed suitable:

> They [the Turks] respected my father like a saint because he was a chanter. The Turks would ask for him: 'Ilia efendim, bird ova oloun.' 'Ilia Efendi, read a blessing.' My father would read a blessing from memory, he'd bless the kannavi and give it to the Turk.[12]

Sacred sites also drew the two communities together. The tombs of Muslim saints, for example, were shrines that were sometimes ascribed sacred power by the local Christians. The testimony of one Zizis Antoniadis of Nikomedia presents a typical case:

> In the Turkish graveyard was a tomb of Agios Ermolaos, which was also the tomb of a hodja. There were two more like this. Turks would pray there and hang ribbons from the gate so illnesses would go away. We'd do the same. We believed that St Ermolaos would cure us, as he was among the healing saints.[13]

Natural sanctuaries were also 'shared', including water fountains or streams that provided holy water ('agiasma') known to cure ailments of various kinds. 'At Horoskoi near Manisa', recalled Michalis Orologas, 'there was a monastery with *agiasma* and a miraculous icon of St Anastasia. People come from as far as Smyrna. Even Turks would come.'[14] Elizabeth Mikalopetraki, also from Alaşehir, recalled the power of a particular holy hillock linked to St John the Theologian:

> There was a hill called Ai Yanni o Theologos. It was about 40 steps. The soil there was always wet…When your eyes were sore, you'd mix the soil with wine and you'd put some on your face. If you had faith you became well. Many have been cured by this soil. The Turks went there also.[15]

Some Turks were said to have placed more trust in the power of the Christian religion than their own Muslim faith. One Pontic woman claimed:

> We were free to practise our religion, and they actually respected our religion. Once one of our Turkish neighbours asked on his deathbed for a priest to preside over his funeral. He came to us every Sunday to receive koliva [sweetened boiled wheat].[16]

Even in times of intercommunal tension or when relations had broken down, the Turks maintained their faith in the sacred power of Christians. One Michalis Triantafilidou of Bodrum (Halikarnassos) recalled the fate of a priest who was forced to bless Turkey and the Turkish army:

> While he was doing it, the priest suffered an illness: his mouth went crooked and he could not speak. Later he went to Kalymnos where he died without ever having recovered the ability to speak.[17]

The oral testimonies also report many cases of interfaith sacrilege, of blaspheming infidels who suffered divine retribution. One woman from near Bergama told a story of some Turks who came to the village intent on disrupting a religious festival. St George taught the intruders a lesson: 'They came and found themselves surrounded by walls. They left and felt like captives. St George performed his miracle.'[18]

As noted earlier, however, religion also had a way of strengthening inter-communal engagement, since Romioi and Muslims could often acknowledge the numinosity of the same holy figure, and given they each believed that they could transcend religious boundaries without committing apostasy. Routine crossings constituted an important part of the fabric of the imperial social order, an ingredient that explained stability and tempered those modern pressures that were otherwise pushing the empire towards greater ethnic segmentation. Here, the norms of what Marshall Hodgson once described as the 'Islamicate', a societal framework that presupposed cultural complexity, and within which identities were well-defined yet flexible, were still in evidence as late as the first decade of the twentieth century.[19]

Anatolia as religious frontier

In the meantime, however, the received image of Turks in Western societies was not at all influenced by the Islamicate as Hodgson described it. Orientalist literature and Western journalism had long been promoting a caricature that depicted a 'race' known for fanaticism, bloodthirstiness, and intolerance.[20] Hence travellers were often surprised by their initial experiences in 'Turkey', and usually framed their writings of encounters with real Turks in terms of a paradox:

> In respect of religious feelings or intolerance, there is a marked contrast between the village Turks and the city Turks. In the villages you rarely see any signs of bigotry or of dislike to Christians. The people seemed never to have the slightest objection to my going freely about their mosques; and, when asked whether I need take off my shoes, they assured me that it was quite unnecessary ... [21]

During his extensive travels among Anatolia's villages in 1883 and 1884, the archaeologist William Mitchell Ramsay claimed that he got to know that world 'more intimately than archaeologists usually see it', finding an inner life that was normally concealed to the casual visitor. Not all of it was useful or to his taste: 'There are depths, too, in village life which I have heard about, and which I wished to avoid attempting to plumb.' He claimed his presence (and money) had a way of generating local excitement and even the removal of the 'restraints of religion', which also meant he was forced to listen to more matters of a parochial nature than he cared to. Ramsay conceded, however, that such discomfiting intimacy did bring him closer to 'history':

> I was not investigating the moral and social condition of the Turks, but seeking for historical evidence; I had not then realised how much ancient history still remains in Turkey, clothed in Mohammedan forms, and called by Turkish and Arabic names. The traveller must always be careful to avoid concluding that what he has not seen does not exist; though it is strange how little the most superficial travellers recognise that.[22]

What readily became apparent to the more intently observant foreigner, and those who were adventurous enough to set out across the Bosporus or venture beyond the precincts of Smyrna, was that Anatolia's interior was essentially a *terra incognita*. Preconceptions were influenced by Classical and biblical literature, by knowledge of such familiar historical landmarks as Troy and the cities ministered to by St Paul, and by an Oriental literary tradition that, as Edward Said famously observed, offered a caricatured image of a Near Eastern world that was as degenerate and dangerous as it was uniform and predictable.[23] In fact, not since the early Crusades had Westerners really penetrated beyond Anatolia's long coastline, and it was only during the nineteenth century, when commercial interests really began to prize open the interior and exploit its economic potential, that this vast landmass was ready to be 'rediscovered'.[24] Even at the beginning of the twentieth century, with railway tracks having been laid between Constantinople and the Arab Levant, most of this vast landmass remained as mysterious and bizarre as any part of colonial Africa or Asia. Sir Edwin Pears' guide to *Turkey and its People* paints Anatolia as a forgotten world waiting to be rediscovered:

> Yezidis and others unattached to any recognized cult, followers of some dervish or Christian heretic, are hidden away and owe their safety to their obscurity and insignificance. They are survivals who have got into backwaters and are out of the main stream of their race's history. In Lycia, in the Taurus mountains, and in many other parts of Asia Minor, they are occasionally encountered. They have kept the habits and customs, the weapons and in many cases the dress of their ancestors. The Holy Places of their remote ancestors in their midst have continuously been reverenced, sometimes under Pagan forms, sometimes under the form of Christian, and later under that of Mahometan sanctuaries. In the province of Konia, at Sinason, where there are no Turks, there is a survival of ancient Greek-speaking people who keep many words and forms of the ancient language which modern Greeks have forgotten. The same district abounds in rock dwellings. There are still troglodytes with many of the characteristics that are attributed only to prehistoric man.[25]

As a long-term resident of Constantinople, Pears could claim substantial experience of Ottoman life, and he held to the standard view that Anatolia's exoticism was a function of the tenacious grip of the ancient past. Backwardness at least had the virtue of keeping a more treasured past in some state of preservation. For its early archaeologists, Anatolia held a particular fascination as a living museum of Graeco-Roman culture that could still be found among the living. Thus the prolific folklorist and linguist Richard Dawkins, Oxford's first professor of Byzantine and Modern Greek studies, noted the tenacity of archaic forms of Greek in various isolated pockets within the central plateau. During an extensive period of fieldwork between 1909 and 1911, Dawkins studied dialects that had survived in regions where Islam and Turkish pre-dated Mehmet the Conqueror's seizure of Constantinople by more than three hundred years.[26] More remarkable still were the residual manifestations of Graeco-Roman paganism among Anatolia's Christians and Muslims. William Ramsay, a renowned authority on early Christian Asia Minor, gave scholarly credence to the idea that there were profound structural continuities in the transition from paganism to Christianity to Islam in the Ottoman East.[27] Holy sites remained holy, only the religion changed. Sacred sites, beliefs, and symbols had a way of migrating to the succeeding faith; pagan temples became churches, which in turn became mosques. For most pundits, however, the preoccupation with 'survivals' had as much to do with the Western obsession with the Classics as it did with the fact that it was the only aspect of popular religion in Anatolia that seemed to make any sense.[28] A seasoned expert of these Oriental religions said specifically of the 'Greeks' that:

> Religion, consequently, as understood by the mass of the people, consists of an agglomeration of superstitious rites concerning times and seasons, fasts and feasts. And, notwithstanding that the Greeks consider themselves Christians par excellence, they have remained in sentiment as essentially pagan as were their predecessors in classic times.[29]

All local religious traditions, in fact, were regarded in this fashion. Syncretism and superstition were seen as having distorted the Abrahamic faiths to the extent that none was thought to be authentic religion. That kind of dismissive attitude was confirmed by popular interest in all sorts of spirits, such as jinns (genies), peris (winged spirits), Charos, kallikantzari, ghosts, and neraides: some of these figures were recognized as survivals from paganism. The 'degenerate' condition of Christianity and Islam in the region was usually attributed to the failure to jettison pagan influences. For Protestant missionaries, even the

Greek and Armenian Churches, whose saints were assumed to be the old gods in new guises, were seen as only 'nominally' Christian.[30]

Frederick Hasluck was among the few who deemed the subject of local religion worthy of academic study, and who could appreciate the logics of many of these traditions. A case in point was the question of transference from paganism to Christianity and then to Islam, a matter that preoccupied him throughout his career. Hasluck took issue with the common idea that there was anything perfunctory about the process, noting, for example, that Muslim conquerors observed guidelines regarding which Christian structures within newly conquered territories should be transferred into mosques.[31] He also noted the importance of contingent factors. Thus any site thought to be haunted was avoided, although churches linked with saints that were revered by Muslims were appropriated, after which the Christians were often permitted continued access. The presence of a hostile spirit was often indicated by frequent building accidents during the renovation process. Most telling was the collapsing minaret; some were reportedly stuck by lightning, or felled by earthquakes, or fell for unknown reasons. In all such cases transference was aborted.[32]

In other words, Hasluck found there to be a rational basis to even the strangest of 'Oriental' beliefs. His studies promised to combat the misleading effects of transference as an automatic process and to bring 'into prominence certain points which have been unconsciously kept in the background by the, in some ways, over-logical methods pursued in recent research'.[33] His view was that by studying these living cultures and the meanings embedded in their beliefs and practices, one might be able to explain the specific circumstances of transference.[34] He sometimes conceded that he had little regard for the kind of 'superstitions' he studied: 'Credulity and almost entire lack of logic as regards religious matters are not peculiar to the Turkish peasant.'[35] In a letter to R. M. Dawkins, he was less circumspect. Regarding Muslim traditions concerning pre-Islamic prophets and saints, which had 'John the Baptist…avenged by Nebuchanezzar!', he wrote that, 'I despair less of being able to eventually unpick the composition of Chidr–S.George–Elias: Nothing is too silly, that is the tip.'[36] His publications, however, were written with a tone of learned detachment, along with scientific rigour that meant he could identify recurring patterns of devotional practice and thought: 'Religious practice…seems to develop within certain broad lines.' The effect of his work was to bring to light something resembling a coherent pattern of religious traditions across Anatolia and the Balkans.[37]

Indeed, more so than any modern text on the Ottoman Empire, *Christianity and Islam under the Sultans* effectively exposed the gap between Islam as formally accepted, on the one hand, and the beliefs and practices of most Ottoman Muslims, on the other, bringing to light phenomena that were commonplace yet discomfiting to established Islamic thinking.[38] In this world, orthodoxies were extensively augmented by heterodoxies. Aside from the standard aspects of Sunni Islam, with its Five Pillars (profession, prayer, fasting, alms-giving, and pilgrimage to Mecca), institutions (mosques, madrasas), and the Ulema (mullahs, imams), along with the standard traditions, prohibitions, and rites (circumcision, dietary norms, etc.),[39] there was also a rich, yet quasi- or unorthodox, tradition of saints, spirits (jinns, peris), mortuary cults, religious orders (sing. *tarikat*), monastic sanctuaries (sing. *tekke*), animistic beliefs, and natural sacred sites. When it came to matters spiritual, ordinary peasants and townspeople often preferred Sufi mystics to the mullahs and imams for their more intuitive and indeed experiential insights into the divine. As was the case generally at the popular level, heterodox rituals and hagiographies among Anatolia's Muslims competed with scriptural exegesis, and were usually found to be more resonant.

Hasluck and popular Islam

Thus, contrary to orthodox Islamic teachings, Anatolians ascribed enormous sacred significance to the tombs of saints and sanctuaries associated with the lives of saints. As an archaeologist, Hasluck had an eye for sacred sites, their uses, and their changing significance, particularly with regard to the *türbe*. These sanctuaries, which centred on the tomb of a saint, were almost as pervasive a feature of Anatolia's sacred landscape as mosques and minarets, and considered popularly to be the most efficacious sources of supernatural power. Pervasive too were the dervish orders (*tarikat*) and the *tekkes*, monastic complexes that each housed a given order and which were often linked to a holy shrine. The *tekke* acted as a hospice and retreat for spiritual contemplation for the faithful. As a close observer of Ottoman religion, Lucy Garnett, whose expertise in the subject rivalled that of Hasluck, noted that mystical traditions were expanding along with Anatolia's burgeoning towns and cities, and that they ranged in size, nature, and popularity.[40]

Garnett's own richly detailed study of the dervishes, *Mysticism and Magic in Turkey* (1912), which was striking for its capacity to get *inside* the subject,[41] noted that while discouraged by orthodox opinion and therefore somewhat concealed, these mystical traditions were nevertheless deeply ingrained in the social consciousness of the mainstream.[42] Sufi mystics, ascetic brotherhoods, and mystical traditions flourished as a substructure within the Ottoman Islamic world; not officially recognized yet tolerated because of their hold on the general Muslim population. Garnett noted that 'the majority of the Turkish nation...always regarded the Dervishes, their Sheikhs, and above all, the Founders of the Orders, as the beloved Sons of Heaven, and in intimate relations with spiritual powers'.[43] Provided its authority was in no sense threatened, the Ottoman state gave a wide birth to such religious movements and traditions. Even the more manifestly heterodox groups like the Bektashis and the Shi'ite Kizilibashis (Alevis), technically deemed to be heretical, were largely left to their own devices.[44]

Official tolerance also had to do with the fact that heterodoxies met a number of basic needs. Thus, mystical traditions provided for the kind of sensory and spiritual experiences that appealed to most subjects, including social elites and even sultans. The links between the state and these movements were often quite close, especially in early Ottoman times when Sufis were at the vanguard of converting newly conquered groups to Islam. The *tarikat*s and their traditions had played a critical part in providing various types of social groups and institutions, including guilds, with a deep sense of corporate solidarity. In such ways, religious brotherhoods and mystical religion were usually stabilizing forces in society.[45] For such reasons, the state's attitude towards benighted popular digressions and to the 'errors' of the non-Muslims was normally sympathetic.[46]

Another negative aspersion usually directed by Western pundits at popular religion was its preoccupation with magic. It was certainly the case that rites were performed for instrumental reasons: to secure good fortune, safeguards against evil, and miraculous cures. It was for such ends that the faithful visited a *türbe*, where the resting saint might perform his miracles. Edwin Pears explained that:

The traveller constantly comes across such tombs, which exist in considerable numbers in Constantinople itself, where articles of clothing have been attached to the railings which surround them in the belief that virtue will come from the holy person who is there buried, and will accrue to the benefit of the person who has deposited the article belonging to him or her. Many of these tombs have literally hundreds of

*such votive offerings hanging upon them, which time and strong winds have torn
into shreds and rags.*[47]

Similar powers were ascribed to particular holy mountains, waterholes,
caves, trees, stones, and other natural features that were linked to saints. Different sites were known to provide for different kinds of miracles. Typical is
a story related by Garnett, who tells of a specific stone into which Khidhr
(Hıdırellez) was believed to have thrust his finger, and which offered a cure
for those suffering from 'profuse perspiration': 'The sufferer inserts his finger into the cavity, strokes with it his forehead and eyelids, and, it is confi-
dently asserted, "goes away cured".'[48] To counter misfortune, individuals
often sought to communicate with the supernatural for warnings or instruc-
tion. As with their Christian counterparts, Muslims practised 'incubation':
sleeping within the precincts of a sanctuary 'with the intention of receiving
the desired communication'.[49] *Kurban* or animal sacrifice was an important
prophylactic that had multiple applications. Although *kurban* was a standard
Islamic ritual conducted during the last month of the religious calendar,
Anatolian peasants performed animal sacrifice 'during sickness, after omi-
nous dreams, in times of danger, and to check fire and pestilence', as well
as during rites of passage ceremonies (circumcision, weddings), before
operations, at the opening of mines, and when men set off to war.[50] Another
means of guarding against evil was 'binding', which involved tying knots on
tree branches near a sacred site. A tight knot was meant to bind the evil
more firmly.

There was more to Muslim popular rites, however, than practical benefit. What foreign observers usually failed to recognize was that Muslim saint
cults were as important as their Christian counterparts in helping believers
find their moral bearings. Every venerable *saint* had a story or associated
traditions that bespoke of selflessness, charity, and faith in God and all other
virtues. Sainthood denoted an intimate connection with the divine that was
attained by rejecting creature comforts and material interests, and by leading the kind of virtuous life thought to bring the faithful closer to God. As
with Christian saints, the Muslim saint was an exemplar of true virtue to be
emulated by the living, and who appealed on a number of levels. As dis-
pensers of miracles they provided living proof of the power of God to those
whose faith was weak or needed strengthening. Saints were deemed to be
the embodiment of Islam and Christianity, which meant that their actions
and words served as a guide to salvation. And as such, they posed a chal-

lenge to official religion, for as humans who had become 'one with God', and whose acts and utterances were therefore deemed sacred, their insights into the divine were often seen to have more value than prosaic theology.

In both religions, saints were people who had renounced the world and regarded all its conventions as ultimately meaningless. Even religious ritual was dispensable. Typical is the story of one Haji Bekir, an Anatolian saint whose resting place was a mystery because he deliberately wanted to avoid 'the posthumous honour of a *türbe*', but his attempts were foiled when his devotees found a solution: 'his spirit is supposed to haunt a mill he frequented in life, where incubation is practised by pilgrims as at a formal tomb'.[51] Despite the lesson the venerable Haji Bekir sought to inculcate, his followers seemed to acknowledge their own limitations and insist that faith had to be reinforced by ritual practices. Proper ritual might tap supernatural power, but its general application was for reaffirming faith.

Sacred geographies and overlapping boundaries

Thus far I have considered the distinctions between 'high' and 'low' culture, between univocal, doctrinally fixed, official religions, on the one hand, and more protean and heteroglossic local variants, on the other. Although mindful of the distortions that come with drawing hard distinctions between popular religion and its ostensible 'true' version, it is clear that the 'really existing' sorts of belief and practice were resplendent with various kinds of heterodoxies, to the extent that one can see the shortcomings of such categories as 'Islam' and 'Christianity' for an understanding of Ottoman society. The existence of the many local 'islams' and 'christianities' also raises questions about that society as a set of vertically organized confessional communities. If one considers religious practice within each of the *millets* from a comparative perspective, one can see notable *horizontal* parallels that point to different kinds of cross-confessional unities.[52]

The discussion thus far has identified some similarities and borrowings that are suggestive of long histories of cohabitation and exchange. The fact that Muslims regularly sought 'readings' from priests and Christians visited miracle-working *türbes* point to local histories of communal interdependence. Clear resemblances could also be seen in attitudes to mysticism and sainthood. It is noteworthy that pious Christians and Muslims were equally drawn to the same kind of mystical man and woman who, unlike the average cleric, was deemed to possess numinous qualities, and who was believed to be a more direct source of spiritual wisdom. The dervish, much like the monk, disavowed the ego, disregarded all creature comforts and social pre-occupations, and deliberately embraced a life of privation and suffering as a means of becoming one with God—the highest state (*hal*) that a dervish could attain was that of 'union with Allah'.[53] The bizarre eccentricities or insane behaviours of certain mystics, particularly the wandering dervishes or monks, were tolerated precisely because these behaviours were con-strued as paranormal. Their poignant utterances were valued as holy wis-dom, which they could conjure without recourse to holy texts because they were more in tune with the other world.[54] In both religious communities, saintly figures emerged from within the everyday and yet stood apart from it. Hence, Christian and Muslim saints cut very similar figures, and as such they often rendered religious boundaries superfluous.

Ritual practices, too, were exchanged. Among the most striking cases was blood sacrifice. Throughout Anatolia and the Balkans, many Greek Orthodox communities had adopted *kurban* as an important initiation rite, despite the protestations of the Church—the Hellenized term was 'kourbania'.[55] It was commonly believed that slaughtering a goat at a building site and placing its severed head among the foundations had the effect of ensuring a solid struc-ture. The adoption of animal sacrifice as a Christian practice clearly horrified the American missionary G. E. White, who was struck by the fact that a Greek woman, whose son was dying of tuberculosis, could vow 'that if my boy recovered I would go to our monastery four days distant and offer a sac-rifice there'. He also reported that the doors of Greek houses in Trebizond were smeared with 'sacrificial blood struck in the sign of a cross, and that it was a frequent custom of Greeks to make such crosses whenever they offer sacrifice'.[56]

In such ways the *millet* boundaries were found to be overlapping, and the blurring of distinctions had a way of generating common experiences and memories. At some points in time, intimate communal coexistence even allowed for limited forms of religious melding. Rainmaking was one exam-ple. Over time, neighbourhoods, villages, and rural localities with mixed confessional populations produced a common fund of insights about the locality and developed common rituals in response to natural disasters such as dearth, pestilence, and drought. Kleodimos Landos recalled that in his village of Tsliflikaki, locals followed a rainmaking custom in which com-munities hedged their hopes:

Rarely did we see lots of rain. If we had drought, the Turks and Christians together would perform a litany. Christians and Turks together. We'd go to a mountain, to a field or an orchard. No candles or icons. We'd just go and pray according to our religion. And it always rained.[57]

Local sacred geographies are important factors when considering the entangled nature of Ottoman religious history. As the Mediterranean historians Peregrine Horden and Nicholas Purcell have noted, locality is a space defined by various kinds of interactions between inhabitants and their native ecologies, and sacred sites were particularly vital to local mental mapping. Sacred geographies determined how 'fatherlands' were imagined and later remembered.[58] When the refugees were prompted to describe their particular *patrida*, it was the churches, rural chapels, and other sacred sites that provided the principal communal markers. When asked to describe his *patrida*, Andonis Tisizis of Livisi recalled the chapels that effectively served as communal boundary markers:

From the spring of Tourapi we proceeded to the road dividing the plain from the castle, but before we get to the bridge, on the plain side and about 150 metres further up there is a small chapel dedicated to St George. Climbing higher above the bridge towards the courtyard of Tsoumbo, and about 100 metres away from the bridge there was a small chapel painted red. It was the Virgin Mary (Panayitsa). Proceeding from St George, following the same road and towards the plain we come across a chapel, the Virgin of Zambali. We proceed by foot on these two diverging paths and when we reach the bakery, a bit to the left about 20 metres high up we find the old fortress, [where] there is an old church of St Anthony. Right of the central road you'll find St Marina. 200 metres away is St John.

Tisizis went on to describe many more chapels, including those dedicated to St Tharanos, St Basil, two more to the Virgin Mary, as well as to St Anastasios, St Sotiris, and St Pelagia.[59] The Romioi of Livisi had close contacts with all the neighbouring Turkish villages, with whom they shared knowledge regarding the location of malevolent spirits such as jinns and *neraides*. They all knew the local sources of holy water and other natural sanctuaries. Each of these sites served as an interface between the locality and the supernatural.

These sacred geographies sometimes overlapped and intersected with those of other communities. Mosques that were once churches associated with a miracle-working Christian saint continued to draw Christian devotees, while the local Muslims sometimes believed that the these 'pre-Islamic' saints were holy. Lucy Garnett reported the case of St Dimitrios, whose bones were believed to be held in a 'beautiful basilica' in Salonica which had long since been converted to a mosque, but where 'Greeks and other Christians are now allowed to visit this shrine freely':

> ... *and the old Mevlevi Dervish, who acts as a caretaker of the mosque, appears to have no less faith in the miraculous powers of St Dimitri than have the numerous members of the Orthodox Church who make pilgrimages to his shrine".*[60]

Hasluck describes similar phenomena in Anatolia. At Domuz Dere near Keshan, where a church once dedicated to St George was usurped by Bektashis, Hasluck noted that the Christians continued to perform their annual festival:

> *At the present time the feast day of S. George is still celebrated at the Domuz Dere by a* panegyris *of a social character, which is frequented both by Turks and Greeks; the representatives of the two religions do not mix together more than is necessary. The original church of S. George has been divided by the dervishes into several compartments, including living rooms and a tomb-chamber for the abbots' graves; the compartment including the original 'sanctuary' still preserves the upper part of the screen* (templon), *and on its north wall is an ancient* eikon [icon] *of S. George flanked by lighted lamps. This has been actually seen by my informant.*[61]

The retention of some aspects of the supplanted shrine, including the icon which the dervishes clearly held sacred, suggested a belief in sacred continuity. Hasluck showed that transference could happen for many reasons, but that Muslims generally understood Islam to be the *succeeding* faith, thus presupposing that there was residual sacred value in the religion that had been overtaken. Christians also often assumed the some of their true religion carried through into Islam. Thus, one Aglaia Kontou of Menemen recalled that the grace of St Theodore could be accessed in a Muslim shrine of a saint named Nempi Hodja. The shrine

> *had the Imam's tunic. In his memory* [St Theodore's], *we'd go there and give out koliva, breads, which the Turks liked. They honoured the shrine too, that of Nempi Hodja. We'd take oil there, and there was an old Turkish lady there who kept a candle lit.*[62]

Another Christian woman from the same region recalled making irregular visits to a local mosque for similar reasons:

> *The mosque had a memorial with plaques around it and a pine tree on top. We'd go to it every St Paraskevi Day to pray there and light a candle and do incense. Women would gather and go to it now and then. The mosque was built there because they* [the Turks] *liked to build on church foundations to make it solid.*[63]

Such accounts of communal habit suggest that Anatolians took for granted the fact that local Muslim and Christian sacred geographies coincided at important junctures. There was also the implication that infidels could be God's children, and that 'correct' faith was not absolutely necessary for receiving God's grace.

Sources of holy water (*agiasma*), which were pervasive in Ottoman Anatolia and the Balkans, were also important interfaith junctures.[64] Although regarded as marginal zones that were often haunted by *neraides*, there were specific water sources known for their miracle-working powers, and each religious community paid homage to these sites. Persephone Tsotridou of Kouvouklia recalled the existence of an *agiasma* source in a nearby village, where the inhabitants had once been Christians, but had long since converted to Islam:

> There was a Turkish village named Göbelye, where there was the agiasma of the Holy Virgin (Panagia). It was a Greek village that became turkified, but the agiasma was still there. The locals continue to use it. Our girls would go there on Saturdays and light a candle at the spot. Turkish women did the same.[65]

St George and Hıdırellez

The convergence of sacred geographies was facilitated by the fact that Muslims and Orthodox Christians each enjoyed a similar level of latitude when it came to shaping their sacred environments. *Tekke*s and saint cults were functions of popular piety and were created at the local level. Muslim popular cults could in fact emerge more quickly because no official endorsement or input was required. As Hasluck put it: 'The Turk is quite at liberty to choose or even invent the patron of a mountain or spring or build a tomb...' He believed that Muslim saint cults reflected popular piety at its purest, for unlike most Christian saints, 'the cult of the Turkish saints is purely popular in origin and development'.[66] Lucy Garnett gave a sense of the process of a communally authorized beatification in a story she heard regarding a new cult linked to a mystic in Cavalla [Kavala]. The sheikh astonished his followers by predicting his own death with uncanny precision: on the appointed day he lay in his tomb and, despite appearing in good health, passed away:

The fame of his holy life and the circumstances of his death soon became widely known in the neighbourhood; the devout watchers did not fail to see supernatural lights hovering over his grave; and before long miracles of healing were reported to have been performed at the shrine of the Sheikh of Cavalla.[67]

As was typical of saints, the 'Skeikh of Cavalla' when alive had been capable of paranormal powers and continued to dispense miracles to pilgrims long after his death. His *türbe* became a site of pilgrimage.

Aside from their focus on tombs and the absence of *official* interest, saint cults in local Muslim cultures were not much different from Christian ones, for apart from having achieved unity with God and dispensing divine wisdom, saints in both traditions continued to influence temporal matters long after death. And there was enough correspondence to allow certain saints to be conflated and shared. The linkage made between the most popular Christian saint, St George, and the most popular Muslim saint, Hıdırellez, represents a striking convergence of the two faiths.[68] Western observers assumed that the cults of St George and Hıdırellez had been amalgamated, or that Muslims had simply adopted the Christian St George. Another notable pairing was St Dimitrios and Kasim. In the oral testimonies, refugees frequently drew a connection between these respective pairings,[69] and of relevance here is the fact that each pairing was (and continued to be) celebrated on days that marked seasonal change: St George/Hıdırellez (6 May) announced the beginning of spring, while Kasim and St Dimitrios marked the beginning of the colder months.[70]

The historical reasons why St George was linked to Hıdırellez is a matter of speculation, although Hasluck usefully showed that Hıdırellez was always considered a higher grade of saint who catered to a range of important religious needs, and that in Anatolia his association with St George (and with the Prophet Elijah) pre-dates the Ottomans. Hasluck further notes that all Muslim sects revered him:

Accepted as a saint by orthodox Sunni Mohammedans, he seems to have been deliberately exploited by the heterodox Shia sects of Syria, Mesopotamia, Asia Minor, and Albania – that is, by the Nosairi, the Yezidi, the Kizilbash, and the Bektashi – for the purposes of their propaganda amongst the non-Mohammedan populations. For the Syrian, Greek, and Albanian Christians Khidr is identical with Elias and S. George.[71]

To this day, many Turks regard St George as a manifestation of Hıdırellez. On the island of Büyükada near Istanbul, where a famous monastery continues to function, Turkish pilgrims visit the church annually in vast numbers.[72] Not all Ottoman Muslims, however, included church visits as part of the day's celebrations. In places like Aphisia in the South Marmara region, and Omarkölü near Samsun, interest was limited to the after-church festivities.[73] At Kasaba, Anna Hatzisotiriou claimed that although Muslims did not attend church, they believed that the festival itself could be a source of miracles:

> They'd pay their respects to St George not by going to church but by having a good time [at the festival]. Workers, judges, lots of people came. We'd see them passing by our window. They called him Hıdırellez. They would say that he was their saint. Where did THEY find him? They'd come to St Anastasia celebrations too. When they'd arrive the bells would toll. They'd then gather: the mute, the insane, and miracle cures would make them better. You should have seen the gifts they brought with them: olives, oil, and cheeses. On Good Friday the Turks would gather before the Epitaph. They'd remove the fez when it passed. For days before they'd ask: Where do you keep the beautiful candles?[74]

Such cases of interfaith interest in saints and shrines were hardly unique to Ottoman Anatolia and the Balkans. Westerners also noted the preponderance of such interactions in the Levant—Hasluck claimed that the identification of 'Khdir' (Hıdırellez) with St George was even greater in Syria. As the anthropologist Glen Bowman has shown regarding interactions at 'mixed shrines' in present-day Palestine and the Former Yugolsav Republic of Macedonia, Muslims and Christians consciously play down their religious identities and instead focused on their bonds, for 'The focus of their interest...seemed for the most part to be the pleasure of communal mixing per se.'[75]

For the refugees, this culture of religious engagement was recalled nostalgically because it evoked the spirit of intercommunality, but there was also a purely religious reason. For the Romioi also believed they had led more pious lives in Anatolia, and the fact that the Turks did so as well was no coincidence. While living side by side, the two communities believed they lived closer to God. The explanation given by the refugees was that in those days, people had deeper faith.

Faith and substance

In some senses the supernatural realm as imagined in Anatolian popular thought bore some resemblance to that of pagan Classical Greece, where gods were capricious, petulant, and malicious. In chapters entitled 'Chris-

tian Sanctuaries frequented by Moslems' and 'Mohammedan Sanctuaries
frequented by Christians', Hasluck makes the observation that for Muslims
'Christian saints, like Christian magic, have power and may be offended or
placated', and that people were ready to believe the power of any holy
shrine so long as it was a source of miracles.[76] In such cases, argues Hasluck,
'the attraction of healing miracles goes far to overcome all scruples, and
Greek no less than Turk admits the idea that, if his own saints fail him, an
alien may be invoked.'[77]

However, Hasluck has also pointed out elsewhere that there was more to
local belief than mere instrumental need. Ordinary people also wrangled
with theological questions, and it mattered that their ideas and practices had
a rationale. As historian Stuart Schwartz has shown in his study of early
modern Spain, Portugal, and the New World, where the Inquisition supervised religious conformity, ordinary people were often charged with committing the error of relativism and other offences that involved questioning
official dogma through reason. Despite official intolerance of religious difference, many humble Catholics thought it unreasonable that only those
who followed Church strictures would be saved. They thus claimed that the
grace of God surely extended to good people who happened not to be
Catholic. Much of this deliberation had to do with so many Spanish subjects
being converts or the children of converts, and to do with encounters with
new peoples and faiths in the New World. 'All can be saved', was the
adage.[78]

Given their proximity to and familiarity with other peoples, the Romioi
could also appreciate that pious people existed within other faiths. In the
transcripts the refugees sometimes claimed that their Muslim neighbours
were 'blessed' people (*evlogimeni*), whose conduct in life was surely pleasing
to God, and who often demonstrated greater piety than Christians. 'They
were blessed the Turks', asserted Sofia Lazaridou from Pontus: 'They were
people of God.'[79] When it came to considering who counted as children of
God, therefore, many refugees emphasized the importance of faith (*pisti*). As
the saints clearly demonstrated, unequivocal belief opened a direct relationship with God. Ritual practice was of no account unless it was underscored
by faith.

Turks with deep faith could therefore access the blessings and benefits
that God, Jesus, the Virgin Mary, and the saints could offer. Muslim women
in particular were praised for their unerring faith. There is very little in the
oral transcripts on Muslim women, except when the refugees turned to the

issue of miracles and belief. Interviewees recall Muslim women approaching Christian sacra and successfully attaining cures for their sick children because of their absolute belief that a cure could be procured. The following story related by Avgerinos Spanopoulos was typical:

> I recall there was one time when the daughter of our Turkish neighbour was seriously ill and was taken by her mother to the monastery. She was sprinkled with holy water of Ai Yanni [St John] and she became well: we saw this with our own eyes![80]

The power of pure faith is addressed more directly in the following anecdote from the testimony of Tassos Giannaris of Nea Phokies (Yenifoça) who tells the story of a woman who was tricked into thinking she had been given holy water:

> Around town were numerous chapels, all of which were the venue for celebration on saints' days. One particular chapel had two springs, and women who could not express milk were sent there and drank its holy water and milk came immediately. One Turkish woman didn't have milk and asked one of our people: 'Why don't you get me some holy water so I can drink?' The child set off but on the way he came across someone from Phokies who told him not to bother, and to just give her some water from the village well. The child took the water to the woman, and yet the miracle still happened![81]

The woman had her miracle cure because of the power of belief. More routinely, Muslims sought out priests so they might 'read over' their sick, although in the following case the interviewee was careful to disclaim any suggestion of reciprocity:

> We'd regularly lend farm tools to Turks in other villages. We had few religious connections, as we were so different. Yet they believed in the power of our religion. They came to receive Bible readings from the priest for their sick. We never went to a hodja.[82]

Giorgos Bambourakis claimed that Turkish women continued to believe in the power of Orthodox sacra long after the Romioi had been expelled from Anatolia. When he returned to visit decades later, he claimed that the local women continued to place their trust in miracle-working chapels:

> I recently returned to the chapel [St John Vatatzis], and found a candle lit. Turkish women said that they don't take their children to doctors but take them instead to the chapel to get well.[83]

Although such stories were often meant to prove the power of Orthodox faith and its superiority to Islam, the more substantive point tended to be about the power of belief per se. And on this matter, Muslims and Christians were of the same view. The mystical traditions of each faith emphasized spiritual connection with God without reference to doctrine, 'correct' ritual, and sacred material (texts, churches, mosques, shrines). In both cases, saints were people of pure faith. Their lives demonstrated that their pure faith bestowed on them the power of prophecy, miracles, and other paranormal feats.

The end of sacred time

Pure faith therefore had the potential to make difference superfluous. The Romioi could appreciate the spiritual resolve of Muslim women and pious Muslim men, and see them as 'people of God'. It was yet another reason for arguing that the Romioi and the Turks were compatible peoples.

But as with all other aspects of intercommunal living in Anatolia, religious connections were suspended with the Balkan Wars. News of Muslim communities being persecuted by Balkan Christian armies changed the political and social climate within Constantinople and western Anatolia completely. It quickly became apparent to Muslims and Christians that intercommunal living was in conflict with the new Ottoman vision of society, and as the violence continued, the chances of resuming the old ways of relating became increasingly difficult.

5

Catastrophes

Nationalism and the War Years (1908–22)

At the Smyrna disaster I was with my parents on the harbour at Punta. I was dragged from their arms. And I was left behind in Turkey, a prisoner.

It was midday when I was taken away with the others. Night fell and the patrols were still bringing men to the barracks. Near midnight the guards came in. We were crammed up against one another and they were hitting us right and left with sticks, kicking those of us who were sitting on the ground, our knees drawn up. Then they picked out as many as they wanted and led them away, cursing us as they went.

We were scared they'd do away with us all.

One of the clerks, who had his office beside the door, heard our pitiful words and beckoned us to come to him.

'The next time they come and start calling out, stay at the back', he said. 'But not a word to anyone.'

From that night on, they took people from the barrack rooms every night. When we heard the gunfire from Kadife Kalesi we said to each other, 'It's firing practice'.

After days spent in fear, an officer came with forty soldiers and took charge of us. They took us into the yard and separated us from the civilians. That's when I saw my brother. They put us in lines of four and ordered us to kneel. So they could count us.

The officer, who was mounted on his horse, looked us over and said, 'I'll see to it that your seed is wiped out!'

Then he gave the order to march.

There must have been two thousand men in our column.

They marched us straight into the marketplace. A Turkish mob that was waiting there like a horde, fell on us. From all sides they threw tables, chairs, glasses— whatever they could lay their hands on. There were European sailors with them in the coffee houses and they were looking on for a bit of fun.

When we reached Basmahane a hafiz, a reciter of the Koran, came out and stood in front of us. He looked at us:

'Allah! Allah! What's going on here!' he called out to the asker aga, the officer in command. The officer stopped.

'Captain, over here', he called again.

Clip, clop. The captain's horse went over. The captain saluted him.

'Is this what our Book says?' the hafiz asked him.

The captain saluted him again.

And we passed again before them in lines.[1]

The opening passage of Stratis Doukas' *Istoria enos Echmalotou* presents us with an Anatolian world that has been turned upside down, and one that bore no resemblance to that discussed in the previous chapters of this book. The setting is the immediate aftermath of the Greek–Turkish War, the autumn of 1922. Turkish Nationalist troops have claimed control of those regions of Anatolia that had been occupied by the Greek army. Following the Battle of Dumlupınar in late August 1922, the demoralized Greek troops fled to the coast, leaving a path of destruction in their wake. Villages were torched, and Muslim civilians caught in their path were killed or maltreated. By that stage, relations between the Muslim and Rum population had long since broken down, but the exceedingly barbarous behaviour of the retreating Greek troops meant that the prospects of reconciliation now seemed virtually impossible. Neither the Turkish Nationalists nor the average Anatolian Muslims were prepared to countenance the idea. Once the last of the Greek troops had been evacuated from Anatolian shores, the surviving Romioi were to be expelled. The latter not only had to pay for the sins of the Greek occupation but also had to account for their collaboration with the invaders. The narrator of Doukas' story is a Romios, one of thousands of young men who had enlisted with the Greek occupiers, and who were now treated as traitors.[2]

In *Istoria enos Echmalotou*, Muslims and Rum appear to have become pure communal actors. Identity boundaries are such that the only meaningful sort of engagement involves violence. For the Turks, 1922 marks the beginning of 'national' time and of a monocultural Turkish future. The Turkish officer vows menacingly to extinguish any trace of the Rum presence in Anatolia, while ordinary Muslims who have been brutalized and impoverished by war and Greek persecution, attack the POWs in revenge. It now appears that Muslims are ready to become 'Turks', much as the Rum seem to have already become 'Greeks'. There are also indications in Doukas' story, however, that nationalism's victory is not complete. The Turkish clerk secretly advises the Greek prisoners on how they might survive, and there is also the *hafiz*, the ethically autonomous figure who remains true to his faith and demands that the POWs be treated as any of God's children. The officer does not act on the demand, but he does not dispute the *hafiz*'s moral authority.

For the narrator, the Turks are not evil. The times have made them barbarous, while Greek barbarity played a determining role in provoking this

Turkish behaviour. Ethnic antagonism is made comprehensible but it is not dismissed as a function of culture. Doukas dedicates the fifth edition of his book to the 'common ordeals of peoples' (Αφιερωνεταί στα κοινά μαρτύρια των λαών),[3] suggesting that the root cause of evil does not lie with 'the people': the cycle of violence that culminated in the torching of Smyrna and the hellish captivity experienced by Doukas' protagonist was not started and perpetuated by 'peoples' (λαοί).

Kosmas Politis was more pointed about who was responsible. In his *Stou-Hatzifrangkou*, set during Smyrna's halcyon years at the very beginning of the century, and yet when memories of recent Greek–Turkish wars of the late nineteenth century are still fresh and cause for reflection, Reis effendi and Papa Nikolas discuss politics. As the narghile-puffing Turk laments the loss of his homeland in Thessaly and how the Greeks have obliterated all trace of centuries of Muslim life, the Greek tells him that these national/ethnic wars are sadly a matter of fate. In the same breath, however, the priest admits fate has nothing to do with it:

> Reis effendi, for all that the fault lies with the borders and with religion. We are all humans. God is one, regardless of who his prophet might be. And when it suits them, the great ones get along.[4]

The political message of the last sentence is deeply subversive. The priest first offers ideology, but it is immediately conceded to be false. The 'fatality' of the nation and national struggle is acknowledged as a deception.[5] As with other celebrated 'Asia Minor' writers, Politis read the Greek–Turkish War as an imperialist struggle, a position that was largely informed by Marxism and the politically polarized atmosphere of the middle decades of twentieth-century Greece. It was the blood of ordinary people that paid for the wars perpetrated by elites, who were motived by their own economic and political reasons. Outside of historiography, there was considerable agreement on this point, even among non-leftists. The refugees were certainly in common agreement. The general view among them was that the political elites were responsible for the violence and the destruction of Asia Minor. The Young Turks and the Kemalists were nearly always cited, while some also indicted the Great Powers, especially Germany.[6] Paraskevi Tsaloglou of Kayseri claimed the Armenian Genocide was plotted by the Ottoman Empire's domineering ally: 'It was the finger [conniving influence] of Germany that was responsible, so the Germans could seize Armenian lands and so they could receive loans to pay for their war.'[7] Careful not to appear unpatriotic, the refugees were less vehement in their criticisms of the role of the Greek state.

'Ethnic' conflict

Before discussing the 'long war' (1912–22), as historians of Turkey sometimes describe it, some clarification is needed regarding the concept of ethnic conflict, and especially the issue of responsibility. After all, were not the 'oppressed peoples' mentioned in Doukas' dedication involved in the violence? Did not Doukas himself enlist and join the imperialist war?[8]

It is certainly the case that ordinary Anatolians did participate in the violence, and that animosities between Christians and Muslims did indeed arise soon after the Balkan Wars. The wars that raged between 1912 and 1922 undoubtedly fed off certain pre-existing tensions, but there is little to suggest that ethnicity was the energizing force that underlay the entire crisis, as anthropologist Andrei Simić has claimed of the Yugoslav crisis of the 1990s.[9] When discussing such crises, pundits tend to see 'ethnic' violence as revelatory rather than constitutive, and see animosities as having been 'exposed' rather than created. Samuel Huntington's 'Clash of Civilizations' thesis is but the extreme version of this very commonplace approach, but even within academically respectable debates on genocide, ethnic cleansing, and ethnic/religious conflict one can find scholars falling for the intuitively resonant and symbolically efficient culturalist explanation.[10] The problems with it are many, including the fact that using an ethnic category as the determining cause of ethnic violence makes causal analysis virtually unnecessary. The complex origins of conflicts are reduced to being the function of difference.

Another effect is to make ordinary people, the humble Greek, Turk, Serb, Croat, Bosnian, Kosovar, etc., as culpable for the 'ethnic' violence as their political elites and paramilitary elites. If ethnic conflict is about ethnic groups and their incompatibilities, then Anatolia's elderly people, children, women, and humble menfolk, who simply tried to live their everyday lives as best they could, people who were essentially subaltern, were authors of their own destruction. What can be obscured by the blind use of ethnic categories is the question of who perpetrates the violence. One can indeed argue that the 'ethnic' violence of that period cannot be characterized as 'communal violence', namely the variety that sees villages mobilized against other villages, neighbours against neighbours, where old friends suddenly become murderous assailants. If anything, the violence is usually anti-civilian. Armed groups brutalize, kill, and drive away the unarmed civilians who are linked to the enemy. As the refugees often claimed, it was 'outsiders', namely foreign troops, paramilitaries, nationalists, refugees, and political authorities, who destroyed their *patrides*. It was not their neighbours.

Seeing such 'ethnic' conflicts as struggles between uniform and bounded objects (*the* Greeks and *the* Turks) is yet another instance where a category of practice is confused with one of analysis.[11] In working with these false models of reality, the effect usually is to reduce the often complex sources of tension within society to mere questions of intolerance.[12] To the victims of ethnic conflict and ethnic cleansing, however, unearthing the essential causes was more than an academic exercise. For those whose lives were destroyed, who lost family, homes and communities, and who experienced traumas and chronic destitution, causality was vital for settling questions of justice and accountability. It was also important for combatting the imputation that 'peoples' should be lumped with the responsibility of having destroyed their own homelands. Ordinary Anatolian Christians were adamant that neither they, nor their Turkish neighbours, caused the breakdown of intercommunality and the catastrophe that befell the Anatolian world.

Of course, for ordinary Muslims and Christians, Turks and Greeks, ethnicity *was* a category of 'practice' that helped them make sense of the breakdown of the Ottoman multiethnic order. Thus Turks were often critical of the Romioi for rejecting intercommunality and the generous state offer of full citizenship following the Young Turk Revolution in 1908. The key accusation levelled later against the Romioi was that they collaborated with the empire's enemies during the Balkan Wars, the First World War, and during the Turkish War of Independence.[13] 'The Romioi' are read here as a single entity. It is certainly true that Pontic Greek paramilitaries did fight with the Russians, while Rum males enlisted with the Greek army and were thought to have taken part in the outrages committed against Muslims. For Ali Onay, a Cretan Muslim resettled in the Aegean coastal town of Ayvalık, the Romioi were disappointing because they succumbed to the inducements of nationalism, and thereby sacrificed their neighbours in the bargain:

> *This was sad because Christians and Muslims had lived together for four hundred years ... Unfortunately the Rums forgot the tradition of Christian-Muslim friendship*

after 1919. Before the Greek Army came to Anatolia, the Rums were not nationalists, they were Christians who were loyal Ottomans. But when the Greek army came here and did terrible things to the Muslim community, and the Rums collaborated with them, then it was all over. If only those terrible things hadn't happened, the Rums would still be living here now.[14]

Claims of Rum disloyalty during the Greek–Turkish War of 1919–22 gave the Kemalist government a pretext for mass expulsion on security grounds, while also giving ordinary Muslims a moral justification for the removal of 'bad' neighbours. It also gave them their own excuse for adopting nationalism. Having betrayed the intercommunal compact, the Romioi (and the Armenians) gave the Muslims no choice but to become nationalists themselves. Ottoman benevolence was misplaced, as Christians betrayed the empire when given the chance, thus revealing their true selves. Muslims emerged from the war years as the victims of Christian violence, but also as people who remained faithful to the principles of intercommunality, and thereby emerged with their moral credibility intact.[15]

The Romioi, for their part, always blamed the Turkish nationalists, the Young Turks, and the Kemalists (Turkish Nationalists) for corrupting the good Muslims of Anatolia and for destroying Ottoman society. And while Greek refugees rarely questioned the moral standing of Anatolian Muslims, they could agree on the malign influence of nationalism per se. Well before 1908, both communities recognized that calls for exclusive national homelands meant war and ethnic cleansing, since recent precedents had been set in the Balkans and the Caucasus. Although Greek nationalism in Anatolia did appeal to the urban middle classes, these people were also aware that a secessionist agenda like that pursued by Armenian nationalist groups could destroy the community. As Çağlar Keyder put it, 'most Ottoman Greeks seem to have realized that the dispersal of their population made territorial annexation by Greece problematic',[16] while the humiliating military debacle in 1897 confirmed that the Greek kingdom did not have the wherewithal to challenge the Ottoman Empire.[17]

Muslim Cretans: portents of the nation

A different situation and a very useful one for comparative purposes obtained on the island of Crete. When it was conquered in the mid-seventeenth century from the Venetians, a sizeable proportion of the largely Orthodox population converted to Islam, and for centuries the normal forms of communal coexistence applied between these very familiar groups, although tensions became more apparent during the course of the nineteenth century. While roughly equal in size in 1800, Muslim numbers thereafter began to shrink, and by the 1890s the Muslims, known in Greek as *Tourkokritiki* or *Tourkokrites*, formed about 30 per cent of the population. The causes of Muslim population decline are many, but the principal reasons included radical changes to land laws, to military service requirements, the reduction of Muslim access to administrative posts, and Christian land purchases.[18] As Christians and their notables increased their holdings, and armed Christian groups extended their influence in the countryside, Muslims withdrew to the towns. Imperial decline had a profound influence on the estrangement of Cretan Christians and Muslims. Given the island's relative distance from the Ottoman mainland, and the empire's diminishing international standing, Christian leaders became increasingly confident in their claims for more power and autonomy. The Greek revolt of 1821 left the island in ruins, and by the end of the century there had been eight more rebellions that saw Christians pitted against the Ottoman state and local Muslims. These conflicts inevitably drew international attention and saw various power-sharing arrangements imposed, including an elected assembly (1868). One of the effects of this assembly, where notables aired grievances over power inequities and other communal disputes, was the further politicization of the population.[19]

While Muslims remained stolidly loyal to the Sultan, Christian leaders were manoeuvring to secure secession from the empire and unification with Greece. By the 1890s, Christian and Muslim paramilitaries were terrorizing the countryside and sharpening communal divisions. The 1897 rebellion precipitated a war between Greece and the Ottomans, and while the former was roundly defeated, the Great Powers nevertheless determined that Crete should be autonomous, albeit under Ottoman sovereignty. Muslims greeted the prospect of Christian domination with great trepidation, given that Christian leaders often made it clear that the next step was unification with Greece whenever the next political opportunity presented itself.

During the 1897 conflict rural Muslims had been driven from their ancestral homes in the countryside and restricted to the main towns.[20] Fearing for their future, many Muslims migrated to Anatolia. More expatriations followed the political disturbances of 1908 and 1909, and especially after 1912, when the island was annexed by Greece. The remnants of the Muslim community were transferred under the terms of the Treaty of Lausanne.

In Anatolia, Cretan resentment was channelled towards the local Christians, who in turn described these Cretan Muslims as the most implacably hostile Turks.[21] The author of a useful study of Anatolia's human geography, Pantelis Kontogiannis, noted at the time that, 'during the Christian deportations and expulsions just before the First World War, and indeed during that war, the Cretan Turks were the most merciless and aggressive persecutors of the Greeks'.[22] The noted feminist and writer Halide Edib offered confirmation from a Turkish perspective:

> No Moslem hates the Greek as the Cretan. Having suffered from the Greek oppression in Crete and having seen frequent Moslem massacres, the Cretan is bitter against the Greek as the Armenian is against the Turk.[23]

The Cretans settled along Anatolia's Aegean and Mediterranean coastal areas, and it appears that local Muslims and Christians initially closed ranks against these outsiders. The Cretans were not Turkish-speakers and they were widely viewed as troublemakers. One Euripides Martoglou recalled that they were likened to infidels:

> The locals [Anatolian Turks] hated the Cretans. They would not give them their daughters in marriage or jobs, and they did not communicate with them. They called them giavour [gâvur, infidel] because they spoke Greek. The giavourides left and then came worse giavourides![24]

However, the mere presence of these displaced peoples, the victims of a failed intercommunal order, was bound to have an unsettling effect. Most troubling was the fact that the Cretans talked politics, which meant the politics of nationalism. The Cretan habit of talking incessantly about political affairs was both irritating and disconcerting:

> They were criticized for constantly talking about politics. They were accused of doing nothing else, as if they had nothing else to do. They did this from morning through to night. Of course, they were constantly talking about the politics of Greece.[25]

Communal accommodation required active social engagement as well as political silences. In merely talking politics the Cretans were refusing to observe an important social convention of communal coexistence that required the studied avoidance of contentious subjects that might draw too much attention to differences. The Cretans, however, had no interest in intercommunal accommodation; their aim was to awaken their Muslim brethren to the kind of political realities that Muslims were facing elsewhere. Cretan leaders often promoted punitive action against the Romioi in retaliation for Greek nationalist activities on Crete.[26] They were the most ardent supporters of state-orchestrated boycotts of Rum businesses in 1909, which were to be repeated with much more success after the Balkan Wars. Along with other displaced Muslims, particularly the Macedonian Turks who essentially founded the Turkish nationalist movement, the Cretan Muslims were among the earliest foot soldiers of Turkish nationalism. An interviewee from Menderes riverine region, where much of the Muslim Cretan population was resettled, believed that these 'bad' Turks became useful to the state from 1912 when it began to persecute the Christian population:

> Before the Cretan Turks came we got on very, very well with the local Turks. Whenever we went to the Turkish villages we would be given cheese pies. Although it was obvious that the Cretan Turks wanted to get rid of us, and it was also obvious to us that they were being encouraged by the government.[27]

The Romioi read this Cretan threat by using the idiom of communal values and especially cultural stereotypes. Thus the Cretan Muslims were typecast as very different in character to the humble Anatolian Turks, in that they were shrewd, cunning, and unfriendly. They were prone to zealotry and thus were unsuitable partners in any communal arrangement. For such reasons, claimed many interviewees, Muslim Anatolians initially rejected these cantankerous outsiders, but the 'bad' Turks did eventually manage to corrupt the 'good' ones.[28] Although the Anatolian Muslims were said to have preferred the familiar Romioi to the Cretans, their *agathotita* or humble innocence also meant that they were highly impressionable and vulnerable to manipulation. In Bodrum, often the first port of call for Muslims fleeing Crete, the newcomers were treated with great suspicion, and yet as Kostas Halkitis claimed, the interlopers eventually drew the locals to their side:

> In the beginning the [local] Turks didn't accept them. They could not even tolerate their company... They [the Cretans] were very shrewd, however, and slowly, slowly they prevailed upon our innocent Turks and influenced them. They were given the best jobs [as state employees].[29]

After the First Balkan War, the Balkan Muslims would also play the role of anti-Rum bête noire. Although consisting of a range of cultural groups, the Muslims of the central Balkans, particularly those in the countryside, were also affected by the armed paramilitary struggles of rival Orthodox Christian groups (Greek, Bulgarian, IMRO), but were shocked by the sudden and conclusive victories of Serb, Bulgarian, Montenegrin, and Greek armies. Much more numerous than the Cretans, the Balkan Muslim refugees inevitably made a far greater political impact on Anatolian society:

> We lived together in a brotherly fashion with the Turks until 1912. With the Balkans Wars and the exodus from Macedonia came the haters. They were anti-Greek. So too were the Cretan Turks.[30]

> The Turks did not pressure us. We loved them, they loved us. But the Macedonian Turks came through here and they were fanatics and they spoiled them [tous halasane].[31]

> Until the Hurriet we enjoyed a blessed life with the Turks. Then came the refugees from Crete and Bulgaria. They were fanaticized against Greeks, and every so often they propagandized the locals to hate us.[32]

> Then came the Pomaks, Turkish refugees from Bulgaria, beastly people . . .[33]

These newcomers were therefore seen as having corrupted the Anatolian Turks by politicizing them. In Greek refugee memory, the fanatically aggressive and anti-Christian refugee served as a foil to the pious and humble Anatolian Turk. It was this ardently hostile 'foreign' Turk, who was not unlike the irremediably villainous 'Turk' of Greek nationalist lore, who destroyed Anatolia.

However, the refugees were not captive to such crude stereotypes. The interviews show that they were well aware that the Muslim Cretans had been victims of nationalist politics, and that traumas perpetrated against them by other Romioi had made them 'bad' Turks. As Nikolas Diakanis pointed out quite evocatively, Muslim hostility was itself a product of abject violence and human suffering:

> The Turks were good people. Only after 1912 did our relations with them suffer, for the Turkish refugees from Macedonia and Crete would say 'they've pushed us out'. They'd say [to the Anatolian Turk], 'hey you. You have THESE people as your "brothers"? Do you realize what the Greek army did to us?'[34]

Diakanis' words do not necessarily shift the blame for the cycle of violence onto the Romioi and the Greeks, but like most interviewees he recognizes the circumstances that create communal conflicts. The Anatolian Turks might have been 'good people', but under certain conditions many among them would also begin to behave as the Cretans and Balkan Turks.

Recent studies conducted among Turkey's Cretan Muslims also confirm that they too were capable of reading history without a nationalist ideological frame, despite a reputation for waving 'the Turkish flag more enthusiastically than many others'. In an insightful work on the Greek–Turkish population exchange that draws mainly on Turkish popular memory, Bruce Clark notes how the Cretans of Ayvalık praise Kemal for having 'saved the Greeks from the Turks, and Turks from the Greeks', and who therefore give the impression that they completely endorse the remaking of the Ottoman world into ethnically exclusive nation-states.[35] As with the progeny of other non-Anatolians, however, the Cretans refused to yield to many of the demands of Turkish nationalism. After all, the Greek language was retained until relatively recently as the vernacular within Cretan households, having overcome a great deal of pressure to desist and speak only Turkish—all non-Turkish-speaking minorities were targeted during the early Republic by an oppressive 'Citizen Speak Turkish' campaign. The dialect, which is simply described as 'Cretan' (*Kritika*), survived, although nowadays it has all but disappeared due to natural attrition.[36] Today, one can also see maps of Crete on the walls of shops owned by Cretans, who often speak nostalgically of the 'homeland'. In such ways they refused to give themselves completely to Turkish nationalism. As Clark points out, they 'are not supposed to feel nostalgia for their homeland, or for its Christian inhabitants, yet they do'.[37]

The implications of such transgressions are significant. In mediating the demands of Turkish national culture with the need to retain emotional ties with the lost homeland and even its Christian inhabitants, the Cretan Muslims developed an identity based on antithetical values that were nevertheless resonant and meaningful.[38] This *disemic* condition, where the formal national identity was in permanent tension with communal Cretan identity, limited the cultural purchase of nationalism, denying it, for example, exclusive claim to the term *homeland* (*patrida, anavatan*). As for the other dislocated communities, the authentic *patrida* of the Cretan Muslim lay outside the nation, and would in all likelihood remain an absence. While this authentic *patrida* has been lost, the displaced and their progeny have been known to do pilgrimage to these lost homelands in order to retain at least some familiarity with them. Such nostalgia-based traditions have problematized the nation-building project in that they defy the nation's capacity to gloss over the violence that went into its making. Clark notes that for the otherwise 'flag-waving' Muslim Cretans, Turkish nationalism was essentially a necessary evil, something they were forced to take up in reaction to Greek nationalism.[39]

The ambivalent meanings of post-Ottoman refugee traditions also have implications regarding the disintegration of the empire. If Muslim Cretans accuse their former Orthodox Cretan *patriotes* of forgetting the *patrida* and succumbing to political manipulation, then from where did these divisive political influences emanate? What was producing the kinds of conditions that pitted Christian against Muslim, Muslim against Christian? Whose project was it to remove peoples from their homelands? The oral traditions of all displaced groups, whether Armenian, Muslim or Orthodox, Anatolian, Macedonian, Cretan, Rum, or Russian Muslim refugees, suggest that the wars and political turmoil that saw peoples removed from their homelands were contrivances of high politics. If the 'great ones' get along 'when it suits them', as the priest of Politis' *Stou Hatzifrangkou* implies, then it is the great ones who are the authors of wars and catastrophes. Deep down, therefore, cultural difference was understood to be a ruse employed by the powerful in a much larger power play.

'We lived well until "Freedom" (*Hürriyet*)', 1908–12

Implicitly condemning European-born nationalism, they often say that it was the Great Powers who brought the hatred, the 'stupid politicians' who made them hate one another.[40]

According to Yale scholar Tolga Köker, himself the progeny of refugees from Macedonia, this bottom-up critique of political elite culpability is the commonplace discourse one hears among 'Balkan immigrants to Turkey from Albania, Bulgaria, Greece, the former Yugoslavia, as well as among Turkish Cypriots'.[41] Köker presents these discourses to support his damming appraisal of the effects of forced population transfers and the engineering of culturally coherent states, which he describes as among the many failures of modernity. Ethnographic studies conducted in Greece and the oral testimonies collected at the Centre for Asia Minor Studies show that the refugees from Anatolia made precisely the same claim.[42] Every survivor of 'the Catastrophe' believed in their bones that they were victims of high politics, of nefarious political programmes hatched within the centres of power. The question that a historian might wish to ask is: what can these 'feelings' tell us about the history of the period and its larger questions? What light might such popular subjectivities shed on twentieth-century Europe's first great phase of ethnic cleansing and mass killings?

The traumatic experiences that were detailed in the oral transcripts were conveyed with reference to what anthropologist Anna Tsing has labelled 'global positioning', as Anatolian refugees framed their personal travails in reference to their own political marginality.[43] While the conceptual tools employed to convey local meanings (social idioms, stereotypes) might give the impression of a world view that is 'mythical' and symbolic rather than realistic and practical, as David E. Sutton has argued, ground-level perspectives are privy to the pointed or frayed end points of political power. Such perspectives can reveal truths about the local effects of power structures that the more educated pundits recognize much later (if ever).[44] In the case of Ottoman Anatolia, they offer qualitative assessments of the ground-level effects of state power and interstate power play, and the extent to which these effects politicized, nationalized, and thereby modernized the people affected. It is at the everyday level where the practical outcomes of political visions can often be seen.

The remaining sections of this chapter deal with the nexus between high politics and the everyday, and how the deterioration of the Ottoman Empire's international position and its ultimate collapse affected relations at the communal level. Ordinary Ottomans were well aware that their welfare was linked inexorably to what diplomats and historians once called 'The Eastern Question' of international relations, the protracted international struggle over the fate and ultimate dismemberment of the Ottoman Empire. All subjects had long understood that the empire was weak and vulnerable to the machinations of more powerful states and their clients (i.e. Italy, Greece, Serbia, and Bulgaria). What happened at the international level had major knock-on effects within the empire, which affected the way the state related to its Christians. While the arrival of displaced peoples in Anatolia (i.e. Cretans) was a mere portent of the politicization of culture, the advent of the Young Turk regime brought about its inception. Within a few years, the very future of 'minorities' became a matter of political negotiation, with Armenians and Romioi becoming objects of an increasingly hostile state. All these developments were beyond the control of most Ottoman subjects, each reaffirming a sense of fatalism associated with being the periphery of a periphery.

This sudden change in fortune is one important reason why the interviewees presented the preceding Hamidian era as the Ottoman golden
years. 'The greatest period of Christianity', as Antonis and Elisavet Georgiadis put it, 'was the age of Hamid.' Another reason for nostalgia for the
reign of Sultan Abdülhamid was that international developments could
actually bring blessings to the periphery. Antonis and Elisavet Georgiadis,
along with every other Rum subject, were well aware of the significance of
Russian power in the region:

> We Greeks had freedoms that were not pleasing to the Turks. We were protected by
> Russia; so we could pull the beards of the Turks in the marketplace without fear of
> retribution. We infidels were the masters. We never had to go to war.

Regretting the conceited and ungracious insinuations in these words, the
couple reassured the interviewers that: 'We were not ungrateful. We loved
Hamid. We would call him "The Father of the Christians".'[45] Often the
victims of the regime's arbitrary authority—it was with Abdülhamid's assent
that thousands of Armenians were butchered between 1894 and 1896 for the
actions of secessionist rebels—Armenians and Romioi nevertheless recognized the significant benefits of certain inequities in the Ottoman system.
The capitulations and exemptions from conscription were among the chief
reasons why the Romioi wished to remain in the empire.

Most Romioi nevertheless appeared to welcome the overthrow of the
Hamidian regime, for aside from the prospect of power sharing,[46] there also
appeared genuine interest in the restoration of constitutional governance.[47]
Along with other non-Muslim groups, the Romioi were participants in a
general upsurge in civic activism, which saw the formation of numerous
political parties and the launching of 353 newspapers and magazines by
1910.[48] Non-Muslims were encouraged by the fact that they figured in
Young Turk plans for regenerating and remaking the Ottoman polity. The
historian of the Young Turks, M. Şükrü Hanioğlu, emphasizes the point that
the plans of the Committee for Unity and Progress (CUP), the political arm
of the Young Turk movement, for saving the empire from its threatened
demise involved securing the loyalty of the empire's non-Muslims.[49]
Although a form of Turkish patriotism had been influential in the making
and conduct of the CUP, many non-Turks and non-Muslims were registered among its ranks.[50]

Interviewees recalled the outpouring of public joy that was widely
attested at the time. All peoples appeared to revel in the promise of 'hürri-

yet' (liberty), of 'müsavat' (equality), 'uhuvvet' (fraternity), and 'adalet' (justice). The Muslim community at large now seemed to be open to the idea of full equality, which was not the case in the Tanzimat period:

> How could we not be happy? The Young Turks were promising many freedoms. We were embraced by Turks, and they said to us: 'we will no longer call you infidels. We are now brothers born of the same earth.'[51]

> Enver Bey and Nazli Bey had got rid of the king Hamid. At the time it was said we had become one with the Turks, that we had become brothers. There was great fanfare ... we lit torches in the villages, a 'festa' they were called. We would shout 'Yassassin Enver Bey!'[52]

> We were fine until 1908, when we were told that we were now like brothers.[53]

However, the interviewees cited these initial happy moments for ironic effect, since the celebrations augured the beginning of a long period of political crisis that eventually led to sectarian bloodshed. The initial problem centred on the meaning of Ottoman citizenship. Although deeply divided on many issues, most Greek Orthodox leaders fought to preserve communal rights, which many hoped might be guaranteed in a federated state or an electoral system of proportional representation.[54] As such the Romioi were like many subject peoples within the great multiethnic empires prior to the First World War, whose idea of nationality was articulated through calls for cultural autonomy and the preservation of corporate interests.[55] However, that contravened the spirit of the 1908 revolution, as non-Muslims were expected to concede their privileges and assume the same responsibilities as other citizens, including military service.

From the CUP's perspective, dogged recalcitrance from Rum and Armenian leaders fuelled suspicions regarding their loyalty to the state, and it was an important factor behind the CUP's eventual turn to exclusivist Turkish nationalism. This transition must also be seen within the context of chronic political instability in Constantinople and ongoing territorial losses (e.g. Libya in 1911, the Dodecanese Islands in 1912), and yet the CUP officially persisted with the idea of an inclusive polity under Turkish domination. According to Carter Findley, until 1912 the regime was still concerned about 'competitors for its subject's loyalties' and thereby showed no indication of planning ethnic cleansings.[56]

Many interviewees, however, identified the Young Turk Revolution as a dangerous development because it politicized society and posed particular challenges to the spirit of intercommunality at the local level. If community symbolizes cooperation and mutuality, politics by definition refers to the contestation of power and the accentuation of difference. With the Young Turk Revolution, community found itself pitted against the state for the first time: 'For us over there it all began with the Young Turks. Before *The-Hurriyet*,' claimed Anania Zahariadi 'as far as we can remember, we don't think we had historical events: indeed we took not much notice of the happenings of the world.' With 'freedom', however, came 'various bureaucrats, state employees, *kaimakams*, telegraph operators, secretaries, [and Muslims] from Thrace, Crete, Thessaloniki, who knew the Greek language but hated Greeks'. Under the CUP, the state began to interfere in the internal affairs of communities. As Anania explained further, before the CUP the state respected communal rights:

> *The senior figures, the* kaimakams*, the school inspectors, inspected our schools and were aware that we taught Greek history. On the holy day of the Three Hierarchs were held school performances featuring ancient heroes. In the churchyard the young danced at Easter time and shot bullets in the air, and the Turks would watch us without intervening.*[57]
>
> *After the* Hurriyet *(1908 Revolution), however, things changed. First of all they began ripping pages out of our books, pages on religious history, Greek history: The Trojan War, Alexander the Great. Then they lifted our holy history and gave us Turkish religious texts.*[58]

In its attempts to see the empire function like an integrated nation-state, with uniform laws, administration, fiscal order, and education system, the Young Turk regime had to secure Turkish as the national medium, and therefore required Rum schools to teach Turkish and desist from teaching the histories of other states—Anania's claims that the Rum children were required to read the Muslim rather than Christian religious texts is implausible. For the average Rum villager, however, such unaccustomed invasive behaviour by the state made the Young Turks appear anti-Christian:

> *The Young Turks organized the* Comitato Ittihat ve Terakki (CUP), *which was anti-Greek. They sacked our teachers because they were spreading propaganda.*[59]

Rum recalcitrance on such matters, however, tested the patience of the regime, whose ranks suspected that Christians had no intention of committing to the new order or indeed the empire. Military service was widely thought to provide the sharpest test of non-Muslim fealty, especially as the exclusion of non-Muslims from military service was the privilege that non-Muslims prized most. As Michelle Campos notes, conscription was, for the CUP, 'the marker of the limits and boundaries of Ottomanization', and non-Muslim leaders were quick to acknowledge its importance as a declaration of loyalty to the state.[60] However, Muslim families were well aware that military service was a crushing burden, since young males were taken away for many years, very poorly paid, suffered disease and malnutrition, and high mortality, given the frequent number of military conflicts.[61] For many young non-Muslim men, the call to service became an excuse to emigrate:

> After the Constitution, they wanted to conscript us. Some went in the beginning, but others escaped to Mytilene. You'd give a lira to the Turk and he'd give you a wink. In other words, the Greek escaped with Turkish awareness. A thousand escaped with that method, and set off for America... Those left behind stayed hidden because [the authorities] did their rounds, looking for deserters.[62]

> All the boys [of Söke] went missing as of 1908, 1909, 1910, so as to avoid the call up.[63]

> In 1908 all men were told they had 15 days before Christmas to have their names registered. I left for Makri [Fethiye]. Hardly anyone turned up for register. I registered at Makri.[64]

Newly constituted nations always found it difficult to make conscription a compelling duty, but whereas it was easy for state and Rum leaders to extoll the virtues of military service, the fact that Muslim desertion was also endemic suggested that disloyalty was not the only problem:

> From 1908, after the Constitution, they started the call up. Are we to be soldiers? And who returned alive among those who joined the Security Battalions? 'Lets get away!'. We'd change residence, change names, and we'd live as strangers among strangers during our time of service.[65]

For such reasons the interviewees often identified the Young Turk Revolution as the beginning of the troubles. The Romioi resented the growth of state interference, and the fact that many of the officials charged to carry out state directives were Cretan Muslims and muhacir.

In reality, the early years of CUP rule did not see dramatic changes at the local level. Aside from the threat of conscription, life for ordinary people in the localities did not change a great deal. Rum schools were still free to teach Greek, and Rum communities continued planning their new schools and churches. Intercommunal relations appeared to be unaffected. The standard social practices, of Hıdırellez/St George festivals, house visits, and wedding invitations, continued as before. All this was to change with the First Balkan War.

The Balkan Wars (1912/13) and first expulsions

On 8 October 1912 an alliance of Balkan states—Serbia, Bulgaria, Greece, and Montenegro—launched a military invasion into the last remaining Ottoman provinces in Europe. Within a few months, Ottoman forces had been defeated on several fronts. Bulgarian troops caused the greatest damage, having forced the Ottomans to retreat to a fortified ridge near the town of Çatalca, only a few kilometres west of Constantinople. The war featured a scramble for territory. The Greek army quickly seized the prized port city of Salonica, the city of St Dimitrios, while the Greek navy mopped up the rest of the Aegean island archipelago. By December, the empire had effectively been defeated, but the Bulgarians felt cheated in the division of territorial spoils, and thus a second Balkan War soon followed in June 1913 between Bulgaria and its erstwhile allies. The Ottomans seized the chance to recoup some territory, including the former medieval capital Edirne, but that only slightly mitigated what amounted to the empire's greatest modern disaster to date. Macedonia and the territories south of the Maritsa River, which included the provinces of Yanya, Monastir, Selanik and Edirne, had been core territories since the fifteenth century, and also happened to be home to a disproportionate number of CUP leaders. As such, losing the Balkan provinces was much more painful than losing Libya (1911) or the Dodecanese Islands (1912). The war also displaced some 177,000 Muslim civilians, mostly from territories seized by the Serbs and Bulgarians—the Greek government needed to assuage the fears of Muslims caught behind their lines in order to limit retaliation against Romioi in Constantinople and Anatolia.[66] Even so, the news delivered to readers in Constantinople and Smyrna by the Ottoman press told of numerous atrocities against Muslim people, while refugees streaming into the capital were also able to tell their own stories.[67]

For such reasons the First Balkan War shook the empire to its core. The mere fact that it suffered comprehensive defeat at the hands of petty Balkan kingdoms and former subject peoples made it all the more humiliating and infuriating. Of great relevance was the fact that these minor powers were Orthodox Christian states that had cultural links with the *millet-i Rum*. The Ottomans strongly suspected political links as well. On this occasion it was commonly thought that Christian recruits were to blame for the military defeats,[68] as was the belief that the Romioi had been sending money to Greece to support its war effort.[69] The mere fact that Christian Serbia,

Bulgaria, and Greece had been persecuting and evicting Muslims, however, was enough to turn Anatolian Muslim opinion generally against the local Christians. The CUP, which had lost power prior to the war, seized it again early in 1913, this time instituting a one-party dictatorship that was determined to deal once and for all with the Christian minorities. With support from the Turkish language press and patriotic organizations, the new government sought to create a secure Anatolian homeland composed overwhelmingly of loyal ethnic Turks. No longer a 'multicultural project', Ottomanism now involved the eviction of the Greek Orthodox and the Armenians. An inter-government agreement with Bulgaria in September 1913 for a limited population exchange provided an early indication that the CUP solution would involve mass evictions.[70] Talks with the Greek government about a more extensive exchange programme were afoot during the first half of 1914, although by that stage a major Christian exodus from Anatolia was already in train.[71]

Many interviewees identified the First Balkan War as the event that ruined everything (*halasane ta pramata*). Among state officials, the Turkish-language press, and Muslims in the streets, there was serious talk of ridding Anatolia of the Romioi. The initial method to induce an exodus was boycotts and job dismissals. In Bursa, for example, Rum teachers and public servants were sacked, while boycotts became progressively harsh and were forcing many businesses to close.[72] The Turkish press and patriotic movements called upon Muslims to boycott Christian businesses and employ only Muslims. The former governor of Salonica, Hüseyin Kazim Bey, argued that the boycott was really an awakening; for while the disloyal Romioi deserved to be punished, he also argued the empire needed a Muslim business sector to restore the empire's parlous financial condition.[73] While the boycotts appeared to be an expression of popular anger, they were coordinated by government officials such as Rahmi Bey in Smyrna and Nazim Bey, secretary general of the CUP.[74] The movement appeared to enjoy broad community support, but agents on the ground were ordered to enforce the boycott, and punish those who failed to observe it.[75] A Rum resident of Kios/Gemlik recalled how these 'fanatical' operatives were out in force: 'If they ever saw a Turk approaching a Greek shop to buy goods, they apprehended him and gave him a beating with sticks.'[76] The most conspicuous enforcers of the boycotts and other anti-Rum activities were Muslim Cretans and Macedonians: Rahmi Bey reported that the over enthusiastic Cretans were difficult to control.[77]

The consequences for Rum shopkeepers were devastating, but the Romioi also had to deal with political violence. The CUP regime created the *Teşkilat-i Mahsusa* or 'Special Organization', which was charged with prosecuting a terror campaign. The immediate aim was to remove the Romioi from strategically sensitive regions along the Aegean shoreline and transfer the vacated properties to Muslin refugees. The methods ranged from simple warnings of an impending pogrom to actual attacks by armed militias, which were usually composed of refugee Muslims. Chryssavgi Korakis of Bodrum recalled how most of the Rum community fled by boat to the nearby island of Kos when Muslim neighbours reported rumours of an imminent attack by armed men from deep inside Turkey. The suggestion was that the local Turks would never do such a thing.[78]

Those who refused to leave Anatolia, however, were vulnerable to militia attacks organized by the *Teşkilat-i Mahsusa*, or from roaming bandits or local roughs who could attack Rum communities with impunity. As early as April 1914, reports filed by foreign consular staff were painting a hellish picture. Particularly affected were zones deemed to be strategically sensitive, such as Thrace and the Aegean coastal region, as well as the environs of Constantinople and the South Marmara region. Rum residents of the villages and towns near the northern littoral of the Sea of Marmara, such as Rodosto (Tekirdağ), Köseilyas, and Kumbağ, were forced to take flight.[79] Between January 1914 and July 1915, over 60,000 Rum residents were removed from eastern Thrace.[80] June 1914 witnessed violent attacks by militias all along the Aegean seaboard and further inland. During the first week of June, 45,000 Greeks were reported to have fled the region of Çeşme, and another 50,000 fled Edremit, Burhaniye, Bergama, Kınık, Dikili, and Foça.[81] Hardly any Romioi were left in either Bergama or Kınık: most appear to have escaped to the island of Lesbos.[82] Inland villagers, such as the Romioi of Görükle, Karacaoba, and Uluabat, were forced to seek refuge in larger towns like Bursa and Bandırma, where they were sheltered and fed by the Church.[83] In late June, there was much property theft and damage at Tire, Aydın, Tachman, Çeşme, and Ahmetli. Rum peasants were reportedly starving because they had been driven from their homes and fields.[84] The Danish consul at Smyrna reported the following militia attack on Foça on 25 June:

> [W]ithin a quarter of an hour after the assault had begun every boat in the place was full of people trying to get away and when no more boats could be had the inhabitants

sought refuge on the little peninsula on which the lighthouse stands. I saw eleven bodies of men and women lying dead on the shore. How many were killed I could not say, but trying to get into a house of which the door stood ajar I saw two other dead bodies lying in the entrance hall. Every shop in the place was looted and the goods that could not be carried away were wantonly destroyed.[85]

Consulates were receiving almost daily reports of killings, looting, and arson in the region of Smyrna. Thus, on 13 July one Thomas Bourdouroglu was reportedly shot by a Cretan in Bournabaşi; a coffeehouse proprietor named Dimitri Livieris was flogged at Kokaryalı; the shop of Stelio Massopoulos in Salabatli was looted, and at Agasoluk several Romioi were found dead in their fields. On 14 July two girls were raped in Engelonissi, on 16 July the homes of a Mr Maragoudakis in Miressi and Mr Katsikaris of Chigli were burned to the ground, and on 18 July Romioi houses were pillaged in the town of Urla.[86]

An important factor behind these widespread attacks on Rum communities as summer approached in 1914 was the sharply deteriorating relationship between Athens and Constantinople. A third Balkan War was widely anticipated, as the Ottoman government was demanding the return of the Aegean islands, feeling confident that it could win a war at sea once it received delivery of two Dreadnoughts. Meanwhile, the Greek government under Eleftherios Venizelos was trying to induce Russia into the conflict before the battleships could be delivered.[87]

Hostilities between the Ottoman Empire and Greece abated temporarily with the outbreak of war in Europe in August 1914, as did the persecutions, although by then more than 200,000 Rum had already fled from western Anatolia. According to Ottoman statistics the South Marmara region alone witnessed the flight of 164,000 Rum to Greece.[88] Christians who had abandoned their villages were officially encouraged to return to their homes, which in most cases had been looted, torched, or occupied by Muslim refugees. The violence resumed, however, once the Ottomans entered the war on the side of Germany in November. After French naval craft had shelled the town of Bodrum, the remaining Rum residents were forced to evacuate the town after a gun battle with local Muslims.[89] Around the town of Livisi, villagers were being robbed and raped as they tried to get to the relative safety of the town. Among the typical stories were those of Calliope Cosma and Mary Joannou of the village of Trimli, who:

had managed to escape from their persecutors when Trimli fell into the hands of another band of peasants near Kestapi. The [sic] were allowed to leave only after they had been subjected for eight days to the most infamous of outrages, as a result of which one of them died.[90]

Reports on the new round of persecutions across Anatolia were compiled by the Ecumenical Patriarchate in Constantinople, which published its findings after the war in a tome entitled *I Mavri Biblos* or *The Black Book*.

'They became angry'

The violent interlude between the Balkan and First World wars marks an important rupture in the history of Ottoman intercommunal relations. The refugee testimonies link the golden days of intercommunality to a specific time frame (the reign of Abdülhamid II) and with a specified terminus. Some interviewees claimed that the terminus was the First Balkan War, while others nominated the empire's entry into the First World War. Nikos Vezirgiannis was typical when he claimed that the relationship deteriorated suddenly: 'With the Turks of the village we had great relations until 1912'.[91] Anestis Varsitopoulos, whose native Foça had been destroyed by a militia attack on 25 June 1914, gave the impression that the harmonious nature of intercommunal relations might have continued had it not been for the First Balkan War:

> *It was only with the war did we see each other as enemies. The cause was the Balkan War...Before 1912 they'd come to our weddings and baptisms. We did* koumparies[92] *...after 1912, such things no longer happened. We were at daggers [sta maheria].The Turks no longer trusted us.*[93]

Kleodimos Landos said that there was *omonoia* (harmony) until 1912, and that the disharmony that followed was caused by outsiders: 'In 1912 everything changed because of the Cretan Turks. They liked to kill in secret. The people started leaving...Before the Macedonian [Balkan] War our relations were first rate (*aristes*).'[94]

Others sensed that relations with neighbours went sour only after the declaration of war in November 1914. In Bozdoğan, where Kostas Phinikopoulos recalled that there had been 'only good relations with the Turks' and that these Turks were humble people (*agathi*) and 'of the community'(*tou laou*), the hatred took over slowly:

> *After the Seferberlik* [general mobilization in 1914] *the change came slowly, slowly. The troubles started. First we began fighting over water. Before, our women would go to the wells together. Even our men were welcomed in their homes. It seems they were*

always jealous of us, our money. The began pouring petrol into our sugar, and such things.[95]

Other interviewees also identified 1914 as the year when everything changed. As usual, the sources of discord were said to have emanated from outside:

Until the 1914 war we had good relations. Went to their homes, they came to ours…but whenever the Allies bombarded the coastline, they would become angry with us.[96]

In 1914 we were not allowed to trade in the shops. Turks were not allowed to employ Greeks. They would not buy from us. The hatreds started with the Young Turks.[97]

The communities therefore ceased to have regard for one another. They no longer paid visits to each other, socialized, went to the same coffeehouses, and even avoided bartering. Relations were no longer friendly. On the contrary, the refugee transcripts begin to refer to 'the hatreds' (*to misos*). Most commonly they refer to the Muslims as having become hostile: 'the Turks became angry' (*i Tourki agriepsane*) was the most commonly used phrase. The choice of the word 'angry' is telling. The actual Greek term 'agriepsane' (αγριέψανε) literally means 'they became wild', suggesting an implacable hatred and a refusal to see reason. The image was also in keeping with the popular stereotype of 'the Turk' as prone to fanaticism and punitive violence. Neighbours were no longer willing to treat each other as 'people of God', but as treacherous antagonists. Whereas Greek nationalists might claim the Turks were reverting to type, however, the refugees were aware that their neighbours were not being their true selves. The change happened under specific conditions created by the rapid deterioration of the empire's international position, and, critically, because the empire's principal enemies happened to be Orthodox Christians. The interviewees could see why local Muslims might suddenly treat them as fifth columnists.

In the oral transcripts the 'wildness' or 'implacable hostility' of the Turk after 1912/1914 is firmly historicized. The transformation from ideal neighbour to intransigent enemy is made explicable in that it occurs at a specific historical juncture, and happens in response to persecutions suffered by Muslims at the hands of fellow Orthodox Christians. In other words, the Rum refugees regarded the resentment and antagonism directed towards them as rational, accepting to some degree the logic of collective guilt. 'If you think about it,' conceded Oddiseus Diakos and Sergios Toutaros, 'it is WE who did not treat THEM well.'[98]

1914–18

Wartime provided a cover for numerous crimes against civilian populations by all the belligerent powers during the First World War, although nothing in Europe really compared with what happened in Ottoman Anatolia. The atrocities committed here foreshadowed developments that were more in keeping with the 'bloodlands' of the 1930s and 1940s.[99] Historians and polemicists have written a great deal about eastern Anatolia, but of the rest of Anatolia and eastern Thrace we know relatively little. How extensive, for example, was the problem of banditry? To what extent did regional 'warlords', such as Topal Osman of Giresun, control Anatolia? And how does one explain the variety of conditions faced by urban and rural Christians during the war period? Smyrna, for example, would remain a relatively safe haven for Christians and foreigners, largely because it was under the authority of the boycott-promoting Rahmi Bey, the *vali* of Izmir, who appeared intent on maintaining an atmosphere of 'business as usual', and who refused Enver Pasha's orders to deport the Armenians into Anatolia's interior, largely because of his personal animus for the CUP leader. As Philip Mansel has put it, the cosmopolitan entrepôt and its 'Levantine synthesis survived'.[100] Similarly, the memoirs and oral histories of the Karamanlides of central Anatolia, whose homelands were barely touched by the conflict, suggest a relatively benign wartime experience.

Most of the Romioi, however, lived in regions that could be designated as strategically sensitive, namely the coastal regions but also along the railway lines. Throughout 1915 and 1916, such communities were relocated into the less vulnerable regions of central and eastern Anatolia, but most of these journeys involved marching long distances across rough terrain. At short notice, villagers and towns people, now mostly women, children, and the elderly, were rounded up and expected to walk in extreme weather conditions and with inadequate provisions. Angeliki Kaminou was living in the relative safety of Bursa, but recalled the time when Romioi from the coastal areas were being herded through the outskirts of town, selling their dowries just to stay alive: 'Women sold *mandilia* [small sacks of valuables] for two trays of wheat':

> We opened our homes to them of course, to many Ai Valiotises [women from Ayvalık] but others had already died along the way from the hardships. To kill the Armenians they simply deported them. At the time we did not understand these things.[101]

Thracians were among the earliest peoples to be evicted. As many as 60,000 Romioi from Thrace were shipped across the Marmara Sea and sent marching towards interior locations. The marches had the effect of culling the least physically able, particularly the elderly and the sick. In 1915 another 40,000 Romioi were removed from South Marmara, and by the end of 1916, most of the remaining communities along the Black Sea coast were being herded through the steep alpine Pontic ranges, often in the dead of winter. The survivors had to fend for themselves in the parched landscapes of the interior. Dimitri Phitopoulos claimed that all 700 people of his village (Akagia) were ordered to march out on Christmas Day, 1916. There were four guards at any one time: one who walked ahead, one on the side, and two behind. The guards changed as they passed each village. Along the way, more Christians were added: 'The herd of people kept growing as we marched towards death.' They were marched by day and slept in the snow at night. They were not allowed to go into settlements to speak to anyone. There was hardly any food, and little time was allowed for rest. 'We'd sit for a little to eat and the Turk would say "you get up, giavour".' Countless people died on the road. Phitopoulos claims people's feet were full of balloon-sized blisters and full of cuts. The only hope was for some help from the Christian Karamanli villages: 'We got to a village called Fel [Felâhiye?]. There were Christians there who gave us shelter, but many of us died of typhus. I lost two brothers there.' Eventually, the Romioi were allowed to settle in an area. Those who plied trades like shoemaking set up businesses to earn money. Phitopoulos took the unusual step of trekking back to his village, moving through the mountains to avoid detection, which he did for two months, and then enlisted in the Ottoman army. After the war, when he eventually resettled in his village, Phitopoulos claimed that all but 120 members of his community were dead.[102] Overall, it was these forced marches that accounted for the high civilian death toll. Regardless as to whether authorities intended to cull the Romioi in this fashion, the effect of the forced marches was genocidal.[103]

Meanwhile, all able-bodied Rum males were drafted into labour battalions, in which mortality rates were high due to overwork, malnutrition, and disease. Among the survivors was Yannis Mehagioglou:

Their aim was to move us in order to kill us off, with hardships and privations. Labouring on roadworks, work with the military, work in transporting, breaking stones, working charcoal, work, hunger and beatings. What courage I had! How often did I have

*no water? I would hear about my father and my heart would bleed. I was young and
could cope.*[104]

The worst excesses were experienced in the Pontos region. While many
lost their lives in the marches, others managed to flee across the Russian
border or took to the mountains with their guns. Here they endured a precarious existence, keeping one step ahead of Turkish soldiers while robbing
Muslim villages for provisions. Pontic Greek tradition has likened this experience to a partisan war, although the actual aim was survival.[105] The Pontus
region was particularly unstable owing to the fact that it was a military
front. The Russians occupied the eastern areas and held Trabzon from April
1916 through to the end of 1917. Rum civilians on either side of the Russian front faced very difficult challenges: on the Ottoman side they were
deported, while on the Russian side they feared what might happen if the
Russians withdrew. One Yannis Holetsidis recalled that the enthusiastic
reception his community gave to the Russian troops when they entered
Trabzon incensed the Muslims. One said sarcastically: 'Your *godfather* has
arrived, you're *so* happy.'[106] Fearing reprisals, many Pontians followed the
departing Russian army when it withdrew in 1917.[107]

Aside from state-orchestrated persecutions, villagers in every part of
Anatolia were terrorized throughout the war and in the post-war years by
Muslim bandits or chettes. These bands were often linked to a regional
warlord or to other local authorities who took a share of their spoils. Many
Pontian interviewees from the central Black Sea region recalled attacks that
were sometimes personally led by Topal Osman, whose militias appeared to
have more power in the region of Giresun than the state. Efcharis Deligian-
nidou recalled the day when Topal Osman's men came to her village of Atta.
She claimed to be the only survivor:

> Of all the people in my village, I was the only one to be spared the knife and the fires.
> I remember such things and I still tremble. The chettes of Topal Osman came and we
> were lost. First they killed, then they looted, and then they burned. Two or three
> women escaped, but they chased them and killed them. Only then did they rape them!
> I was hidden near the river, inside bushes. I heard them mocking [the dead
> women] 'Aren't you ashamed . . . ' They had killed the priest. First they knocked on
> his door. They broke in and nailed him to the door of the Church. There were many
> women in Atta that had fled from other villages.[108]

Banditry thrived in these wartime conditions. As with most cases of ethnic
cleansing in the twentieth century, the task of clearing undesirable popula-

tions was left to armed gangs of young males and criminal elements who saw an opportunity to rob and live out their sadistic fantasies. Chettes and warlords targeted Christian villagers with impunity, looting and raping while claiming to be fighting the enemy. As Ryan Gingeras points out, Muslim bandits in the south Marmara region extorted and killed Muslim villagers as well, while Christian bandits were also roaming the country-side, targeting Muslims.[109] Lawlessness characterized every part of rural Anatolia.

The violence committed against Anatolia's Christians during the First World War was pivotal in shaping political culture and promoting secession-ist nationalism. The cumulative effect of these traumatic experiences on the Greek Orthodox population was to transform the Romioi into enemies of the Ottoman Turkish state. Ordinary Romioi were praying to be rescued by Christian armies and for the destruction of the empire. And while the Ottoman homefront was a living hell for Christian minorities, it also had the effect of politicizing the Muslim population, which feared retributive persecution at the hands of Christian troops in the event of Ottoman defeat. Given the history of expulsions (*sökürün*) from Europe and the Caucasus since the 1870s, Anatolia's Muslims feared that they too might be the vic-tims of ethnic cleansing. In eastern Anatolia, where Armenians hoped to create an ethnic homeland, and in the western regions coveted by the Greek state, local Muslims would indeed be given a small taste of *sökürün*.[110]

For such reasons the state managed to rally large sections of Ottoman society behind the war effort, including women, who volunteered for fund-raising and factory work. As in the other combatant countries, however, food shortages and other privations made life as difficult for Ottoman civilians as it was for people in Russia or say Italy, where state food rationing and welfare effectively did not exist. The cumulative impact of the privations and high casualty rates was to further harden and politicize identity boundaries. The progressively dire material conditions, which leading figures like Enver Pasha and Kemal Mustafa conceded in 1917 had the entire country in despair and near collapse, also served to crystallize antipathies between groups.[111]

Independence/catastrophe, 1919–22

On 30 October 1918 the Ottomans signed an armistice and effectively con-ceded defeat. Two weeks later, on 13 November, French, Italian, and British troops occupied Constantinople. Discredited by the catastrophic defeat, the CUP regime had relinquished power and left the country under the leadership of the sultan, Vahdeddin or Mehmet VI. As news of the armistice spread, the survivors of the forced marches made the long journey back to their homes, while armed Pontic Greeks descended down from the mountains.[112] Those who had taken refuge in Greece during the war were more cautious and waited until conditions in Anatolia were safe. Commissions were set up by the victorious powers to assist in the repatriation of Romioi and Armenians, to rebuild homes, churches, shops, and mills.[113] The people who did return fully expected to see their homes looted, torched, or occupied by Muslim refugees. Some were surprised to find that Muslim friends and neighbours had secured their properties and belongings, a sign that not everything had changed.[114] Polybios Narliotis recalled that his father's friend, Rhemzi Bey, had saved his sewing machines and his materials, and thus he was able to restart his tailoring business.[115] Returning to Adramitti (Edremit), which was occupied by Greek troops between 1919 and 1922, Anna Pari recalled having to evict the Bosnian refugees now living in her home:

> *Everyone went back to their own houses. We began, slowly, slowly, to restore our domestic pride* (na stinoume to nikokirio mas). *The local Turks were all sweet with us now. They paid outstanding debts, because now they needed us, given we were under Greek occupation.*[116]

Conditions varied even within regions. In south-western Anatolia, for example, the inland towns appear to have fared better than those on the coast. At Kuşadası, the Greek quarter had been gutted. Only 1,300 of the original 7,000 Romioi returned, and all of them were living in abject squalor. In Bodrum, 255 of the estimated 750 Rum homes were ruined, a further 50 only moderately so, while the habitable homes had been distributed among 3,000 Muslims who had come from as far as Lake Van. Those returning to Milas were accused by Allied authorities of exaggerating damages in order to procure more assistance, while material conditions for the Romioi in Muğla were reportedly good, as indeed were relations with local Muslims.[117]

Recent memories of Turkish persecutions left the Romioi anxious about the future, however, with many local leaders along the Aegean coastal region calling openly for Greek rule. The Romioi of Gallipoli (Gelibolu) caused great consternation among their Muslim neighbours when on 10 April they gave a Greek naval vessel a flag-waving reception, while further south at

Makri (Fethiye), intercommunal ructions were reported when the Greek Red Cross was also received with Greek flags and cries of 'zito' (hooray).[118] Local Romioi were emboldened by the fact that these regions were being considered at the Paris Peace Conference as concessions to Greece. In Manisa the local Romioi held a plebiscite calling for their town to be 'liberated'.[119]

Muslims also had reasons to be anxious. The future of the empire was being decided at the Paris Peace Conference, where sympathies lay with the Christian minorities, and where there was no Ottoman representation. Muslims generally expected to lose their Arab territories (Iraq, the Hijaz, Syria), but there was broad agreement that Anatolia should remain a Turkish homeland. All previous experiences with European treaty-making, however, had them expecting a punitive peace. Muslims feared that much of eastern Anatolia would become an independent Armenian state, and that Greece would be rewarded with parts of the Aegean coastal area, including Smyrna. The prospect of Anatolia's dismemberment became the new rallying call for Turkish nationalism.[120]

If the more politically active elements in Ottoman society were energized by the treaty discussions, many more yearned for a return to some semblance of normality, as indeed did most Europeans at the close of 1918. Uppermost in people's minds was the need to rebuild lives and restore communities. Iakovos Koulouheris of Samsun recalled that among the first tasks of those returning from exile was the reopening of schools:

From our exile, which lasted until 1918, those who could escape did so secretly, as I did with my sisters. When the armistice of the First World War was signed, only half of us [villagers] managed to return. All the rest, indeed most, had died of typhus or from the depravations or the marches. It was doubtful that half of us had returned. Given the shortage of men, those who had experience as community officials played these roles again . . . I had the responsibilities of the secretary. We gathered together and did what we could. We searched for teachers and made our priest the principal. He was from another small town, Kavakia. We found two female teachers who taught before the expulsions, and that is how we operated a school which before the war had seven grades.[121]

The respite was all too brief. Avgerinos Spanopoulos returned to his village in May 1918, and received a small government subsidy to rebuild his home, which he did slowly, 'but as soon as we could say "God be praised", the Greek–Turkish War started'.[122] Sectarian violence resumed with the Greek landing at Smyrna in May 1919, and escalated significantly with the signing of the Treaty of Sèvres (August 1920), which confirmed that the Turks would be left as little as one-third of Anatolia. Greece was allocated Smyrna and its environs, subject to a plebiscite within five years, while Armenians were allocated vast areas of eastern Anatolia stretching from Trabzon to Lake Van.

Historians of Turkey are agreed that it was the arrival of the Greek occupation force in Smyrna on 16 May 1919 that polarized Anatolia's Muslim and Rum communities irretrievably. Şina Akşin claims it is impossible to exaggerate the importance of this moment since the Greeks were expected to persecute Muslims and expel them as they had done in the Balkans: 'No matter how war weary they were, such a threat could only motivate them to rearm in defense of their right to survive.'[123] As the expeditionary force was greeted by tens of thousands of flag-waving Rum Smyrniots, elsewhere in Anatolia protesting Muslims filled the streets in far greater numbers.[124] Mustafa Kemal said of the landing: 'If the enemy had not stupidly come here, the whole country would have slept on heedlessly.'[125] Under his leadership, the Turkish Nationalist movement eventually managed to rally Anatolian Muslims against all foreign occupiers, but in the meantime many other elements were mobilized, including discharged soldiers, officers, CUP operatives, and various other Turkish civilian organizations.[126]

The new war that flared in the environs of Smyrna saw Muslim irregulars pitted against Greek soldiers in a vicious guerrilla campaign in which civilians suffered most. The Allies received reports of civilian atrocities by Greek soldiers throughout the summer months of 1919, of widespread killing and raping. Thus on 4 July Greek soldiers invited the villagers of Buluk Kaya to lay down their arms, after which the men were executed and the women raped. The following day Greek troops were responsible for a massacre in Aydın. On 17 July Greek troops were driven out of Nazilli, after which Muslim irregulars moved in to rob and kill the remaining Christians.[127] Even if many of these stories and body counts were exaggerated, as consular officials often suspected, the circulation of these stories could only raise tension in other parts of Anatolia.

By 1921 Greek forces had moved well beyond the designated occupation zone, marching as far as Eskişehir and coming within 100 km of Ankara, the centre of the Nationalist resistance. The stated aim of these military operations was to crush resistance and enforce the terms of the Treaty of Sèvres, although it was also clear that the Greek government was seeking to extend its territorial acquisitions to the Marmara region. In the Izmit and Yalova areas, for example, it appears that between 24 and 27 June the Greek army had undertaken an ethnic cleansing operation.[128] It was the heavy toll on civilian lives that convinced the historian Arnold J. Toynbee, acting as correspondent for the *Manchester Guardian* at the time, that the Greeks were as unfit to rule mixed populations as the Turks.[129] It was patently obvious to observers, in fact, that the Greek authorities and Turkish Nationalist or Kemalists were colluding with paramilitary groups, and that they were even creating such groups. Horace Rumbold, the then British Ambassador in Constantinople, asserted that the Turkish Nationalists and chettes were difficult to distinguish.[130] Meanwhile, an Allied commission of inquiry found that Greek authorities were not protecting local Muslims from Greek bandits, and suggested there was collusion between the said bandits and the authorities. One Michalis Scholias of Tepecik near Alaşehir recalled his days in a 200-strong bandit group that wore Turkish uniforms in order to penetrate Muslim villages more easily. He later enlisted in the Greek ninth army.[131] It is clear that much of the activity was focused on looting. Close observers of Greek operations in Ayvalık, Kasaba (Turgutlu), and Nazilli advised that much of the disorder was attributable to Rum and Muslim bandit groups who were robbing indiscriminately. Some of the Christian bandits were operating from the island of Samos.[132] Further east in the Black Sea region, Pontian communities were being devastated by vicious attacks by irregulars or *bashi-bazouks*. In the central Black Sea area, a Major Emin and Colonel Kemal Bey recruited 3,000 irregulars to form a special extermination squad. When they entered the town of Bafra on 5 July 1921, they killed all Rum males and raped all the females; the prettier ones were reserved for the officers.[133] Meanwhile, Topal Osman and his *bashi-bazouks* were again killing Christians in the vicinity of Giresun. Topal himself was observed killing some victims with his bare hands.[134]

August–September, 1922

The purpose of this detailed recounting of the dialectic of violence that began with the Balkan Wars, and which ravaged large parts of Anatolia for a decade, is to clarify the exceptionally violent circumstances that brought the peaceful order of coexistence to an end. The commonplace claim found in the oral testimonies that the culprits were 'outsiders' is borne out by the evidence. Soldiers, paramilitaries, and bandit groups, who paid special attention to killing off or driving away civilian populations, carried out the destruction. Sectarian animosities certainly played a role in the struggles, but the violence could not be defined as 'communal' violence, since it was rarely carried out *between* communities. However, the sustained and cumulative effect of the violence had the desired political effect of crystallizing differences and making reconciliation appear nigh impossible. Thus, after years of suffering at the hands of Muslim paramilitaries and bandits, and having seen their communities decimated by the forced marches, the Romioi of Anatolia welcomed the empire's enemies as saviours. Meanwhile, the Treaty of Sèvres and the Greek occupation made ordinary Muslims receptive to the callings of Turkish nationalism. The decisive conclusion to the Greek–Turkish War, which ensured Kemal Mustafa became 'Ata Türk' (i.e. Father of the Turks), and which gave Greece its greatest national catastrophe, appeared to complete that process of mutual disaffection and nationalization in the most dramatic fashion.

The Kemalists won a decisive military victory near Afyonkarahişar on 26 August 1922. The Greek front collapsed in disarray, but in retreat the defeated left a path of destruction, killing, raping and burning as they made their way to the sea for evacuation. The wanton violence, which included burning women and children in mosques, and which devastated much of north-west Anatolia, reflected the extent to which the Greek soldiery had dehumanized the Other. The following report by a foreign observer gives some indication of what happened in the war's final days:

> Passing the Oushak [Uşak], one saw a horrible spectacle. The town burning, and various vagabonds [Greek soldiers] with a hanoum [Turkish woman] a piece, outraging her on the railway line... The same thing was repeated in the rest of the Turkish villages. To escape the above, the inhabitants of the villages came out with sweets and food, in order to placate them. But alas they found the same fate. In general, the whole country between Afion-Karahissar and Smyrna was completely devastated.[135]

A Catholic missionary said at the time that the 'Greeks have lost any right now to speak of Turkish barbarism'.[136]

The spiteful deeds of the retreating soldiery gave the victorious Kemalists excuses to carry out punitive actions against the remaining Rum population.[137] Much was made of Rum collaboration, as it is clear that Rum males did enlist in or fight alongside the Greek army, and Rum civilians did give

aid and comfort to the invaders.[138] For most Turks, this claim of Rum collaboration is significant because it also provided the moral justification for
the unmaking of the multiethnic order. Rum wartime behaviour was
painted in terms of betrayal and ingratitude: betrayal because the Greeks
sought to expel the Muslims from their Anatolian homeland with Rum
support; and ingratitude because the empire had treated them benevolently
in the past.[139] As Gingeras has pointed out, most scholars and commentators
in Turkey have also blamed Ottoman Christians for being the chief domestic catalyst of the war and the ensuing human catastrophe in the period
1919–22.[140] The destruction of the Christian quarters of Smyrna by fire (13
and 22 September), where over 200,000 Rum Smyrniots and villagers from
the region had been awaiting deportation, was regarded as a form of just
retribution.[141]

Meanwhile, the destruction of Smyrna provided ammunition for
Greek scholars and commentators to accuse the Kemalists and Turks of
crimes against humanity. The standard Greek approach has been to focus
on the sacking of Smyrna. Rum Smyrniots and refugees were left at the
mercy of Turkish paramilitaries, who went on a killing and raping spree,
often in full view of Allied naval personnel whose ships were moored
offshore.[142] The Greek and Armenian sections were then set ablaze, leaving civilians at the mercy of an inferno. The destruction of Smyrna has
since remained the focus of Greek national memory, symbolizing the
end of 'Greek civilization' in Asia Minor but also the rank barbarity of
the Turk.

National memory in both countries has since persisted in reading the
war in terms of a simple good-versus-evil schema. As Ayşe Osil has pointed
out, most Turkish historians have either ignored or paid mere lip service to
the crimes committed by their own side.[143] The same claim can be made of
most of their Greek counterparts. The oral sources, however, are often
more balanced and 'self'-critical, confirming that neither Greeks nor Turks
had a monopoly on war crimes, while also being deeply critical of their
own political elites. The refugees occasionally admitted to a sense of betrayal,
for not only had the Greek occupation forces exacerbated tensions between
religious communities with their malicious behaviour, but they also felt
they had been abandoned to the oncoming Turks. Many complained of the
fact that civilians had been kept in the dark about the military collapse so as
not to cause another exodus, giving families no time to gather their belongings and make an escape:

Then came the accursed August. What horrors! What havoc! Who could have expected it all? To be told nothing as we watched the soldiers return! They didn't even tell us what was happening. To watch the villagers leaving their homes and coming down to Smyrna! It was from them that we learned of the bitter truth.[144]

Such complexities would not be allowed to disturb the standard Turkish and Greek narratives. The War of Independence (İstiklâl Harbi), as it is known in Turkey, and the 'Asia Minor Catastrophe' (Mikrasiatiki Catastrophi) as it is known in Greece, has been read as a war between two distinct peoples, Greeks and Turks, with each side drawing lessons of national victimhood and enemy turpitude. Refugee memory, on the other hand, points to a far more complicated and nuanced picture, and which is confirmed (and indeed further complicated) by an important monograph that focuses on the south Marmara region. In *Sorrowful Shores*, Ryan Gingeras shows that Kemalists were also pitted against Muslim refugee groups (Circassians, Pomaks, Albanians) and forces loyal to the Sultan, and that ordinary Muslims did not necessarily rally behind Kemal. In fact the violence perpetrated in the region reflected a range of political interests and witnessed shifting alliances. He further notes that Rum paramilitaries were a feature of the endemic violence, usually working under the auspices of the Greek military command, but often pursuing personal vendettas.[145]

The conventional 'Turks versus Greeks' frame has also obscured the disjuncture between civilian interests, on the one hand, and those of state and nationalist groups, on the other.[146] As noted earlier in this chapter, ordinary Ottomans, particularly women, children, and the elderly, were the principal victims of the violence that characterized the 1912–22 period, and yet national narratives likened the struggle to a 'people's war', where neighbour was pitted against neighbour, community against community. Former neighbours did indeed harm each other during these terrible years, as some interviewees were prepared to admit, but the evidence does not suggest that there was endemic bloodletting between former neighbours.[147] As Cathie Carmichael has argued, it may 'be somewhat naïve to argue that popular consciousness of difference was not a factor in ethnic cleansing', but 'consciousness of perceived difference is not enough to create situations of crisis and violence'.[148]

Rather, the conventional focus on the war as a struggle between nations also had a way of giving the nation immunity from criticism by its citizenry. Even the refugees found it difficult to vent their anger against the Greek army:

The Greek soldiers did many dreadful things to the unarmed Turkish population. It's better we don't discuss it . . . [149]

To Eskishehir our men advanced without resistance, then the Turks resisted. The horrors started, by Greeks and Turks. Ours [Greek soldiers] *took the Turkish women into the mosques and set them alight. The Turks saw all this. They also then started to burn and slaughter.* [150]

The interviewees were slightly less reticent about criticizing Greek state authorities, particularly those linked to the pro-Monarchist regime that replaced that of Venizelos in late 1920, and which was to shoulder the blame for the military debacle. Aside from failing to warn the civilians of the military collapse in the last days of August 1922, the Greek authorities were also held responsible for failing to provide adequate assistance to evacuate civilians from Anatolia's shores, and for encouraging them to stay put. Anna Paris noted in her interview that she was only alerted to the fact that the Greek front was teetering on collapse through personal connections, and hence she was able to make an early escape to Mytilene. She was outraged that Greek officers at the time were telling civilians that the situation was stable, and she told one particular officer that he would choke on the blood of innocents. 'My curse was effective,' she said, for sometime later 'that officer choked on a Turkish delight at *Zaharotou* [a well-known pastry shop] in Athens.'[151]

In fact the Romioi in north-western Anatolia *were* abandoned to their fate. Those who were apprehended by irregulars were doomed. Giorgos Kefalas was a survivor of the inland village of Kagiatziki, where most members of the seven families still living there at the time were killed, including six members of the Yannis Zeimbek family, five of the Kokona Kalaitzi family, seven of the Anastasis Meimaroglu family, five of the Iordanis Deligiannis family, and eight of the Yannako Axarlis family.[152] One Yannis Mimikos of Bergama lost his wife and five children.[153] Harilaos Tsairis reported that Turkish irregulars killed his two sisters, a brother, and his mother at Narli: 'What did they do to deserve slaughter?'[154] Many of the interviewees described the scramble to escape. Typical was the story of Vasilia Roumelioti of Urla, whose father was killed while working in the fields. She fled with her mother, but was almost taken by a Turk who grabbed her by the arm, only to be saved and handed back to her mother by another Turk.[155] Many Anatolian families were separated in all the confusion, and if they were lucky they were reunited later in Greece, often with the help of the Red Cross.

Becoming national, forgetting community

For Anatolia's Christians, the war years were cataclysmic. Overall, the number of Greek Orthodox Christians who fled or were expelled between 1913 and 1924 was 1,221,849, including 626,954 from Asia Minor, 182,169 from Pontus, 256,169 from eastern Thrace, and 38,458 from Constantinople.[156] The number of those who died from the forced marches, random killings, attacks by paramilitaries, soldiers, disease, and hunger is difficult to estimate, but it appears that somewhere between 640,000 and 920,000 lost their lives prematurely. Perhaps as many as half of the Pontic Greek population perished during these years.[157] Aside from a handful of individuals who had been given exemptions by the Nationalist regime, the Romioi had been completely expunged from Anatolia by 1925.[158]

This chapter has sought to give a non- or anti-'statist' depiction of the war years, during which time the political violence had the effect of politicizing and homogenizing civilians. By appropriating their pasts, national narratives of the Turkish War of Independence/Asia Minor Catastrophe sought depictions that served their respective national interests exclusively. I have hinted on occasion in this chapter, however, that these strategies had only partial effect. Although the war years did certainly succeed in creating new identities, that success in many cases was partial. As with the Cretans and Macedonian Muslims in Turkey, the Anatolian refugees in Greece did develop a reputation for being fiercely hostile towards the Turkish state, but as has been noted extensively in this study, and in important monographs by Rénee Hirschon and Bruce Clark, the refugees were also notorious for harbouring affection for the Turks.[159] Former Ottoman subjects were certainly 'nationalized' by the war years, and they did appear to adopt some of the concepts and analytic frames of statist ideology, but they also remained wary of the fact that the same ideology was responsible for ruining their lives. Thus the very process that constituted nationalism also gave its subjects the ammunition for its disavowal. In holding mutually contradictory positions, the refugees confirmed the power of nationalism but also revealed the powerful effects of the traumas caused by the nationalizing process.

Thus, as the victims of violent statist strategies perpetrated by operatives, soldiers, and paramilitaries, the refugees could retain a critical perspective of the Greek–Turkish conflict from an ethically independent standpoint. As people who identified with their communities as moral environments, they were affronted by state and paramilitary strategies that sought to invert the values of these environments. The refugees recognized that the base activities of soldiers and paramilitaries, the tortures, sexual assaults, and malicious damage by bands of adult males acting deliberately without any moral scruples, were essentially aimed at destroying the moral environment and creating national spaces.

Put another way, the oral sources suggest that the violence against civilians produced a 'civilian' perspective on these terrible years. That much is suggested by the frequent references to friends and neighbours who did not reject the older values of intercommunality, and who came to their aid in desperate times. Those interviewees who claimed that friendship meant more to Turks than to Greeks, often had in mind the assistance that such friends provided during the darkest hours.[160] Yannis Nikolaidis and Yannis Karpidis said that in their village (Kiriharam) there were always Turkish friends 'even to the very end':

> The Turks themselves, our friends, would learn of terrible developments and imminent attacks and would counsel us to get up and leave, to go to Nikodemia [Izmit] where we'd be safe.[161]

The perpetrators of violence were nearly always described as outsiders: Kemalists, Young Turks, chettes, and Cretans. In that way the interviewees could distance the locality as a moral space from the community-wrecking states and their operatives. 'It wasn't our Turks who brought about all the troubles and dangers,' claimed Polybios Narliotis:

> It was these Turkish soldiers, wild men, who knows from what part of Anatolia they came from. It was they who did all the robberies and killings . . . Even the Turks didn't like them. They too suffered at the hands of these bandits.
>
> In 1922 it wasn't our Turks who started the massacres in the nearby villages. They were chettes . . . unruly soldiers . . . thieves, bad people, they had been let out of the jails and they extorted anyone they came across.[162]

Interviewees often noted that neighbours could not help them because they feared for their own lives, especially as paramilitaries were also known to harass and extort Muslim communities. In some cases, however, Muslims were prepared to take serious risks for their Rum friends. Michalis Aslanidis spent the war years in the Pontic highlands, where survival sometimes depended on these friendships:

> We had Turkish friends. They came secretly and would bring us food. They informed us about the whereabouts of Turkish soldiers. They brought us arms, which we paid for.[163]

When the Romioi were in the process of being deported, many recalled the acts of friendship and common decency. Ourania Spanopoulou said that as she and her fellow villagers were leaving, her Turkish 'patriots' looked after them and let them sleep in their homes.[164] Interviewees often noted acts of kindness that reflected purely ethical motives. Yannis Holetsidis had spent his second period of internal exile nears Kars, where he survived by plying his trade as a barber. When the war ended he returned briefly to Trabzon for two days, before being deported permanently to Greece:

> *I will never forget the hospitality and kindness shown to me by a Turkish lady when I was in Trabzon for two days. An old neighbour insisted I stay with her. She gave me clothes, bathed me, gave me a bag full of* pide *(flat bread), eggs, lemons, garlic and cigarette paper.*

Such simple acts of kindness by a former neighbour signified that the ethical consensus that once underpinned the intercommunal order had not been completely effaced. Friendship and neighbourliness still had meaning. In this case the Muslim woman was prepared to clean and feed an adult Christian male in her own home because she had not forgotten her moral duties as a neighbour.[165]

In Greece and in Turkey, such seemingly innocuous memories of the Other point to the limitations of statist ideological hegemony. In later years, such memories were recalled in private or in the company of other refugees, and they constituted a form of counter-memory, given that in each state there was immense pressure to conform to statist norms and to ignore anything that problematized these norms. Nostalgic memories were useful for maintaining a critical distance and to retain a sense of an authentic self that had been constituted in the pre-national homelands. For refugees on either side of the Aegean, being Greek or Turkish was disemic in the sense that both groups emerged from the war years as genuine flag-waving patriots, while holding to personal values and memories that grated with the tenets of patriotism.

The turmoil for ordinary Anatolians certainly did not end with the conclusion of the Greek–Turkish War. The Treaty of Lausanne (24 July 1923) allowed for an internationally supervised population transfer between Greece and what became the Republic of Turkey (29 October), with 356,000 of the remaining Muslims in Greece being exchanged for 290,000 Rum still in Anatolia.[166] The Kemalist regime especially insisted that the exchange be compulsory, to the consternation of foreign officials involved in the process, which greatly disappointed the thousands of Muslims who remained in Macedonia until all efforts to fight deportation had been exhausted, and many Karamanlides, who hoped to stay in their homes as Turkish Orthodox Christians.[167] As the threat of violence diminished, civilians facing deportation and the refugees who had already made their way across the Aegean experienced other hardships that also figure strongly in popular memory. Rum refugees in particular suffered from malnutrition and disease, and an extremely high mortality rate. Foreign observers frequently described their condition as desperate.

The death toll among Greek soldiers and Rum adult males still held captive in Turkey was also very high. Able-bodied males were detained by the Kemalist regime, and they were often set upon by local peoples or massacred by chette bands. Yet even in this bleak world of captivity, the identity boundaries that had been hardened by years of malicious violence seemed incapable of maintaining their rigidity. In odd moments, commonplace norms of sociability often came to the surface. Elias Venezis of Ayvalık was a young man of eighteen when he was dragooned into a labour battalion of 3,000 men when the war ended, and was one of only twenty-three who survived. He went on to become a major Greek novelist, and was linked to a significant group of writers whose oeuvre was shaped by their experiences in Anatolia. A sense of that experience of captivity is conveyed in *The Number 31, 328*, where at various times each day the disjuncture of the political and the social is made plain:

> *With time without realizing it, blindly, we began, along with the mafazaves, to get close. To come together. At night they come more often to keep company with us. We talk about our troubles together. And in their conversation they no longer call us 'yesir'. With their heavy Anatolian voice they pronounce full of warmth and kindness:* 'Arkantas' *(comrade).*
>
> *During our labours they no longer beat or curse us. When there is no Romios tsaous around they pretend not to see and let us sit down. They shiver at the sight of the tsaous because they report them to officers.*
>
> *At noon . . . we sit down together under the sharp sun and eat our bread. We speak amicably, and often the time allocated for rest passes. Then they, fearful, get us up gently gently, as if pleading with us, 'Come on, comrades, get up'.*[168]

At other times they consciously adhere to their 'scripts' and behave as enemies. The Turkish guards tap the POWs on the shoulder and lament their common predicament:

> '*What can we do, arkanta, may God take pity, on you and us* (Ο Θεός να μας λυπηθή, κ'εσάς και εμάς).'
>
> '*He should take pity, "on you and us"'*. *They say it virtually independently. They began to find it difficult to distinguish between the two sides, theirs and ours.*

Epilogue

For many years after the population exchange, Anatolian refugees held out some hope that they might still be allowed to return to their homelands. Those who found sanctuary on the island of Kastellorizo, for example, kept listing properties in Kaş, Livisi, Fethiye, and in other parts of southern Turkey in dowry agreements throughout the 1920s.[1] Many of those now living in Thessaloniki and Piraeus hoped that a change in the political climate might pave the way for a return to the homeland. As the Greek historian Antonis Liakos notes, the 'lost homelands' were not considered irretrievable until the Greek and Turkish governments signed an agreement in 1930 that finally settled issues of compensation, and when Venizelos, then in his final term of office, nominated Kemal Mustafa Atatürk for the Nobel Peace Prize.[2] Until that point, therefore, many of the refugees still believed that they could live within a Muslim-dominated land, and perhaps even restore those intercommunal links that made the Anatolia of memory so attractive.

Some refugees did return much later on private visits, in search of children or siblings who had been left behind, or simply to see their homelands. Haralambos Gerasimidis went back to find his sister. In 1921 his mother and five-year-old sister died in exile somewhere near Biltis, where a Turkish woman had adopted his other infant sister. In 1962 he set out to find her, to kiss her one more time. 'Many went back to find their people,' he said, and they 'found them as Turks'. He claimed he received a great deal of local help, including from a hotelier who drove him around in his own taxi, but he could not remember the village where his sister was adopted, and despite some clues from local converts in the area, he could not find her. He said he returned to Greece with a broken heart.[3]

Those who wished to glimpse their beloved homeland once more usually enjoyed the experience. The reception of the local Turks was always warm, particularly from those who themselves had been forcibly transferred from the empire's former European territories.[4] Thus in 1954, Giorgos Bambourakis and other expatriates went back to Kemalpasha (Nymphaio/ Nif), some 30 km east of Izmir (Smyrna), where locals welcomed them and organized a dinner. Giorgos gave a speech about common progress and friendship to an audience of Turks who had mainly come from Greece, and they liked what they heard: 'They would not let us spend any money'. Unfortunately he could not find his house, and there was no sign of the old church, even though 'it was one of the few villages that the Greek soldiers did not put to the torch'.[5] In August 1960 Thomas Stefanidis travelled with his nephew from United States to his old town Ahmetli, on the railway line between Manisa and Alaşehir. When he got off the train he did not know anyone and could only recognize the Turkish school and the house of a local notable. Thomas admitted that the new town was much nicer. After asking about the whereabouts of certain people, he encountered two old neighbours in the street coming towards him, who were shocked and embraced him with much emotion (*me poli sigginisi*). He also found an old school friend:

> When he saw me he hugged and kissed me. I was received in such a way that one can-
> not describe it. He would not let me leave, but I'd organized with my nephew that
> I would be back in Smyrna. He made me promise to come back. If my health holds up,
> I will.[6]

By the 1980s and 1990s, pilgrimages to the lost homelands were continued by the children and grandchildren of the refugees, who throughout childhood had been forced to listen to the stories of Anatolia while also being drilled in aspects of the homeland culture (food, dance, music). Thus the progeny often came to share the sensory and emotional experiences of the lost homelands, and usually found the actual visit to Anatolia quite moving.[7] The warm reception of locals also seemed reminiscent of a lost culture of intercommunality. During a visit to Safranbolu in 1988, a Greek women shed a tear for her recently deceased father, who would have loved to have been able to see his 'topos' (place). Locals learned of the visiting Yunan (Greek) and returning 'local', and one particular old man who could remember her forebears came forward:

> 'A!! Allah, Allah, Aferim!' And he turned his head to the sky. 'Elisaios, Alekos,
> Anastas! Olga!' He struggled to think of others... He took us by the hand, to take us
> to his home... People emerged from the shops and the coffeehouses to greet us. At one shop

where we sought Safranbolu's famed locum *the shopkeeper said that he heard from his mother that they, the Turks, lived lovingly with the Christians.*[8]

Children and grandchildren of the 'refugees' have often admitted to being surprised by the friendliness of the Turks, given the troubled relationship of their respective nations, but also given what they had been taught about each other in schools and through the media. In a detailed study of an organized 'return' visit of the descendants of the Romioi of Phokies/Foça, many of whom now lived in a town renamed Palea Phokia,[9] anthropologist Eleni Papagaroufali described a second and better-organized visit when the Turkish community there was ready to receive them:

> *The Greek Fokaeis* [Phokiani] *met with many people who became witnesses of their grandparents' and their own past: with old women and men who 'knew' exactly where Fokaeis' grandparents lived and worked, and who took guests 'by the hand' to show them these places; with Turkish newcomers who lived now in Fokaeis' parents' houses and were still keeping the legitimate owners' keys by the door's side; with grandchildren of Muslims who lived in Greece before 1922 (before being 'exchanged' with Christians living in Turkey) and who still spoke Greek. All of them reassured Fokaeis that their forefathers were good persons and used to live with Turkish Fokaeis 'like brothers'. This time, Fokaeis tasted Turkish/Foca dishes and realized they were the same as the ones their mothers and themselves cooked. Foca women reassured them that the recipes were 'originally Greek'—'theirs'. Music and dances performed for their own sake also sounded very similar, almost the same—a further sensorial testimony that their forefathers used to live with Turkish Fokaeis 'like siblings'. One day, while listening to Foca music, Mrs Koula started crying: 'I remembered my parents singing and dancing their pain in exile.' A young Turkish man approached her and told her: 'I know why you are crying…I am crying too inside me.' He then took her arm, put it along his, and said: 'Our veins are run by the same blood.'[10]*

There is much about the twentieth century, about the limits of nation formation, ethnic cleansing, and state acculturation, that can be gleaned from such moments. Although there was much about the 'reunion' that was orchestrated, it is clear from the mutual outpourings of emotion and tender gesturing that spontaneously ensued that both sides wished to communicate with each other on an intimate level. Through reliving a sense of that older intercommunality the two groups sought to reaffirm that the local trumps the national,[11] that the moral environment of the community is superior to that of the nation, and that difference does not necessarily require exclusivity. Although the people in question did not actually know each other, their sense of the histories that had generated the traumas that had blighted the lives of their ancestors had to be confronted together.

Mutual recognition of common victimhood was one way in which they were able to 'really feel' their local histories as opposed to their divisive national ones. Papagaroufali claimed that through a new process of 'adelfo-poesis' (literally 'brotherhood-making'), the 'Fokaeis [Phokiani] who performed the *adelfopoesis* found themselves feeling or "touching" time more as open-ended than one-sidedly marked by linear ordered events, invested with fixed nationalistic feelings'.[12]

After a seventy-year absence, my own grandfather and namesake was welcomed back to his neighbourhood in Bodrum by descendants of Cretan refugees and by others who were too young to have known him. The encounter was typically 'sygginitiko' (emotional). Local ladies shed a tear and kissed his hands, and he was invited into people's homes. It is easy to mock such moments by drawing attention to violent episodes in the past, to what 'Greeks' and 'Turks' have done to each other, to recall the violence that supposedly revealed the true nature of the relationship. Yet the rarely examined assumptions that inform the 'clash of civilizations' models of the world naively ignore the extent to which the animosities in question had been based on political contrivance and manipulation. If, as the priest in Politis' *Stou Hatzifrangkou*, wistfully claimed, everything is predicated on the powerful, who get along when it suits them, and if the nation is a modern invention, then such touching moments between 'enemy' peoples speak to a reality that is more historically and locally grounded. As Benedict Anderson forthrightly claims, 'nation-ness' remains the most 'universally legitimate value in political life in our times',[13] but it cannot seem to obliterate the values that pre-date and do not recognize nation-ness, and which in times past have proved useful whenever peoples of difference have had to coexist within the same societies.

Glossary[1]

agathos – innocent, gullible (G)

agiasma – holy water (G)

agrammati – the illiterate (G)

amorphoti – the uneducated (G)

anavatan – Turkish for motherland, equivalent of the Greek *patrida*

bayram – religious festival (T)

bey – sir or master, often appended to a man's name as a gesture of respect (T)

beylik – early Turkic principality (T)

Çerkes – Circassian (T)

chette (*çete*) – Turkish bandit

Charos (*Charon*) – in modern Greek folklore, he is the angel of death who takes the recently deceased to the other world

chiflik (*çiflik*) – private landed estate (T)

dhimmi (*zimmi* **in Turkish**) – non-Muslim subjects under Muslim rule

disemic – refers to holding mutually contradictory meanings and ideologies

efendi – gentleman, ascribed to eminent and influential men (T)

Ellines – refers to Greek nationals (G), *Yunan* in Turkish

gaza – Turkish for holy war (T)

gâvur – infidel (T), rendered as 'giavourides' in Greek

glendi – refers to a festive scene (G)

hanım – Turkish for woman/lady, pronounced 'hanoom' in Greek

Hıdırellez – very popular and widely revered Muslim saint

hodja (*hoca*) – spiritual teacher (T)

Hıristiyan – Christian (T)

Intercommunality – refers to the spirit and practices of communal coexistence

istories – literally means histories, but means travails (G)

jinn – genies, powerful spirits (*cin* in Turkish)

---

1. (G) – denotes Greek, (T) – denotes Turkish

kaymakam – provincial administrator (T)

kallikantzari – goblin-like creatures (G)

Karamanlides – Turkish-speaking Greek Orthodox Christians of central Anatolia (G)

Karamanlidika – Turkish dialect spoken by Greek Orthodox Christians of central Anatolia (G)

kefi – means festive mood (G)

koinotita – community (G)

koliva – sweetened boiled wheat distributed at Greek memorial services

kurban – animal sacrifice (T)

laos – people (G)

mahalle – town or village neighbourhood (T), rendered as *mahallas* in Greek

Megali Idea – refers to Greek national goal of reclaiming Constantinople and Asia Minor

millet-i Rum – the Greek Orthodox Community (T)

Mikrasiates – Greek Orthodox Christians of Asia Minor

misos – hatred (G)

morphomeni – educated people (G)

morphosis – learnedness (G)

muhacir – immigrant, also denotes Muslim refugees received in Anatolia (T)

muhtar – official neighbourhood or village leader (T)

mufti – Muslim cleric, interpreter of Islamic Law (*müftü* in Turkish)

neraides – Nereids, water nymphs (G)

patrida – fatherland or ancestral locality (G)

Romioi – Greek term for Greek Orthodox Ottoman subjects (G)

Rum – literally 'Romans', denoted the empire's Greek Orthodox subjects (T)

tarikat – religious order (T)

tekke – dervish lodge (T)

türbe – the tomb of a saint (T)

vali – governor of a province

vilayet – Ottoman province (T)

vrikolakas – vampire-like creature (G)

xenitia – living abroad (G)

Yörük – Yurouks, nomadic Turks of Anatolia and Balkans

Yunan – Greek nationals (T)

Endnotes

PREFACE

1. Pantelis Kontogiannis, *Geographia tis Mikras Asias* (Athens, 1921), 267; 'Statistikos pinax tis eparchias Kizikou', *Xenophanes*, 3/2 (1905), 92.
2. Aron Rodrigue, 'Difference and Tolerance in the Ottoman Empire', *Stanford Humanities Review* (1995), 81–92.
3. KMS Bithynia, Michaniona: Dimitris Maoutsidis.
4. Rogers Brubaker, 'Aftermaths of Empire and the Unmixing of Peoples', in Karen Barkey and Mark von Hagen (eds), *After Empire: Multiethnic Societies and Nation-Building: The Soviet Union and the Russian, Ottoman, and Habsburg Empires* (Boulder, CO, 1997); Donald Bloxham, 'The Great Unweaving: The Removal of Peoples in Europe, 1875-1949', in Richard Bessel and Claudia B. Haake (eds), *Removing Peoples: Forced Removal in the Modern World* (Oxford, 2009).
5. Michael Herzfeld, *Anthropology through the Looking Glass: Critical Ethnography in the Margins of Europe* (Cambridge, 1987).
6. For example, Herzfeld, *Anthropology through the Looking Glass*, 41ff; *A Place in History: Social and Monumental Time in a Cretan Town* (Princeton, 1991); David E. Sutton, *Memories Cast in Stone: The Relevance of the Past in Everyday Life* (Oxford and New York, 1998); Loring M. Danforth and Riki Van Boeschoten, *Children of the Greek Civil War: Refugees and the Politics of Memory* (Chicago, 2012).
7. L. L. Farrar Jnr, Kiernan McGuire, and John E. Thompson, 'Dog in the Night: The Limits of European Nationalism, 1789–1895', *Nations and Nationalism*, 4 (1998), 547–68.

INTRODUCTION

1. Fernand Braudel, *Civilization and Capitalism, 15th–18th Centuries*, vol. 1, *The Structures of Everyday Life: The Limits of the Possible* (London, 1981), 29.
2. KMS, Ionia, Giatzilari: Maria Birbili.
3. *Seinfeld*, NBC, 'The Pitch', Series 4, Episode 43.

4. Quoted from Penelope Papailias' interview with Christos Samouilidis. See Penelope Papailias, *Genres of Recollection: Archival Poetics and Modern Greece* (New York, 2005), 113.

5. Jane Burbank and Frederick Cooper, *Empires in World History* (Princeton, 2010). On the management of difference in the Ottoman Empire, the key text is Karen Barkey, *Empire of Difference: The Ottomans in Comparative Perspective* (Cambridge, 2008).

6. G. W. F. Hegel, *Lectures on the Philosophy of World History: Introduction*, trans. by H. B. Nisbet (Cambridge, 1974), 79.

7. Fernand Braudel, *The Mediterranean and the Mediterranean World in the Age of Philip II*, vol. 1 (London, 1972), 21.

8. Braudel, *Civilization and Capitalism,* 29.

9. Eric R. Wolf, *Europe and the People without History* (Berkeley, CA, 1982), 6–7.

10. See Bruce Masters, *Christians and Jews in the Ottoman Arab World: The Roots of Sectarianism* (Cambridge, 2001).

11. Peter Sluglett (ed.), *The Urban Social History of the Middle East, 1750–1950* (Syracuse, NY, 2008); Biray Kolluoglu and Meltem Toksöz (eds), *Cities of the Mediterranean: From the Ottomans to the Present Day* (London, 2010); C. A. Bayly and Leila Fawaz (eds), *Modernity and Culture: From the Mediterranean to the Indian Ocean* (New York, 2002).

12. See Philip Mansel, *Levant: Splendour and Catastrophe on the Mediterranean* (London, 2010), but also Bayly and Fawaz, *Modernity and Culture*. See also Hervé Georgelin, *Le fin de Smyrne: du cosmopolitisme aux nationalismes* (Paris, 2005) and especially the work by the aptly named Marie-Carmen Smynelis: *Une societe hors de soi: Identités et relations sociales à Smyrne aux XVIIIe et XIXe siècles* (Paris, 2005).

13. Donald Quataert, *The Ottoman Empire 1700–1922*, 2nd edn (Cambridge, 2005), 175.

14. Quataert's claims are based on an appraisal of residential patterns and (mainly urban) workplace relations: *The Ottoman Empire 1700–1922*, 174–94.

15. Michelle U. Campos, *Ottoman Brothers: Muslims, Christians, and Jews in Early Twentieth-Century Palestine* (Stanford, CA, 2011).

16. Christopher A. Bayly, *The Birth of the Modern World 1780–1914: Global Connections and Comparisons* (Oxford, 2004), 451–73.

17. Sia Anagnostopoulou, *Mikra Asia, 19os ai.–1919: i Ellinorthodoxes koinotites apo to Millet ton Romion sto elliniko ethnos* (Athens, 1997); Gerasimos Augustinos, *The Greeks of Asia Minor: Confession, Community, and Ethnicity in the Nineteenth Century* (Kent, OH, 1992).

18. Fred Burnaby, *On Horseback through Asia Minor* (London, 1877), 148.

19. William Mitchell Ramsay, *Impressions of Turkey during Twelve Years Wanderings* (London, 1897), 34–5.

20. Mansel, *Levant*, 174.

21. Carla Sinopoli, 'Imperial Integration and Imperial Subjects', in Susan Alcock et al. (eds), *Empires: Perspectives from Archaeology and History* (Cambridge, 2001), 195. See also Barkey, *Empire of Difference*; Burbank and Cooper, *Empires in World History*. Much of the emerging literature has focused on frontiers, where identities were much more unstable and relations more fluid. The principle work here is Richard White, *The Middle Ground: Indians, Empires, and Republics in the Great Lakes Region, 1650–1815*, 2nd edn (Cambridge, 2010).

22. Barkey, *Empire of Difference*; Rodrigue, 'Difference and Tolerance in the Ottoman Empire'; Daniel Goffman, *The Ottoman Empire and Early Modern Europe* (Cambridge, 2002).

23. Goffman, *The Ottoman Empire and Early Modern Europe*, 92.

24. Goffman, *The Ottoman Empire and Early Modern Europe*, 90.

25. Edward Muir, 'Introduction: Observing Trifles', in E. Muir and G. Ruggiero (eds), *Microhistory and the Lost Peoples of Europe* (Baltimore, 1991), xxi. On the history of everyday life, see Alf Lüdtke (ed.), *The History of Everyday Life: Reconstructing Everyday Experiences and Ways of Life* (Princeton, 1995).

26. For example, Thalia Pandiri, 'Driven out of Eden', in Peter Isaac Rose (ed.), *The Dispossessed: An Anatomy of Exile* (Boston, 2004), 54.

27. Anagnostopoulou, *Mikra Asia*, 30.

28. Gerald W. Creed, 'Reconsidering Community', in Creed (ed.), *The Seductions of Community: Emancipations, Oppressions, Quandaries* (Santa Fe, NM, 2006), 4ff.

29. Charis Exertzoglou, *Ethniki Taftotita stin Kosntatinoupoli ton 19 ai: Ellinikos Philologikos Syllogos Kostantinoupoleos, 1861–1912* (Athens, 1996); Vangelis Kechriotis, 'Greek-Orthodox, Ottoman Greeks or Just Greeks? Theories of Coexistence in the Aftermath of the Young Turk Revolution', *Etudes Balkaniques*, 1 (2005), 51–72.

30. Christos Soldatos, *I Ekpedeftiki kai Pnevmatiki Kinisi tou Ellinismou tis M. Asias (1800–1922)* 2 vols (Athens, 1989).

31. Samuel P. Huntington, *The Clash of Civilizations and the Making of the New World Order* (New York, 1996).

32. Wolf, *Europe and the People without History*, 6.

33. William H. McNeill, *Polyethnicity and National Unity in World History* (Toronto, 1986), 34.

34. Geoff Eley, *A Crooked Line: From Cultural History to the History of Society* (Ann Arbor, MI, 2008), 202–3.

35. Antonis Liakos, 'Eisagogi: to 1922 kai Emis', in Antonis Liakos (ed.), *To 1922 kai i Prosfiges: mia nea matia* (Athens, 2011), 12.

36. Nicholas G. Pappas, 'Concepts of Greekness: The Recorded Music of Anatolian Greeks after 1922', *Journal of Modern Greek Studies*, 17 (1999), 353–73.

37. Charis Exertzoglou, 'I Istoria tis Prosfigikis Mnimis', in Liakos (ed.) *To 1922 kai i Prosfiges*, 191ff; George Th. Mavrogordatos, *Stillborn Republic: Social Coalitions and Party Strategies in Greece, 1922–1936* (Berkeley, CA, 1983), 182ff.

38. Renée Hirschon, *Heirs of the Greek Catastrophe: The Social Life of Asia Minor Refugees in Piraeus*, 2nd edn (New York and London, 1998).
39. Papailias, *Genres of Recollection*, 96.
40. The *Archeio Proforikis Paradosis* has been the subject of some discussion. See Ioanna Petropoulou, 'I Ideologiki poria tis Melpo Merlier, to Kentro Mikrasiatikon Spoudon kai i sigkrotisi tou Archeiou Proforikis Paradosis', in A. Moutzouvi (ed.), *Martiries se ichitikes kai kinoumenes apotiposis os pigi tis Istorias* (Athens, 1998); Georgios A. Yiannakopoulos, 'The Reconstruction of a Destroyed Picture: The Oral History Archive of the Centre for Asia Minor Studies', *Mediterranean Historical Review*, 8.2 (1993), 201–17; Evi Kapoli, 'Archive of Oral Tradition of the Centre for Asia Minor Studies: Its Formation and its Contribution to Research', *Ateliers du LESC*, 32 (2008), http://ateliers.revues. org/1143 (accessed 12 January 2012).
41. Papailias, *Genres of Recollection*, 101.
42. Hirschon, *Heirs of the Greek Catastrophe*, 29–30.
43. Renée Hirschon, '"We got on well with the Turks": Christian-Muslim Relations in Late Ottoman Times', in David Shankland (ed.), *Archaeology, Anthropology and Heritage in the Balkans and Anatolia: The Life and Times of F. W. Hasluck, 1878–1920*, vol. 2 (Istanbul, 2004), 325–43.
44. Exemplary are Luisa Passerini, *Fascism in Popular Memory: The Cultural Experience of the Turin Working Class* (Cambridge, 1987); and James Fentress and Chris Wickham, *Social Memory* (Oxford, 1992).
45. Papailias notes that relatively little is known about the interviewers either, although her own investigations show that these were committed people who developed a great deal of sympathy for their interviewees. See her *Genres of Recollection*, ch. 3.
46. Exertzoglou, 'I Istoria tis Prosfigikis Mnimis', 194.
47. The case against the Greeks, Armenians and other Christian groups is 'prosecuted' in Justin McCarthy, *Death and Exile: The Ethnic Cleansing of Ottoman Muslims, 1821–1922* (Princeton, 1996) and in the author's other works.

CHAPTER I

1. Herman Melville, *The Writings of Herman Melville, Northwestern Newberry Edition: Journals*, ed. Howard C. Horsford, with Lynn Horth (Chicago, 1989), 58, 60–1.
2. Melville, *Journals*, 58.
3. Melville, *Journals*, 62.
4. Timothy Mitchell, *Colonising Egypt* (Berkeley, CA, 1988), 5.
5. Melville, *Journals*, 61.
6. Written scripts presented additional complications. Thus Jews sometimes used Hebrew script to write Greek, Albanians used Arabic, Greek, and Latin (presumably reflecting their particular religious identities), while some Catholics

used Latin script to write in Greek. As late as the 1950s, Catholic religious texts were still being published in so-called 'frankohiotika'. Richard Clogg, 'Some Karamanlidika Inscriptions from the Monastery of the Zoodokhos Pigi, Balıklı, Istanbul', in Clogg (ed.), *Anatolica: Studies in the Greek East in the 18th and 19th Centuries* (Brookfield, VT, 1996), ch. 12, 56.

7. Christine Philliou, *Biography of an Empire: Governing Ottomans in an Age of Revolution* (Berkeley, CA, 2011), 69ff.

8. H. G. Dwight, *Constantinople: Old and New* (New York, 1915), 332–4.

9. William Gladstone, *The Bulgarian Horrors and the Question of the East* (London, 1876), 16–17.

10. Wheatcroft, *The Ottomans*, 233ff.

11. Lucy Mary Jane Garnett, *Turkey under the Ottomans* (New York, 1914), 1.

12. See Rodrigue, 'Difference and Tolerance in the Ottoman Empire'.

13. Will Kymlicka claims that even those thinkers 'who lived in polyglot empires that governed numerous ethnic and linguistic groups' wrote 'as if the culturally homogeneous city-states of Ancient Greece provided the essential or standard model of the political community': *Multicultural Citizenship: A Liberal Theory of Minority Rights* (Oxford, 1995), 2.

14. Dominic Lieven, *Empire: The Russian Empire and its Rivals from the Sixteenth Century to the Present* (London, 2002), 156; Burbank and Cooper, *Empires in World History*, 345, 348, 394.

15. David D. Laitin, *Nations, States, and Violence* (Oxford, 2007), 11.

16. For example Ashutosh Varshney, *Ethnic Conflict and Civic Life: Hindus and Muslims in India* (New Haven, CT, 2002); Paul Brass, *The Production of Hindu-Muslim Violence in India* (Seattle, 2005), 1–9.

17. Timothy Snyder, *Bloodlands: Europe between Hitler and Stalin* (New York, 2010).

18. Annamaria Orla-Bukowska, 'Maintaining Borders, Crossing Borders', in Antony Polonsky (ed.), *Polin: Studies in Polish Jewry*, vol. 17: *The Shtetl: Myth and Reality* (2004), 172.

19. Orla-Bukowska, 'Maintaining Borders, Crossing Borders', 172–2.

20. Barkey, *Empire of Difference*, 279.

21. Speros Vryonis Jnr, *The Decline of Medieval Hellenism in Asia Minor and the Process of Islamization from the Eleventh through to the Fifteenth Century* (Berkeley, CA, 1971), 35.

22. Vryonis, *The Decline of Medieval Hellenism in Asia Minor*, 55.

23. Vryonis, *The Decline of Medieval Hellenism in Asia Minor*, 48.

24. D. A. Korobeinikov, 'Raiders and Neighbours: The Turks (1040–1304)', in Jonathan Shepard (ed.), *The Cambridge History of the Byzantine Empire* (Cambridge, 2008), 697.

25. Vryonis, *The Decline of Medieval Hellenism in Asia Minor*.

26. E. A. Zachariadou, 'Co-Existence and Religion', *Archivum Ottomanicum*, 5.15 (1997), 124. See also E. A. Zachariadou, 'À propos du syncrétisme Islamo-Chrétien

dans les territoires Ottoman', in Gilles Veinstein (ed.), *Syncrétismes et hérésies dans l'Orient seljoukide et ottoman (XIVᵉ–XVIIIᵉ Siècle)* (Leuven, 2005), 395–403.

27. Goffman, The *Ottoman Empire and Early Modern Europe*, 42.

28. Cf .White, *The Middle Ground*.

29. Cemal Kafadar, *Between Two Worlds: The Construction of the Ottoman State* (Berkeley, CA, 1995), 72.

30. Barkey, *Empire of Difference*, 59.

31. Michel Balivet, 'Culture ouverte et échanges inter-religieux dans les villes ottomans due XIVᵉ siècle', in Elizabeth Zahariadou (ed.), *The Ottoman Emirate (1300–1389)* (Rethymnon, 1993), 3; Barkey, *Empire of Difference*, 61.

32. Barkey, *Empire of Difference*, 115.

33. Goffman, The *Ottoman Empire and Early Modern Europe*, 91.

34. Barkey, *Empire of Difference*, 113–14.

35. Barkey, *Empire of Difference*, 132, 146ff.

36. On the Greek Orthodox Church and its regular extortion by the Sultanate, see Steven Runciman, *The Great Church in Captivity: A Study of the Patriarchate of Constantinople from the Eve of the Turkish Conquest to the Greek War of Independence* (Cambridge, 1968).

37. Ranajit Guha, *Domination without Hegemony: History and Power in Colonial India* (Cambridge, MA, 1997), xii.

38. Randall Collins, *Macrohistory: Essays in Sociology of the Long Run* (Stanford, CA, 1999), 87.

39. See Bruce McGowan, 'The Age of the Ayans, 1699–1812' and Donald Quataert, 'The Age of Reforms, 1812–1914', in Suraiya Faroqhi, Bruce McGowan, Donald Quataert, and Şevket Pamuk (eds), *An Economic and Social History of the Ottoman Empire*, vol. 2 (Cambridge, 1994), 770ff.

40. Bayly, The *Birth of the Modern World, 1789–1914*.

41. Masters, *Christians and Jews in the Ottoman Arab World*, 156ff.

42. Donald Quataert, *Social Disintegration and Popular Resistance in the Ottoman Empire, 1881–1908: Reactions to European Penetration* (New York, 1983), 91.

43. Western style reforms were also a condition of massive loans that were to pay for modern infrastructure projects: Eugene Rogan, *The Arabs: A History* (London, 2009), 105–7.

44. David Brewer, *Greece, the Hidden Centuries: Turkish Rule from the Fall of Constantinople to Greek Independence* (London, 2010), 184ff.

45. Masters, *Christians and Jews in the Ottoman Arab World*, 130ff; Carter Vaughn Findley, 'The Tanzimat', in Reşat Kasaba (ed.), *The Cambridge History of Turkey*, vol. 4, *Turkey and the Modern World* (Cambridge, 2008), 28.

46. Campos, *Ottoman Brothers*, 32ff.

47. Masters, *Christians and Jews in the Ottoman Arab World*, 130.

48. M. Şükrü Hanioğlu, 'Turkish Nationalism and the Young Turks, 1889–1908', in Fatma Müge Göçek (ed.), *Social Constructions of Nationalism in the Middle East* (Albany, NY, 2002), 94.

49. A. L. Macfie, *The End of the Ottoman Empire, 1908–1923* (London, 1998), 29.

50. William Mitchell Ramsay, *The Intermixture of Races in Asia Minor: Some of its Causes and Effects* (London, 1917), 32.

51. William M. Ramsay, *The Historical Geography of Asia Minor* (London, 1890), 25.

52. Ramsay, *Impressions of Turkey*, 132.

53. J. W. Childs, *Across Asia Minor on Foot* (Edinburgh and London, 1917), 57.

54. W. S. Monroe, *Turkey and the Turks: An Account of the Lands, the Peoples, and the Institutions of the Ottoman Empire* (London, 1908), 82.

55. Molly Greene, *A Shared World: Christians and Muslims in the Early Modern Mediterranean* (Princeton, 2000), 205.

56. It was certainly the case that Greek Christians and Armenians formed the majority of registered merchants operating in the imperial capital before the First World War. See Quataert, 'The Age of Reforms, 1812–1914', in Inalcik and Quataert (eds), *An Economic and Social History*, 840; Fatma Müge Göçek, *Rise of the Bourgeoisie, Demise of Empire: Ottoman Westernization and Social Change* (New York, 1996), 115.

57. Mansel, *Levant*, 168–9.

58. Gerasimos Augustinos, *Consciousness and History: Nationalist Critics of Greek Society, 1897–1914* (Boulder, CO, 1977), 128–30.

59. Kemal Karpat, *Ottoman Population 1830–1914: Demographic and Social Characteristics* (Madison, WI, 1985).

60. Donald Quataert, 'The Age of Reforms, 1812–1914', in Suraiya Faroqhi et al. (eds), *An Economic and Social History of the Ottoman Empire*, vol.2, *1600–1914* (Cambridge, 1994), 782.

61. Servet Multu, 'Late Ottoman Population and its Ethnic Distribution', *Nüfusbilim Dergisi/Turkish Journal of Population Studies*, 25 (2003), 11.

62. Paschalis Kitromilides and Alexis Alexandris, 'Ethnic Survival, Nationalism and Forced Migration: The historical demography of the Greek community of Asia Minor at the close of the Ottoman era', *Deltio: Kentro Mikrasiatikon Spoudon*, 3 (1984–85), 28. See also Alexis Alexandris, 'The Greek Census of Anatolia and Thrace (1910–1912): A Contribution to Ottoman Historical Demography', in Dimitri Gondicas and Charles Issawi (eds), *Ottoman Greeks in the Age of Nationalism: Politics, Economy, and Society in the Nineteenth Century* (Princeton, 1999).

63. Yiannakopoulos, 'The Reconstruction of a Destroyed Picture', 207; Ioannis F. Kaztaridis, *I Exodos ton Ellinon tou Kars tis Armenias (1919–21)* (Athens, 1996).

64. Regarding the movement of labour in the region, see Christopher Clay, 'Labour Migration and Economic Conditions in Nineteenth-Century Anatolia', *Middle Eastern Studies*, 34.4 (1998), 1–32.

65. A good demographic survey is provided in Anagnostopoulou, *Mikra Asia*, 137–60.

66. Nedim Ipek and K. Tuncer Çağlayan, 'The Emigration From the Ottoman Empire to America', in A. Deniz Balgamiş and Kemal H. Karpat (eds), *Turkish Migration to the United States: From Ottoman Times to the Present* (Madison, WI, 2008), 31.

67. Argiris P. Peronitis, 'Hazioustalar (Hacıustalar): O Protomastoras Hatzi-Antonis kai i dio mastori aderfia tou', *Mikrasiatika Chronika*, 20 (1995), 197–260.

68. Kiriaki Manomi and Lida Istikopoulou, *Somatiaki Organosi tou Ellinismou sti Mikra Asia (1861–1922)* (Athens, 2006), 223–4.

69. Ioannis Kalfoglous, *Istoriki Geographia tis Mikrasiatikis Hersonisou* (Istanbul, 1899, repr. Athens, 2002), 96.

70. Manomi and Istikopoulou, *Somatiaki Organosi tou Ellinismou sti Mikra Asia*, 248–9.

71. Augustinos, *The Greeks of Asia Minor*, 152ff.

72. Manomi and Istikopoulou, *Somateiaki Organosi tou Ellinismou sti Mikra Asia*, 50; Kalfoglous, *Istoriki Geographia tis Mikrasiatikis Hersonisou*, 148.

73. Sia Anagnostopoulou, 'Greek Diplomatic Authorities in Anatolia', in Evangelia Balta and Matthias Kappler (eds), *Cries and Whispers in Karamanlidika Books* (Wiesbaden, 2010), 67.

74. For example Philliou, *Biography of an Empire*, 166ff.

75. Anthony Kaldellis, *Hellenism in Byzantium: The Transformation of Greek Identity and the Reception of the Classical Tradition* (Cambridge, 2007), 42.

76. *Xenophanes*, 1 (1896), 3–6, and 2 (1905), 18–30; Theodosis Pylarinos, 'To "Biblio" ton Ipotrophon tou Syllogou Mikrasiatikon "I Anatoli"', *Mikrasiatiko Chroniko*, 21 (2002), 98–100.

77. For example, see Pieter Judson, *Guardians of the Nation: Activists on the Language Frontiers of Imperial Austria* (Cambridge, MA, 2007), 2.

78. Irini Renieri, '"Xenophone Nevşehirlis...Greek Souled Neapolitans": The Persistent yet Hesitant Dissemination of the Greek Language in 1870s Nevşehir', in Balta and Kappler (eds), *Cries and Whispers in Karamanlidika Books*, 31–44.

79. For example, KMS, Pisidia, Isparta Kosmas Manologlou; KMS Bithynia, Nicaea, Thomas Athanasiadis; KMS, Bithynia Leventekoy, Anastasia Hatzigeorgiou.

80. KMS Pontus, Derezik: Iraklis Ioannidis.

81. Ussama Makdisi, *The Culture of Sectarianism: Community, History and Violence in Nineteenth-Century Ottoman Lebanon* (Berkeley, CA, 2000), 94.

82. Frederick Cooper with Rogers Brubaker, 'Identity', in Frederick Cooper, *Colonialism in Question: Theory, Knowledge, History* (Berkeley, CA, 2005), 62–3.

83. Cooper with Brubaker, *Colonialism in Question*, 77.

84. Goffman, *The Ottoman Empire and Early Modern Europe*, 91.

85. Makdisi sees the greatest fallacy of Ottoman Lebanese historiography as the reproduction of 'the notion of the pure communal actor': *The Culture of Sectarianism*, 69.

86. Kentro Mikrasiatikon Spoudon (ed.), *Telefteos Ellinismos tis Mikras Asias* (Athens, 1974), 197, 204–5.

87. Thanasis Bravos, 'Ellinismos kai (Neo) Tourkiki Antilipsi peri Mionotiton, 1912–1922', *Mikrasiatika Chronika*, 22 (2007), 5; Alexandris, 'The Greek Census of Anatolia and Thrace', 54. The lower figure is taken from Karpat, *Ottoman Population*, 45.

88. Anthony Bryer, 'The Pontic Greeks before Diaspora', *Journal of Refugee Studies*, 4 (1991), 327.

89. Bryer, 'Pontic Greeks before Diaspora', 322.

90. Bryer, 'Pontic Greeks before Diaspora', 320ff: Greene, *A Shared World*, 103ff

91. R. M. Dawkins, *Modern Greek in Asia Minor: A Study of the Dialects of Silli, Cappadocia and Pharasa, with Grammar, Texts, Translations and Glossary* (Cambridge, 1916), 6–9.

92. Anagnostopoulou, *Mikra Asia*, 222.

93. Clay, 'Labour Migration and Economic Conditions in Nineteenth-Century Anatolia', 6.

94. Geoffrey Horrocks, *Greek: A History of the Language and its Speakers*, 2nd edn (Oxford, 2010), 400–1.

95. Bryer, 'Pontic Greeks before Diaspora', 321.

96. Margarita Poutouridou, 'The Of Valley and the Coming of Islam: The Case of the Greek-Speaking Muslims', *Deltio*, 12 (1997–8), 62.

97. Richard Clogg, 'A Millet within a Millet: The Karamanlides', in Gondicas and Issawi (eds), *The Ottoman Greeks in the Age of Nationalism*, 123.

98. Anagnostopoulou, *Mikra Asia*, 234.

99. Christos Hadziiossif, *Sinasos: Istoria enos topou horis Istoria* (Herakleion, Crete, 2005), 247.

100. Clogg, 'A Millet within a Millet', 131–2.

101. Anagnostopoulou, 'Greek Diplomatic Authorities in Anatolia', 67.

102. Christos Hadziiossif, 'The Ambivalence of Turkish in a Greek-Speaking Community of Central Anatolia', and Renieri, 'Xenophone Nevşehirlis ...Greek Souled Neapolitans'.

103. *Telefteos Ellinismos tis Mikras Asias* (Athens, 1974), 147, 153, 156, 163.

104. Dawkins, *Modern Greek in Asia Minor*, 10.

105. Dawkins, *Modern Greek in Asia Minor*, 13–14; Horrocks, *Greek: A History of the Language and its Speakers*, 403; Pantelis Kontogiannis, *Geographia tis Mikras Asias* (Athens, 1921), 150–1. Kontogiannis writes that Fertek had 3,000 Greeks and 300 Turks.

106. Dawkins, *Modern Greek in Asia Minor*, 28; Hadziiossif, *Sinasos*, 325.

107. Dawkins, *Modern Greek in Asia Minor*, 30–5.

108. Dawkins also notes the survival of 'Asiatic' Greek in the village of Livisi on the southern coast, near Kastellorizo, in Gyölde near the Kula, and in Bithynia near Nikomedia and Bursa. See *Modern Greek in Asia Minor*, 37–8.

109. Dawkins believes that these coastal Greeks had migrated from the islands and the Greek mainland, and therefore their Greek dialect was not indigenous to Anatolia. See *Modern Greek in Asia Minor*, 5.

110. *Telefteos Ellinismos tis Mikras Asias*, 278.

111. Dawkins, *Modern Greek in Asia Minor*, 37–8.

112. Karpat, *Ottoman Population*, 47.

113. *Telefteos Ellinismos tis Mikras Asias* (Athens, 1974), 103, 111, 117, 123, 130, 134, 138.

114. Ippokratis K. Makris, 'I Katiki tis Syzikinis Hersonisou', *Mikrasiatika Chronika*, 11 (1961), 211–26; Nikos Milioris, 'Ta Ellinika horia tis periochis Vouron Mikras Asias', *Mikrasiatika Chronika*, 14 (1970), 177–225; Stamatis Hatzibeis, 'I Krini (Cesme) kai i Periochi tis', *Mikrasiatika Chronika*, 11 (1961), 227–45.

115. Anagnostopoulou, *Mikra Asia*, 191.

116. Cf. Michael Palairet, *The Balkan Economies c.1800–1914: Evolution without Development* (Cambridge, 1997), 201.

117. Anagnostopoulou, *Mikra Asia*, 200.

118. Anagnostopoulou, *Mikra Asia*, 209.

119. Anagnostopoulou, *Mikra Asia*, 200.

120. Giles Milton, *Paradise Lost: Smyrna 1922, The Destruction of Islam's City of Tolerance* (London, 2008), 9.

121. *Ellinikos Odigos: Idioktisia Eterias* (Athens [1920] 1992), 35, 50, 63–5, 69–71, 77.

122. Mansel, *Levant*, 164, 166.

123. Gaston Deschamps, *Sur les routes d'Asie* (Paris, 1894), 151–2.

124. Wolf, *Europe and the People without History*, 6–7.

125. For example Chris Gosden, *Archaeology and Colonialism: Cultural Contact from 5000 BC to the Present* (Cambridge, 2004).

126. Bryer, 'Pontic Greeks before Diaspora', 327.

CHAPTER 2

1. *Exodos*, vol. B, *Martyries apo tis eparchies tis Kentrikis kai Notias Mikrasias*, ed. Paschalis Kitromilides and Yanni Mourelou (Athens, 1982), 152.

2. KMS, Lydia, Parsa: Sofia Delvetoglou.

3. Sofia Anastasiadi-Manousaki, *Kappadokias Mnimes* (Athens, 2002), 25.

4. KMS, Pontus, Zilmera: Sofia Lapasidou.

5. KMS, Lycia, Livisi: Giannis Hatzidoulis.

6. KMS Bithynia, Demirdesi, Alexandros Kontos.

7. For example KMS, Bithynia, Oren: Kiriakos Pachidis: 'We lived well together. They were simple people, farmers like us. They came to our homes on feast days, exchanged eggs at Easter. During Bayram we went to wish them well, they gave us sweets and fresh meat'; KMS, Bithynia, Pilantinos: Sofia Meresetzi: 'In truth, we got on well. We'd invite them to our weddings, and engagements. There were many kind people. Osman Effendi allowed thousands of Greek refugees, who had been exiled from the Marmara Sea to Bursa, to bathe without charge in his baths. He had three sons. One was supportive of the Greeks, another was a Kemalist, and another was neutral.'

8. Svetlana Boyn, *The Future of Nostalgia* (New York, 2001), xvi.

9. For Eastern Anatolia, see Bloxham, *The Great Game of Genocide*; Ugur Ümit Üngör, *The Making of Modern Turkey: Nation and State in Eastern Anatolia, 1913–1950* (Oxford, 2011).

10. For example Steven A. Epstein, *Purity Lost: Transgressing Boundaries in the Eastern Mediterranean, 1000–1400* (Baltimore, 2006); Eric. R. Dursteler, *Venetians in Constantinople: Nation, Identity, and Coexistence in the Early Modern Mediterranean* (Baltimore, 2006); Adnan Husain and K. E. Fleming (eds), *A Faithful Sea: The Religious Cultures of the Mediterranean, 1200–1700* (London, 2007).

11. Kontogiannis, *Geographia tis Mikras Asias*, 310.

12. KMS Ionia, Ypsili: Kostas Kipreos.

13. William M. Ramsay, *The Historical Geography of Asia Minor*.

14. Thea Halo, *Not Even My Name* (New York, 2000).

15. Christos Hadziiossif, *Sinasos*, 149ff.

16. KMS Ionia, Ypsili: Kostas Kipreos.

17. Malcolm Yapp, *The Making of the Modern Near East 1792–1923* (London, 1987), 6–7.

18. Augustinos, *The Greeks of Asia Minor*, 21.

19. KMS, Bithynia, Köprü: Giorgos Akasides.

20. KMS, Bithynia, Geyve: Kostas Berbantoglou.

21. KMS, Ionia, Ypsili: Kostas Kipreos.

22. KMS, Paphlagonia, Tzaitzouma: Iordanes Mavromatis; see also Kontogiannis, *Geographia tis Mikra Asias*, 103.

23. Peter Mackridge, 'The Myth of Asia Minor Greek Fiction', in Renée Hirschon (ed.), *Crossing the Aegean: An Appraisal of the 1923 Compulsory Population Exchange between Greece and Turkey* (New York, 2003), 235. 'Re-mould it nearer to the Heart's Desire' is quoted from the *Rubaiyat of Omar Khayyam*, 32:73.

24. Mackridge, 'The Myth of Asia Minor in Greek Fiction', 239.

25. Dido Sotiriou, *Farewell Anatolia* (Athens, 1996), 17–23.

26. Among the immigrants from the Balkans were Christians from independent Greece and Bulgaria, where national independence had negative economic consequences: Palairet, *The Balkan Economies, c. 1800–1914*. For Greece: Christos Hadziiossif, 'Class Structure and Class Antagonism in Late Nineteenth Century Greece', in Philip Carabott (ed.), *Greek Society in the Making, 1863–1913* (London, 1997), 14.

27. Panagiotis Savorianakis, *Nisiotikes Koinotites sto Aigaio* (Athens, 2000), 86.

28. Savorianakis, *Nisiotikes Koinotites sto Aigaio*, 82, 86.

29. Basili Kouligka, *Kios 1912–1922: Skorpies Mnimes* (Athens and Ioannina, 1993), 85

30. Vangelis Kokkolios, 'Galanadiotes kai Glinadiotes stin Poli kai stin Smyrni (O Kokolios ki o geros Smyrnios, O Avantis)', in N. A. Kefallianidis (ed.), *Mnimes apo tin Anatoli: Anekdota, Imerologia, Tragoudia, Eggrafa* (Athens, 1988), 47.

31. Alastair Bonnett, *Left in the Past: Radicalism and the Politics of Nostalgia* (New York and London, 2010), 9–10.

32. David Lowenthal, *The Past is a Foreign Country* (Cambridge, 1985); Michael Herzfeld, *Cultural Intimacy: Social Poetics in the Nation-State* (New York, 1997), 109ff.

33. Stratis Myrivilis, *Panagia i Gorgona* (Athens, 1956), 17.

34. Lowenthal, *The Past is a Foreign Country*, 4ff.

35. Luisa Passerini, 'Oral Memory of Fascism', in David Forgacs (ed.), *Rethinking Italian Fascism: Capitalism, Populism and Culture* (London, 1986), 186.

36. Dinka Corkalo, Dean Ajdukovic, Harvey M. Weinstein, Eric Stover, Dino Djipa, and Miklos Biro, 'Neighbors Again? Intercommunity Relations after Ethnic Cleansing', in Eric Stover and Harvey M. Weinstein (eds), *My Neighbor, My Enemy: Justice and Community in the Aftermath of Mass Atrocity* (Cambridge, 2004), 145.

37. Myrivilis, *Panagia i Gorgona*, 17.

38. Hirschon, *Heirs of the Greek Catastrophe*; Bruce Clark, *Twice a Stranger: How Mass Expulsion that Forged Modern Greece and Turkey* (Cambridge, MA, 2009).

39. For a clear discussion on social memory and its value for historians, see Fentress and Wickham, *Social Memory*, especially Chapter 3.

40. See Hercules Millas, 'History Textbooks in Greece and Turkey', *History Workshop Journal*, 31 (1991), 21–33; Roger Just, 'Triumph of the Ethnos', in M. Chapman, E. Tonkin, and M. Macdonald (eds), *History and Ethnicity* (London, 1989).

41. Tone Bringa, *Being Muslim the Bosnian Way: Identity and Community in a Central Bosnian Village* (Princeton, 1995).

42. A valuable recent study on intercommunality is Anja Peleikis, 'The Making and Unmaking of Memories: The Case of a Multi-Confessional Village in Lebanon', in Ussama Makdisi and Paul A. Silverstein (eds), *Memory and Violence in the Middle East and North Africa* (Bloomington and Indianapolis, 2006), 134–5.

43. Glenn Bowman, 'A Death Revisited: Solidarity and Dissonance in a Muslim-Christian Palestinian Village', in Ussama Makdisi and Paul A. Silverstein (eds), *Memory and Violence in the Middle East and North Africa* (Bloomington and Indianapolis, 2006), 31.

44. Mark von Hagen, 'The Russian Empire', in Barkey and von Hagen (eds), *After Empire*, 62; Burbank and Cooper, *Empires in World History*, 348.

45. Clark, *Twice a Stranger*, 35.

46. On *morphosis* as cultural capital, see Nicholas Doumanis, *Myth and Memory in the Mediterranean: Remembering Fascism's Empire* (London, 1997), 92ff.

47. Charis Sapountzakis, *Anthologia Pisidias* (Athens, 2000), 115.

48. Sapountzakis, *Anthologia Pisidias*, 121–2. The author of this anthology of testimonies makes note of the fact that the interviewee was a supporter of a controversial attempt by some Turkish-speaking Anatolians to create a breakaway Turkish Orthodox Church led by Papa Eftim.

49. Sapountzakis, *Anthologia Pisidias*, 116–19.

50. Sutton, *Memories Cast in Stone*, 121; Herzfeld, *Anthropology through the Looking Glass*, 42.

51. *I Exodos*, vol. A; Christos G. Andreadis (ed.), *Martyries apo tis eparchies ton Ditikon Paralion tis Mikrasias* (Athens, 1980).

52. Anatolian refugee nostalgia is also described in Renée Hirschon, 'We got on well with the Turks'.

53. KMS, Bithynia Vori: Yannis Mavroudis.

54. Bringa, *Being Muslim the Bosnian Way*.

55. Kalfoglous, *Istoriki Geographia tis Mikrasiatikis Hersonisou*, 132.

56. KMS, Caria, Muğla: Maria and Stefanos Hatzistefanos.

57. KMS, Aeolia, Karagatz: Patroklos Komenoglou.

58. KMS, Ionia, Hatzilari: Kleodimos Landos.

59. Mansel, *Levant*, 172.

60. KMS, Caria, Koitzaki: Yannis Hatziprodromos.

61. KMS, Pontus, Zefonos: Socrates Poslapilides.

62. Another example: KMS, Paphlagonia, Kastamonu: Isaac Simionidis: 'Foreign Turks were bad, especially the civil servants who came here during Hürriyet. They were *Doumedes* [Dönme], Jewish converts from Thessaloniki.'

63. Marc Baer, *The Dönme Jewish Converts, Muslim Revolution and Secular Turks* (Stanford, 2009). Jews are specifically mentioned in testimonies in reference to pre-Lent carnival, when Romioi often burned effigies of Judas, and during which Jewish communities were sometimes harassed. Michalis Triandaphilidou recalled that with the burning of the effigy of Judas during carnival, 'The Jews would hide in their homes all day. Such mania would grip the youth, such hatred, that they sought to seize a Jew, to take him and to try and burn him.': KMS, Caria, Halikarnassos: Michalis Triandaphilidou. On Greek–Jewish tensions, see Mansel, *Levant*, 172.

64. KMS, Ionia, Lotzaki: Andreas Mihos.

65. Iraklis Millas, 'Toukokratia: History and the Image of Turks in Greek Literature', *South European Society and Politics*, 11 (2006), 53-54.

66. 'Kalamaridika' meant official Greek, or the kind of Greek spoken by 'pen-pushing' bureaucrats, since 'kalamaki' (literally 'means 'straw') refers to a quill pen.

67. Kosmas Politis, *Stou Hatzifrangkou: Ta Saranta Chronia mias politias* (Athens, 1965), 40.

68. Politis, *Stou Hatzifrangkou*, 41.

69. Marianthe Colakis, 'Images of the Turk in Greek Fiction of the Asia Minor Disaster', *Journal of Modern Greek Studies*, 4 (1986), 99–106.

70. On attitudes towards Turkey in Greek society, see the special issue 'When Greeks Think About Turks: The View from Anthropology', *South European Society and Politics*, 11.1 (2006).

71. As anthropologists of Greece have shown, this dialectic was manifested in disemic notions of self. See Herzfeld, *Anthropology through the Looking Glass*, 111ff

72. Stratis Doukas, *A Prisoner of War's Story*, trans. Petro Alexiou, with introduction by Dimitris Tziovas (Birmingham, 1999), xiii. I thank Petro Alexiou for drawing my attention to this fact.

73. KMS, Mysia, Narlı: Charilaos Tsairis.

74. KMS, Mysia, Küçükkuyu: Polybios Narliotis.

75. KMS, Bithynia, Karabelit: Stavros Mouratides, Stavros Choulisides, Sofia Paschalidou.

76. KMS, Caria, Koitzaki: Yannis Hatziprodromos.

77. KMS, Bithynia, Kirezli: Alexandros Iosifidis.

78. KMS, Bithynia, Kiriharman: Ion Nikolaidis.

79. KMS, Caria, Koitzaki: Yannis Hatziprodromos.

80. KMS, Ionia, Hatzilari: Kleodimos Landos.

81. KMS Cappadocia, Kayseri: Thomas Milkoglou.

82. KMS, Paphlagonia, Kastamonu: Isaac Simionidis.

83. KMS, Cappadocia, Prokopi: Efstathios Hatziefthimiadis.

84. KMS, Ionia, Karatatzli: Iakovos Kiriazoglou.

85. KMS, Aeolia, Poriatzik: Giorgos Makris.

86. KMS, Pontus, Zana: Pavlos Aslanidis.

87. KMS, Caria, Halikarnassos: Kostas Kaiserlis.

88. For example, Jane Cowan, *Dance and the Body Politic in Northern Greece* (Princeton, 1990), 70ff; Michael Herzfeld, *Poetics of Manhood: Contest and Identity in a Cretan Mountain Village* (Princeton, 1985), 152ff.

89. KMS, Caria, Halikarnassos: Kostas Halkias.

90. KMS, Caria, Halikarnassos: Kostas Kaiserlis.

91. KMS, Mysia, Narzlı: Charilaos Tsairis.

92. KMS, Caria, Bozdoğan: Kostas Phinikopoulos.

93. Herzfeld, *Poetics of Manhood*, 154; see also Euthymios Papataxiarchis, 'Friends of the Heart', in Peter Loizos and Euthymios Papataxiarchis (eds), *Gender and Kinship in Modern Greece* (Princeton, 1991).

94. KMS, Bithynia, Fountouklia: Anastasis Alexiades.

95. KMS, Pontus, Kokse: Lazaros Hisekidis.

96. KMS, Pontus, Zana: Pavlos Aslanidis.

97. Anna Caraveli, ' "The Symbolic Village": Community Born in Performance', *Journal of American Folklore*, 98 (1985), 262.

98. KMS, Ionia, Kioski: Eriphilia Stamatiadou and Elli Volani.

99. KMS, Galatia, Ankara: Kiriakos Kilitzis.

100. KMS, Cappadocia, Sinasos: Angeliki Christidou.

101. KMS, Bythinia, Kios: Fotini Tzamtzi.

102. KMS, Paphlagonia, Tzaitzouma: Iordanis Mavromatis.

103. KMS, Pontus, Şebin Karahisar: Eleni Kolasidou.

104. KMS, Caria, Sokia: Katina Stilidou.

105. KMS, Ionia, Akkioi: Stamatia Fanidou; Aeolia, Poriatzik: Giorgos Makris.

106. KMS, Pontus, Omarkölü: Makoli Theofilos Iliadis.

107. KMS, Aeolia, Borgiatzik: Giorgos Makris.

108. KMS, Bithynia, Fountouklia: Anastasia Alexiades.

109. KMS, Bithynia, Lefke: Ilias Savvas. *Dekapentaugousto*, which literally means '15 August', is the date when the Orthodox celebrate the Assumption of the Virgin Mary. It coincides roughly with the end of Ramadan on 20 August.

110. David E. Sutton, *Remembrance of Repasts: An Anthropology of Food and Memory* (Oxford and New York, 2001), 4–6.

111. KMS, Lydia, Parsa: Evangelia Peristeridou.

112. KMS, Bithynia, Nicaea: Thomas Anastasiadis.

113. *I Exodos*, vol. B, *Martyries apo tis eparchies tis Kentrikis kai Notias Mikraasias* (Athens, 1982), 107.

114. Slavoj Žižek, *Enjoy Your Symptom!: Jacques Lacan in Hollywood and Out* (London, 2001), 8.

115. The exception was the honoured visitor, normally a stranger (*xenos*) who was treated with a form of guest friendship not unlike that practised in antiquity (*xenia*). For example, one interviewee stated: 'We went to their homes, they came to ours. We'd have them sleep over, but not near the icons, and we'd feed them, with the same hospitality we'd give to a Greek.' KMS, Pontus, Alantzuk: Theoharis Alonidis.

116. KMS, Caria, Muğla: Maria and Stefanos Hatzistefanos.

117. KMS, Caria, Karabounari: Urania Aradouli.

118. KMS, Ionia, Meresi: Nikos Verchigiannis.

119. KMS, Karia, Geronta: Victoria Zahariadis.

120. KMS, Bithynia, Lefke: Ilias Savvas.

121. KMS, Bithynia, Kouroudere: Giorgos Tsakirides.

122. KMS, Bithynia, Gieve: Kostas Berbandoglou.

123. KMS, Pontus, Abatzi: Maria Anastasiadou.

124. KMS, Pontus, Askar: Georgios Kaltsidis.

125. KMS, Ionia, Nea Phokies: Tassos Giannaris.

126. KMS, Paphlagonia, Patherio: Kiriakos Deligiannidis.

127. KMS, Ionia, Nea Phokies: Tassos Giannaris.

128. Hirschon, *Heirs of the Greek Catastrophe*, 15–16.

129. KMS, Ionia, Giakakoi: Dimitrios Kavoukas.

130. KMS, Bithynia, Giagketzit: Ilias Papdopoulos.

131. KMS, Mysia, Anaklise: Michalis Athanasellos.

132. KMS, Ionia, Nymphaio: Nestor Dimopoulos.

133. Herzfeld, *Cultural Intimacy*, 111.

134. KMS, Bithynia, Yannis Trichas; KMS, Bithynia, Gonia: Michalis Kirakou.

135. KMS, Bithynia, Karabelit: Stavros Mouratidis, Stavros Choulisides, Sofia Paschalidou.

136. KMS, Pontus, Salamour: Yannis Papadopoulos.

137. KMS Cappadocia: Nevşehir, Anna Georgiadi.

138. KMS, Mysia, Dazlidena: Savvas Kavestos.

139. In reality, all groups profited (and suffered) from the great economic changes. Donald Quataert's studies in late Ottoman economic history demonstrate that there was a marked disparity between perception and reality, and yet perceptions were also important in how communities related to each other. See Quataert, *The Ottoman Empire, 1700–1922.*

140. KMS, Mysia, Adramitti: Anna Pari.

141. KMS, Pontus, Amasia: Maria Anastasiadou.

142. See Herzfeld, *Anthropology through the Looking Glass*, 113.

143. KMS, Bithynia, Fountouklia: Anastasios Alexiades.

144. KMS, Ionia, Phokies: Anestis Varsitopoulos.

145. KMS, Lydia, Parsa: Evangelia Peristeridou: "ένας καφές, χιλια χρόνια χατήρια"

146. E.P. Thompson, *The Making of the English Working Class* (London, 1980), and E. P. Thompson, *Customs in Common* (London, 1991).

147. Bonnett, *Left in the Past*, 10.

CHAPTER 3

1. From Benjamin Barker's *Journal of a tour in Thrace (1823)*, quoted in Clogg, *Anatolica: Studies in the Greek East in the 18th and 19th Centuries* (Aldershot, 1996), xiii, 253–4.

2. Charles Boileau Elliott, *Travels in the Three Great Empires of Austria, Russia and Turkey*, vol. 2 (London, 1838), 90.

3. F. W. Hasluck, *Christianity and Islam under the Sultans*, ed. Margaret Hasluck (Oxford, 1929), 81–2.

4. KMS, Paphlagonia, Tzaitzouma: Iordanes Mavromatis.

5. Selim Deringil, ' "There is no Compulsion in Religion": On Conversion and Apostasy in the Late Ottoman Empire: 1839–1856', *Comparative Studies in History and Society*, 3 (2000), 547.

6. Hasluck, *Christianity and Islam under the Sultans.*

7. J. E. Blunt, *The People of Turkey*, vol. 2 (London, 1878), 241: 'Belief in the evil eye is perhaps more deeply rooted in the mind of the Turk than in that of any other nation, though Christians, Jews and even some Franks regard it as a real misfortune.'

8. See Hirschon, 'We got on well with the Turks', and *Heirs of the Greek Catastrophe.*

9. Charles Tilly, *Durable Inequality* (Berkeley, CA, 1998), 53; Barkey, *Empire of Difference*, 118.

10. KMS, Paphlagonia, Tzaitzouma: Iordanis Mavromatis.

11. KMS Lydia, Hazambeili: Leonidas Davoularis.

12. KMS Lydia, Hazambeili: Leonidas Davoularis.

13. Charles Stewart, *Demons and the Devil: Moral Imagination in Modern Greek Culture* (Princeton, 1991), 76.

14. Vera Shevzov, 'Letting the People into Church: Reflections on Orthodoxy and Community in Late Imperial Russia', in Valerie A. Kivelson and Robert H. Greene (eds), *Orthodox Russia: Belief Under the Tsars* (University Park, PA, 2003), 60; Stewart, *Demons and the Devil*, 246ff; and also Michelle Vovelle, *Ideologies and Mentalities* (Cambridge, 1990), ch. 5.

15. Cf. Michel Meslin, 'Le phenomene religieux populaire' in B. Lacroix and P. Boglioni (eds), *les Religions populaire. Colloque international 1970* (Quebec, 1972), 5–15. See Nikos Kokosalakis, 'The Political Significance of Popular Religion in Greece', *Archives des sciences sociales des religions* 64 (1987), 40. Vovelle's reading of popular religion focuses on alterities: *Ideologies and Mentalities*, 86.

16. Hasluck, *Christianity and Islam under the Sultans*, 255.

17. Stewart, *Demons and the Devil*, 12; Juliet Du Boulay, *Cosmos, Life, and Liturgy in a Greek Orthodox Village* (Limni, Evia, 2009), 8.

18. KMS Bithynia, Papazikoy: Maria Topalidou; KMS, Bithynia, Leventikoy: Anatstasia Hatzigeorgiou; KMS, Bithynia, Kantarikoy: Haralambos Dimopulos; KMS, Bithynia, Otarkioy: Iordanis Akkaoglou. Some reference to these communities is made in Spyridon Zoupoulidis, 'I Eparchia Kolonias', *Xenophanes* (1910), 276.

19. Du Boulay, *Cosmos, Life, and Liturgy*, 304.

20. Kallistos Ware, *The Orthodox Way* (Crestwood, NY, 1995), 15.

21. Ernst Benz, *The Eastern Orthodox Church: Its Life and Thought* (New York, 1963), 36.

22. Du Boulay, *Cosmos, Life, and Liturgy*, 45. See also Benz, *The Eastern Orthodox Church*, 37.

23. Vera Shevzov, *Russian Orthodoxy on the Eve of Revolution* (New York, 2007).

24. KMS Ionia, Aliaga: Stamatina Karakosta.

25. Demons, the Devil, and malign spirits were to be found on the margins. See Stewart, *Demons and the Devil*, passim.

26. Jacques Le Goff, *The Birth of Purgatory* (Chicago, 1984), 4.

27. Christos Samouilidis, 'Kappadokika ethima kai doxasies gia to thanato kai ti zoi', *Mikrasiatika Chronika*, 17 (1981), 233–5; G. F. Abbott, *Macedonian Folklore* (Cambridge, 1903), 193–4. See also Stewart, *Demons and the Devil*, 7; and Margaret Alexiou, *Ritual Lament in Greek Tradition* (Cambridge, 1974).

28. KMS, Caria, Gambei: Apostolos and Maria Stamatiadis.

29. Samouilidis, 'Kappadokika', 250.

30. KMS, Ionia, Giatzilari: Maria Birbili.

31. Simos Lianidis, 'Nekrika kai Tafika sti Santa tou Πontou', *Archeion Pontou* 26 (1964), 161.

32. Alexiou, *Ritual Lament in Greek Tradition*. For Greek rituals and *la longue durée*, see also Loring Danforth, *The Death Rituals of Rural Greece* (Princeton, 1982); regarding 'good death', see Nadia Seremetakis, *The Last Word: Women, Death and Divination in Inner Mani* (Chicago, 1991).

33. Du Boulay, *Cosmos, Life, and Liturgy*, 262–3.

34. Hasluck, *Christianity and Islam under the Sultans*, 217, 413.

35. Abbott, *Macedonian Folklore*, 257–8.

36. See this chapter, note 2.

37. *Persecution and Extermination of the Communities of Macri and Livissi (1914–1918)* (Paris, 1919).

38. Mark Mazower, *Salonica, City of Ghosts: Christians, Muslims and Jews, 1630–1950* (London, 2004), 351.

39. Hasluck, *Christianity and Islam under the Sultans*, 440.

40. The new resting place for the saint is Nea Prokopi. See also Vasso Stelaku, 'Space and Identity: Two Cappadocian Settlements', in Renée Hirschon (ed.), *Crossing the Aegean: An Appraisal of the 1923 Compulsory Population Exchange between Greece and Turkey* (New York, 2003), 186ff.

41. Hasluck, *Christianity and Islam under the Sultans*.

42. KMS, Lycia, Aktse: Nikolas Pisas.

43. Laurie Kain Hart, *Time, Religion, and Social Experience in Rural Greece* (Lanham, MD, 1992), 199, 201.

44. Hart, *Time, Religion, and Social Experience*, 197.

45. Peter Brown, 'The Saint as Exemplar in Late Antiquity', *Representations*, 2 (1983), 4, 6–7.

46. KMS, Bythinia, Kios: Fotini Tzamtzi; a similar kind of story was provided in KMS, Paphlagonia, Askortasai: Avgerinos Spanopoulos.

47. KMS, Bithynia, Kouvouklia: Persephone Tsotridou.

48. KMS, Bithynia, Nikomedia: Zizis Antoniadis.

49. KMS, Ionia, Tsiflikaki: Kleodimos Landos.

50. KMS, Lydia, Hazambeili: Leonidas Davoularis.

51. KMS Caria, Gambei: Maria Stamatiadou.

52. KMS, Bithynia, Bursa: Sofia Spanou.

53. The essential work on this topic is Stewart, *Demons and the Devil*.

54. Stewart, *Demons and the Devil*, 248.

55. KMS, Ionia, Sibrisari: Vasiliki Vardasis.

56. KMS, Aeolia, Karagatzli: Vasilia Kompourakou.

57. KMS Pontus, Koske: Lazaros Hisekidis.

58. KMS, Lydia, Philadelphia: Loukas Loukidis.

59. Du Boulay, *Cosmos, Life, and Liturgy*, 54.

60. KMS, Ionia, Nymphaio: Tikitika Demopoulou.

61. Stewart, *Demons and the Devil*, 10ff.

CHAPTER 4

1. Edwin Pears, *Turkey and its People* (London, 1911), 78.
2. Ziauddin Sardar, *Orientalism* (Buckingham and Philadelphia, 1999), 1–2.
3. Sardar, *Orientalism*, 10.
4. Edward Said, *Orientalism* (London, 1978).
5. Lucy Garnett, *Mysticism and Magic in Turkey: An Account of the Religious Doctrines, Monastic Organisation and Ecstatic Powers of the Dervish Orders* (New York, 1912).
6. Hirschon, *Heirs of the Greek Catastrophe*, 21.
7. KMS, Bythinia, Kios: Fotini Tzamtzi.
8. KMS, Lydia, Kasaba: Anna Hatzisotiriou.
9. KMS, Caria, Giambei: Apostolos and Maria Stamatiadou.
10. KMS, Lycia, Aktse: Nikolas Pisas.
11. KMS, Nymphaio, Ionia: Nestoras Dimopoulou; KMS, Lydia, Kasaba: Isaias Markopoulos: 'We'd send eggs and tsoureki. They considered these things to be holy. I had a Turkish friend who owned lots of chickens . . . and yet he still expected eggs during Easter'.
12. KMS, Paphlagonia, Kastamonu: Ilias Simeonidis.
13. KMS, Bithynia, Nikomedia: Zizis Antoniadis.
14. KMS, Lydia, Philadelphia: Michalis Orologas.
15. KMS, Lydia, Philadelphia: Elizabeth Mikalopetrakou.
16. KMS, Caria, Bodrum, Michalis Triantafilidou.
17. KMS, Pontus, Tutsuz: Stylianos Katzaboudiadis.
18. KMS, Aeolia, Bergama: Yannis Mimikos.
19. Marshall Hodgson, *The Venture into Islam*, vol. 1: *The Classical Age of Islam* (Chicago, 1977), 95–9.
20. Wheatcroft, *The Ottomans*.
21. Ramsay, *Impressions of Turkey*, 31.
22. Ramsay, *Impressions of Turkey*, 33-4.
23. Said, *Orientalism*.
24. Maria Todorova, *Imagining the Balkans* (Oxford, 1997), 62.
25. Pears, *Turkey and its People*, 250.
26. Dawkins, *Modern Greek in Asia Minor*; R. J. H. Jenkins, 'Richard MacGillivray Dawkins, 1871–1955', *Proceedings of the British Academy*, 41 (1955), 373–88.
27. W. M. Ramsay, *Pauline and Other Studies in Early Christian History* (London, 1906); cf. John Cuthbert Lawson, *Modern Greek Folklore and Ancient Greek Religion* (Cambridge, 1910); Frank Trombley, 'The Christianisation of Rite in Byzantine Anatolia: F. W. Hasluck and Religious Continuity', in Shankland (ed.), *Anthropology, Archaeology and Heritage in the Balkans and Anatolia*, vol. 2, 55–75.
28. Michael Herzfeld, *Ours Once More: Folklore, Ideology and the Making of Modern Greece* (Austin, TX, 1983).

29. Lucy M. J. Garnett, *The Women of Turkey and their Folklore* (London, 1893), 105.

30. A. White, 'Survivals of Primitive Religion among the People of Asia Minor', *Journals of the Transactions of the Victoria Institute*, 39 (1907), 151. According to Garnett, 'Religion…as understood by the mass of the people consists of an agglomeration of superstitious rites concerning times and seasons, fasts and feasts…[The Greeks] have remained pagans.' Lucy M. J. Garnett, *Turkey of the Ottomans* (London, 1911), 114.

31. Hasluck, *Christianity and Islam under the Sultans*, 7ff.

32. Hasluck, *Christianity and Islam under the Sultans*, 20ff.

33. Hasluck, *Christianity and Islam under the Sultans*, 122.

34. For example, John S. Stuart-Glennie, 'Essays on the Science of Folklore, Greek Folkspeech, and the Survival of Paganism', in Lucy M. Garnett, *Greek Folk-Poesy* (London, 1896).

35. Hasluck, *Christianity and Islam under the Sultans*, 122.

36. F. W. Hasluck, *Letters on Religion and Folklore* (London, 1926), 157.

37. Hasluck, *Christianity and Islam under the Sultans*, 122.

38. Irene Melikoff, 'Hasluck's study of the Bektashis and its Contemporary Significance', in D. Shankland (ed.), *Archaeology, Anthropology and Heritage in the Balkans and Anatolia: The Life and Times of F. W. Hasluck, 1870–1920*, vol. 1 (Istanbul, 2004), 298. Despite its age, *Christianity and Islam under the Sultans* remains the principal work on Ottoman popular religion.

39. Maurice Gaudefroy-Demombynes, *Les Institutions Musulmanes* (Paris, 1921).

40. Garnett, *Mysticism and Magic in Turkey*, 64.

41. Billie Melman, *Women's Orients: English Women and the Middle East, 1718–1918; Sexuality, Religion and Work* (Ann Arbor, MI, 1992), 106–7.

42. Garnett, *Mysticism and Magic in Turkey*, v.

43. Garnett, *Mysticism and Magic in Turkey*, 191.

44. Hans-Likas Kieser, 'Aveliliki as Song and Dialogue: The Village Sage Meluli Baba', in D. Shankland (ed.), *Archaeology, Anthropology and Heritage*, vol. 1, 356–8.

45. Charles Lindholm, *The Islamic Middle East: Tradition and Change*, 2nd edn (Oxford, 2002), 193.

46. Selim Deringil, *The Well-Protected Domains: Ideology and the Legitimation of Power in the Ottoman Empire, 1876–1909* (London, 1999), 40.

47. Pears, *Turkey and its Peoples*, 79.

48. Garnett, *Mysticism and Magic in Turkey*, 29 n.1.

49. Hasluck, *Christianity and Islam under the Sultans*, 689.

50. Hasluck, *Christianity and Islam under the Sultans*, 260. When *kurban* was performed to greet an important guest, 'sacrifice tends to degenerate into a free meal, since the victim is always eaten and the great man complimented is expected to pay for it: consequently he gains both the spiritual benefit of a *kurban* made in his honour and the merit of charity'.

51. Hasluck, *Christianity and Islam under the Sultans*, 234. Hasluck discusses the types of saints revered by Muslims in Anatolia and their many guises in chapters 18 to 22.

52. Natalie Zemon Davis, 'Some Tasks and Themes in the Study of Popular Religion', in Charles Trinkaus and Heiko A. Oberman (eds), *The Pursuit of Holiness in Late Medieval and Renaissance Religion* (Leiden, 1974), 307–36.

53. Garnett, *Mysticism and Magic in Turkey*, 147.

54. Garnett relates stories about certain dervishes who wondered the streets naked: *Mysticism and Magic in Turkey*, 36. Holy 'foolery' also has a very long history with the Greek Orthodox tradition. There is some brief discussion in Sergey A.Ivanov, *Holy Fools in Byzantium and Beyond* (Oxford, 2006), particularly 241–3 regarding its survival into the modern period.

55. Stella Georgourdi, 'Sanctified Slaughter in Modern Greece', in Marcel Detienne and J.-P. Vernant (eds), *Cuisine of Sacrifice among the Greeks* (Chicago, 1998).

56. White, 'Survivals of Primitive Religion', 153, 154.

57. KMS, Ionia, Tsiflikaki: Kleodimos Landos.

58. Peregrine Horden and Nicholas Purcell, *The Corrupting Sea: A Study of Mediterranean History* (Oxford, 2000) 403–4.

59. KMS, Lycia, Livisi: Andonis Tisizis; Kiriakos M. Hondros, *I Mikra Asia ton Dodekanision* (Rhodes, 2009), 152.

60. Access to Muslim-controlled shrines was not a given, and sometimes denied in the past. Garnett, *Mysticism and Magic in Turkey*, 76.

61. Hasluck, *Christianity and Islam under the Sultans*, 520–1.

62. KMS, Ionia, Menemen: Aglaia Kontou.

63. KMS, Ionia, Loutzaki: Evangelia Mihou.

64. Horden and Purcell, *Corrupting Sea*, 412.

65. KMS, Bithynia, Kouvouklia: Persephone Tsotridou. Another example is given: KMS, Ionia, Loutzaki: Evangelia Mihou: 'At Ai Yanni outside the village there was a brook that sometimes flowed and sometimes lay dry. We regarded its waters as *agiasma*. People would cut rags and tie them to trees nearby...One day a Turk urinated in the water and then bathed, and then saw a hairy hand reaching out from the water. He fled to his home where he suffered swelling and died within two days. Since then the Turks have also deemed it holy.'

66. Hasluck, *Christianity and Islam under the Sultans*, 112, 255.

67. Garnett, *Mysticism and Magic in Turkey*, 169.

68. Garnett presents Hıdırellez as a kind of all-purpose saint who transcends civilizations: 'Supreme among these Saints of the Moslem Calendar is Khizr, or Khidhr-Elias, a mythical personage who from time immemorial has in various forms and under different names, filled a prominent place in the religions of the world. This protean Saint, or Demi-god, appears to be identifiable with the Prophet Elijah, or Elias, as well as with the Christian St. George, who, in his turn, has been identified with Horus': *Mysticism and Magic in Turkey*, 22.

69. KMS, Bithynia, Bursa: Angeliki Kaminou: 'St George they called Hidir Iles, and they worshipped St Dimitrios as Kasim'; KMS, Caria, Bodrum: Kostas Halkias: 'They appeared to love St George, Hidir Iles they call him, more than they did Mohammad'; KMS, Pontus, Ambelia: Maria Tsinaridou: 'We understood that St George heard our concerns and performed a miracle. All the Turks regularly lit a candle to St George'; KMS, Lycia, Aktse: Nikolas Pisas: 'They were more respectful towards our religion than we were. They particularly loved St Dimitrios and St George. We often worked during the holiday [of St Dimitrios and St George], they never did.'

70. Maria Couroucli, 'Empire Dust: The Web of Relations in Saint George's Festivals on Princes Island in Istanbul', in Chris Hann and Hermann Goltz (eds), *Eastern Christians in Anthropological Perspective* (Berkeley, CA, 2010), 224; see also her 'Le partage des lieux saints comme tradition méditerranéenne' and more particularly 'Saint George l'Anatolien, maitre des frontieres', in Dionigi Albera and Maria Couroucli (eds), *Religions traversées: Lieux saints partagés entre chrétiens, musulmans et juifs en Méditerranée* (Arles, 2009).

71. Hasluck, *Christianity and Islam under the Sultans*, 335.

72. Courcouli, 'Empire Dust'.

73. KMS, Bithynia, Aphisia: Angelos Loukakis: 'They loved St. George and worshipped him, but not Christ or Mary. Some even loved St. Nicholas.'

74. KMS, Lydia, Kasaba: Anna Hatzisotiriou.

75. Glen Bowman, 'Orthodox-Muslim Interactions at Mixed Shrines in Macedonia', in Chris Hann and Hermann Goltz (eds), *Eastern Christians in Anthropological Perspective* (Berkeley, CA, 2010), 196; cf. Robert Hayden, 'Antagonistic Tolerance: Competitive Sharing of Religious Sites in South Asia and the Balkans', *Current Anthropology*, 43.2 (2002), 205–31.

76. Hasluck, *Christianity and Islam under the Sultans*, 71.

77. Hasluck, *Christianity and Islam under the Sultans*, 76-7.

78. Stuart B. Schwartz, *All Can Be Saved: Religious Tolerance and Salvation in the Iberian Atlantic World* (New Haven, CT, 2008).

79. KMS, Pontus, Zimera: Sofia Lazaridou.

80. KMS, Paphlagonia, Askortasai: Avgerinos Spanopoulos.

81. KMS, Ionia, Nea Phokies: Tassos Giannaris.

82. KMS, Pontus, Arumteli: Haralambos Eleftheriadis.

83. KMS, Ionia, Nymphaio: Giorgos Bambourakis.

CHAPTER 5

1. Doukas, *A Prisoner of War's Story*, 1–2.

2. Petro Alexiou, 'A Body Broken: A Critical Biography of Alekos Doukas (1900–1962)' (PhD thesis, Macquarie University, 2008).

3. The original read: 'Dedicated to the common ordeals of the Greek and Turkish people': Doukas, *A Prisoner of War's Story*, xxi.

4. As a sign of respect the priest refers to him as 'Reis' even through he is of lower rank: Politis, *Stou Hatzifrangkou*, 42.

5. On Doukas' determination to see humanity obscured by nationalism, see the brief comments in Dimitris Tziovas, 'Introduction', in Doukas, *A Prisoner of War's Story*, xiii. On fatality and nationhood, see Benedict Anderson, *Imagined Communities: Reflections on the Origin and Spread of Nationalism*, 3rd edn, London, 2006), 149ff.

6. KMS Cappadocia, Kayseri: Paraskevi Tsaloglou.

7. Hirschon, Heirs of the Greek Catastrophe, 30

8. Alexiou, 'A Body Broken', 86.

9. Andrei Simić, 'Nationalism as Folk Ideology: The Case of the Former Yugoslavia', in Joel M. Halpern and David A. Kideckel (eds), *Neighbors at War: Anthropological Perspectives on Yugoslav Ethnicity, Culture and History* (University Park, PA, 2000); cf. Bringa, *Being Muslim the Bosnian Way*; Bringa, 'Haunted about the Imaginations of the Past: Robert Kaplan's *Balkan Ghosts*', in Catherine Bestemen and Hugh Gusterson (eds), *Why America's Top Pundits are Wrong: Anthropologists Talk Back* (Berkeley, CA, 2005), 70ff.

10. Samuel P. Huntington, *The Clash of Civilizations and the Remaking of the World Order* (New York, 1996). See the discussion section on Jan T. Gross, *Neighbors: The Destruction of the Jewish Community in Jedwabne, Poland* (Princeton, 2001) in *Slavic Review* 61/3 (2002), 453–89; Daniel Goldhagen, *Hitler's Willing Executioners* (New York, 1997); Richard Pipes, *Russia under the Old Regime* (Harmondsworth, 1974).

11. Cooper with Brubaker, 'Identity', 63; Wolf, *Europe and the People without History*, 6–7.

12. Slavoj Žižek, *Violence: Six Sideways Reflections* (London, 2008), 119.

13. The same war is referred to here as the Greek–Turkish War.

14. Quoted in Clark, *Twice a Stranger*, 35.

15. Clark, *Twice a Stranger*, 35ff.

16. Keyder, 'The Ottoman Empire', in Barkey and von Hagen (eds), *After Empire*, 39.

17. Charis Exertzoglou, 'I Ellinoorthodoxes Koinotites tis Othomanikis Aftokratorias (190s eonas—arches 20 ou)', in A. Liakos (ed.), *To 1922 kai i Prosfiges*, 50.

18. By 1881, 83 per cent of the Cretan countryside was Christian, while most Muslims were concentrated in cities and along the Aegean coastal area: Leonidas Kallivretakis, 'A Century of Revolutions: The Cretan Question between European and Near Eastern Politics', in Paschalis Kitromilides (ed.), *Eleftherios Venizelos: The Trials of Statesmanship* (Edinburgh, 2008), 14–15.

19. Kallivretakis, 'A Century of Revolutions', 12. See also Theochari Detoraki, 'I Ekklisia tis Kritis kata tin Tourkokratia (1645–1898)', in Nikolas M. Panagiotakis (ed.), *Kriti: Istoria kai Politismos* (Heraklion, 1988), 392ff.

20. Pinar Senisik, 'Insights from the Cretan Revolt of 1897', *Journal of Modern Greek Studies*, 28 (2010), 27–47.

21. For example, KMS, Lydia, Theira: Nikolas Diakakis; KMS, Pontus, Zilmera: Sofia Lapazidou.

22. Kontogiannis, *Geographia tis Mikras Asias*, 63.

23. Halidé Edib, *The Turkish Ordeal* (New York, 1928), 8.

24. KMS, Bithynia, Lefke: Euripides Martoglou.

25. KMS, Bithynia, Lefke: Euripides Martoglou.

26. For example, M. Şükrü Hanioğlu, *Preparation for a Revolution: The Young Turks 1902–1908* (Oxford, 2001), 176.

27. KMS, Ionia, Sokia: Nikolas Vogiatzoglou.

28. M. Elliadi, *Crete: Past and Present* (London, 1933), 38.

29. KMS, Caria, Bodrum: Kostas Halkitis.

30. KMS, Pontus, Kavza: Stavros Lazarides.

31. KMS, Bithynia, Dansari: Paraskevas Sotiriadis.

32. KMS, Bithynia, Lefke: Ilias Savvas.

33. KMS, Mysia, Avitzilar: Petros Kostanoglou.

34. KMS, Lydia, Theira: Nikolas Diakanis.

35. Clark, *Twice a Stranger*, 36.

36. The anthropologist Sofia Koufopoulou also notes other Cretan traditions that, along with social memories of the island, were used to underpin a specific Cretan identity within the Republic of Turkey: 'Muslim Cretans in Turkey', in Hirschon (ed.), *Crossing the Aegean*, 209–20.

37. Clark, *Twice a Stranger*, 33.

38. The concept of disemia, see Herzfeld, *Anthropology through the Looking Glass*.

39. Clark, *Twice a Stranger*, 37.

40. Tolga Köker with Leyla Keskiner, 'Lessons of Refugeehood: The Experience of Forced Migrants in Turkey', in Hirschon (ed.), *Crossing the Aegean*, 205.

41. Köker, 'Lessons of Refugeehood', 205, 208 n.33.

42. Hirschon, *Heirs of the Greek Catastrophe*; Hirschon, 'We got on well with the Turks'.

43. Anna L. Tsing, *In the Realm of the Diamond Queen* (Princeton, 1993), 5.

44. David E. Sutton, *Memories Cast in Stone: The Relevance of the Past in Everyday Life* (Oxford and New York, 1998), 168.

45. KMS, Cappadocia, Prokopi: Antonis and Elisavet Georgiadis.

46. Kechriotis, 'Greek-Orthodox, Ottoman Greeks or Just Greeks?', 54.

47. See Fujinami Nobuyoshi, 'The Patriarchal Crisis of 1910 and Constitutional Logic: Ottoman Greeks' Dual Role in the Second Constitutional Politics', *Journal of Modern Greek Studies*, 27 (2009), 14. For a much more detailed account of the response in another culturally complex corner of the empire, see Campos, *Ottoman Brothers*.

48. Carter Vaughn Findley, *Turkey, Islam, Nationalism, and Modernity: A History 1789–2007* (New Haven, CT, 2011), 194–5.

49. Hanioğlu, *Preparation for a Revolution*, 299; M. Şükrü Hanioğlu, *A Brief History of the Late Ottoman Empire* (Princeton, 2008), 148.

50. Erol Ülker, ' "Contextualizing Turkification": Nation-Building in the Late Ottoman Empire', *Nations and Nationalism*, 4 (2005), 613–36.

51. KMS, Cappadocia, Prokopi: Antonis and Elisavet Georgiadis.

52. KMS, Mysia, Derekoy: Achilles Psaropoulos.

53. KMS, Mysia, Ivrinti: Grigoris Anagnostou.

54. Christos G. Andreadis, 'I Vouleftikes Ekloges ton 1908 stin Tourkia kai o Pontos', *Archeion Pontou*, 43 (1990/1), 8; Catherine Bouras, 'The Greek Millet in Turkish Politics: Greeks in the Ottoman Parliament (1908–1918)', in Dimitri Gondicas and Charles Issawi (eds), *Ottoman Greeks in the Age of Nationalism* (Princeton, 2000), 193–8.

55. Geoff Eley and Ronald G. Suny, 'Introduction: From the Moment of Social History to the Work of Cultural Representation', in Eley and Suny (eds), *Becoming National: A Reader* (New York, 1996), 10.

56. Findley, *Turkey, Islam, Nationalism, and Modernity*, 201–2.

57. On 30 January (Gregorian Calendar), the Greek Orthodox Church commemorates Basil of Caesarea, St Gregory the Theologian, and John Chrysostom as the patron saints of education.

58. *I Exodos,* vol. B, 451.

59. KMS, Bithynia, Mihalitsi: Yannis Seitanidis.

60. Campos, *Ottoman Brothers*, 87, 151.

61. Erik-Jan Zürcher, 'The Ottoman Conscription System in Theory and Practice, 1844–1918', *International Review of Social History*, 43.3 (1998), 437–49.

62. KMS, Ionia, Nea Phokies: Tasos Giannaris.

63. KMS, Caria, Sokia: Patroklos Ikonomidis.

64. KMS, Lycia, Livisi: Yannis Hatzidoulis.

65. KMS, Ionia, Beletridzi: Dimitri Nikolitzoglou.

66. Mark Biondich, *The Balkans: Revolution, War, and Political Violence since 1878* (Oxford 2011), 78: Mazower, *Salonica, City of Ghosts*, 300.

67. Arnold J. Toynbee reported that the capital received a quarter of a million refugees: *The Western Question in Greece and Turkey: A Study in the Contact of Civilizations* (London, 1922), 138.

68. Fikret Adanir, 'Non-Muslims in the Ottoman Army and the Ottoman Defeat in the Balkan War of 1912–1913', in G. Suny, F. Göçek, and N. Naimark (eds), *A Question of Genocide: Armenians and Turks at the End of the Ottoman Empire* (New York, 2011), 113–25.

69. PRO FO 195/2459/1465, 13 April 1914.

70. Adanir, 'Non-Muslims and the Ottoman Army', 124–5.

71. Y. Mourelis, 'The 1914 Persecutions and the First Attempt at an Exchange of Minorities between Greece and Turkey', *Balkan Studies*, 26 (1985), 388–413.

72. For example B. Adamantidis, 'Ta Teleftea eti tis Ellinikis Koinotitas Prousas', *Mikrasiatika Chronika*, 4 (1948), 97–8.

73. Mustafa Aksakal, *The Ottoman Road to War in 1914: The Ottoman Empire and the First World War* (Cambridge, 2008), 53–4.

74. PRO FO 195/2458/2864, 4 July 1914; PRO FO 195/2458/2923, 8 July 1914. See also Matthias Bjørnlund, 'The 1914 Cleansing of Aegean Greeks as a Case of Violent Turkification', *Journal of Genocide Research*, 10.1 (2008), 43, 47, 49.

75. PRO FO 195/2458/693, 18 February 1914.

76. Basili Kouligka, *Kios 1912–1922*, 39.

77. PRO FO 195/2458/2923, 8 July 1914.

78. Personal interview with Kalliroi Dimitriadis, daughter of Chryssavgi Korakis.

79. PRO FO 195/2458/1801, 4 May 1914: See also *Mavri Biblos: Diogmon kai Martyrion tou en Tourkia Ellinismou, 1914–1918* (ed.), *The Ecumenical Patriarchate* (Istanbul, 1919), 63–4; Russian sources also note that Ottoman officials were forcing Rum residents in Thrace to sign over property: Akskal, *The Ottoman Road to War in 1914*, 48.

80. Mourelis, 'The 1914 Persecutions', 391–2.

81. PRO FO 195/2458/3080, 21 July 1914; See also *Mavri Biblos*, 190.

82. PRO FO 195/2458/2864, 4 July 1914.

83. PRO FO 195/2458/3080, 21 July 1914.

84. PRO FO 195/2458/2860, 27 June 1914.

85. Quoted in Bjørnlund, 'The 1914 Cleansing of Aegean Greeks', 43; see also *Mavri Bibilos*, 161ff.

86. PRO FO 195/2458/3069, 15 July 1914.

87. Aksakal, *The Ottoman Road to War in 1914*, esp. 42–53.

88. Ryan Gingeras, *Sorrowful Shores: Violence, Ethnicity, and the End of the Ottoman Empire, 1912–1923* (Oxford, 2009), 40; Ayhan Aktar, 'Homogenising the Nation, Turkifying the Economy', in Hirschon (ed.), *Crossing the Aegean*, 83.

89. KMS Caria, Bodrum: Kostas Halkitis.

90. *Persecution and Extermination of the Communities of Macri and Livissi*, 7.

91. KMS, Ionia, Meresi: Nikolas Vezirgiannis.

92. The term *Koumparies* refers to a process of having friends become 'spiritual' relatives, which essentially means having them as godparents or groomsmen.

93. KMS, Ionia, Phokies: Anestis Varsitopoulos.

94. KMS Ionia, Hatzilari: Kleodimos Landos.

95. KMS Caria, Bozdoğan: Kostas Phinikopoulos.

96. KMS Ionia, Agisuluk: Manolis Hatzisavvas.

97. KMS Bythina, Bursa: Angeliki Kaminou.

98. KMS Bythnia, Aloni: Oddiseas Diakos and Sergios Toutaros.

99. James F. Macmillan, 'War', in Donald Bloxham and Robert Gerwarth (eds), *Political Violence in the Twentieth Century* (Cambridge, 2011), 59.

100. Mansel, *Levant*, 199.

101. KMS, Bithynia, Nursa: Angeliki Kaminou.

102. KMS, Pontus, Agkagia: Dimitri Phitopoulos.
103. The question of intent is not important for our specific purposes, but see Suny, Göçek, and Naimark (eds), *A Question of Genocide*. On the question of intentionality and the genocidal effects of certain state practices, see A. Dirk Moses, 'Genocide and Settler Society in Australian History', in A. Dirk Moses (ed.), *Genocide and Settler Society: Frontier Violence and Stolen Indigenous Children in Australian History* (New York, 2004), 28ff. See also Dominik J. Schaller and Jürgen Zimmerer, 'Late Ottoman Genocides: The Dissolution of the Ottoman Empire and Young Turkish Population and Extermination Policies—Introduction', *Journal of Genocide Research*, 10.1 (2008), 11.
104. KMS, Thrace, Chora: Yannis Mechagioglou.
105. For example KMS, Pontus, Agiahlasan: Anastasis Orfanidis; KMS, Pontus, Fountouklou: Ilias Aslanidis.
106. KMS, Pontus, Trabzon: Yannis Holetsidis.
107. The archbishop of Trabzon, whether because he anticipated Russian withdrawal or resented his loss of political power under the Russian occupation, maintained relations with Ottoman authorities, who then appointed him an interim administrator. Michael A. Reynolds, *Shattering Empires: The Clash and Collapse of the Ottoman and Russian Empires, 1908–1918* (Cambridge, 2011), 164; cf. Christos Samouilidis, *Istoria tou Pontiakou Ellinismou* (Athens, 1985), 242.
108. KMS, Pontus, Atta, Efcharis Deligianidou.
109. Gingeras, *Sorrowful Shores*, 65ff. Cathie Carmichael describes the paramilitaries who practiced ethnic cleansing in Yugoslavia during the 1990s as 'extremists and murderers who donned historical names and costumes in a perverse, but thoroughly modern form of warfare'. Cathie Carmichael, *Ethnic Cleansing in the Balkans: Nationalism and the Destruction of Tradition* (London and New York, 2002), 49–51.
110. On *sökürün*, see Kemal Karpat, 'The Transformation of the Ottoman State, 1789–1908', *International Journal of Middle Eastern Studies*, 1 (1972), 272.
111. Reynolds, *Shattering Empires*, 170.
112. KMS, Pontus, Kouzloukiou: Minas Karatisidis; KMS, Pontus, Kurgenpunar: Giorgos Sairdis; KMS, Pontus, Tripolis: Dimitris Thrasivoulos; KMS, Pontus, Tripolis: Michalis Lagidis.
113. PRO FO 286/7026, May 1919; 286/703, 10 May 1919; 286/757/2424, 12 November 1921.
114. For example KMS, Aeolia, Karagatz: Patroklos Komninoglou.
115. KMS, Mysia, Küçükkuyu: Polybios Narliotis.
116. *I Exodos*, vol. A, 228–9.
117. PRO FO 286/703, 23 April 1919, 26 April 1919, 10 May 1919.
118. PRO FO 286/713, 10 April 1919; 14 July 1919: Zito translates as 'hooray', but is largely thought of as a patriotic cry.
119. PRO FO 286/702, 30 April 1919.

120. Hasan Kayali, 'The Struggle for Independence', in Reşat Kasaba (ed.), *The Cambridge History of Turkey,* vol. 4, *Turkey in the Modern World* (Cambridge, 2008), 118ff.

121. Iakovos Kouloucheris, *I Amisos kai ta pathi tis* (Thessaloniki, 1991), 121–22. See also PRO FO 286/702, 6 May 1919.

122. KMS, Paphlagonia, Askortasi: Avgerinos Spanopoulos.

123. Şina Akşin, *Turkey: From Empire to Revolutionary Republic* (New York, 2007), 124.

124. Kayali, 'The Struggle for Independence', 121.

125. Andrew Mango, *Atatürk: The Biography of the Founder of Modern Turkey* (New York, 1999), 217.

126. Kayali, 'The Struggle for Independence', 121.

127. See Çagri Erhan, *Greek Occupation of Izmir and Adjoining Territories* (Ankara, 1999); Dimitris Stamatopoulos, 'I Mikrasiatiki Ekstrateia: I Anthropo-Geographia tis Katastrofis', in Liakos (ed.), *To 1922 kai i Prosfiges*, 95.

128. Gingeras, *Sorrowful Shores*, 113. A French officer saw sixty-four bodies, mostly elderly, with their hands tied, ears cut off, and other signs of torture. See Liakos, 'Eisagogi: to 1922 kai Emis', 19.

129. Arnold J. Toynbee, *The Western Question*; PRO WO 106/1440, 8 September 1922.

130. PRO FO 286/75920, May 1921.

131. KMS, Lydia, Tepejik: Michalis Scholias.

132. PRO FO 286/714, 30 July 1919.

133. PRO FO 286/833, 3 June 1922.

134. PRO FO 286/833, 21 June 1922.

135. Cited from *Tachydromos* in PRO FO 286/804, 25 September 1922.

136. Quoted in Liakos, 'Eisagogi: to 1922 kai Emis', 19.

137. Erhan, *Greek Occupation of Izmir*; Akşin, *Turkey*.

138. PRO WO 106/1440, 28 August 1922.

139. Ayşe Osil, 'Anamesa stin Aftokratoria kai tin Demokratia: I Periodos 1918-1922 stin Tourkiki Istoriographia', in Antonis Liakos (ed.), *To 1922 kai i Prosfiges,* 121–2.

140. Gingeras, *Sorrowful Shores*, 69.

141. Leyla Neyzi, 'Remembering Smyrna/Izmir: Shared History, Shared Trauma', *History and Memory*, 20.2 (2008), 122; Biray Kolluoğlu Kırlı, 'Forgetting the Smyrna Fire', *History Workshop Journal*, 60 (2005), 25–55. On the public pressure to proceed with the Rum expulsions, see Onur Yıldırım, *Diplomacy and Displacement: Reconsidering the Turco-Greek Exchange of Populations, 1922–1934* (New York, 2006), 64.

142. Milton, *Paradise Lost: Smyrna 1922*.

143. Osil, 'Anamesa stin Aftokratoria kai tin Demokratia', 121.

144. Testimony of Hariklia Xenou, in Dimitri I. Arhigeni (ed.), *Martyries apo ti Mikrasiatiki Katastrophi* (Athens, 1973), 49.

145. Gingeras, *Sorrowful Shores*, 69–70, 169.

146. Anagnostopoulou, *Mikra Asia*, 11–14.

147. KMS, Bithynia, Belladari: Kostas Bazaridis; KMS, Bithynia, Karateite: Christos Karageorgiou; KMS, Ionia, Kordelio: Sofia Frangou.

148. Carmichael, *Ethnic Cleansing in the Balkans*, 78. See also Norman M. Naimark, *Fires of Hatred: Ethnic Cleansing in Twentieth Century Europe* (Cambridge, MA, 2001), 10.

149. KMS, Mysia, Avtzilar: Petros Kostanoglou.

150. *I Exodos*, vol. A, 25.

151. *I Exodos*, vol. A, 229.

152. KMS, Lydia Kagiatziki: Giorgos Kefalas.

153. KMS, Aeolia, Bergama: Yannis Mimikos.

154. KMS, Mysia, Narlı: Harilaos Tsairis.

155. Minas Alexiadis, 'Aftobiographia kai Laographia: Kimena apo to Mikrasiatiko Horo', *Mikrasiatika Chronika*, 19 (1995), 181.

156. Others arrived from Russia, Bulgaria, Albania, Serbia, and the Dodecanese Islands: A. A. Pallis, 'Philetikes Metanastefsis sta Valkania kai i Diogmi tou Ellinismou (1912–1924)', *Deltio*, 1 (1977), 79.

157. Pallis, 'Philetikes Metanastefsis sta Valkania kai i Diogmi tou Ellinismou, 82.

158. Yıldırım, *Diplomacy and Displacement*, 106–7.

159. Hirschon, *Heirs of the Greek Catastrophe*; Hirschon, 'We got on well with the Turks'; Clark, *Twice a Stranger*.

160. KMS, Bithynia, Giasigetsik: Ilias Papdopoulos.

161. KMS, Bithynia, Kiriharam: Yannis Nikolaidis and Yannis Karpidis.

162. KMS, Mysia, Küçükkuyu: Polybios Narliotis.

163. KMS, Pontus, Fountouklou: Ilias Aslanidis.

164. KMS, Paphlagonia, Askortasi: Ourania Spanopoulos.

165. KMS, Pontus, Trabzon: Yannis Holetsidis. One can assume that the woman might have been elderly and that other family males were present, as a more salacious interpretation would be out of keeping with the purpose of the anecdote.

166. The Treaty of Lausanne has been the subject of much scholarly attention. See Stephen Ladas, *The Exchange of Minorities: Bulgaria, Greece and Turkey* (New York, 1932); Dimitri Pentzopoulos, *The Balkan Exchange of Minorities and its Impact upon Greece* (Paris, 1962); Yıldırım, *Diplomacy and Displacement*. For the impact of the population exchange on Greece's economy, see Christos Hadziiossif, 'To prosfigiko sok, i statheres kai i metaboles tis Ellinikis oikonomias', in Hadziiosiff (ed.), *Istoria tis Ellados tou 20ou aiona 1922–1940: O Mesopolemos* (Athens, 2002) and Elisabeth Kontogiorgi, *Population Exchange in Greek Macedonia* (Oxford, 2006).

167. Yıldırım, *Diplomacy and Displacement*, 105–9.

168. 'Elias Venezis, *The Number 31,328 (To Noumero 31,328)*, 14th edn (Athens, 1980), 213–14.

EPILOGUE

1. Dowry Registry of Kastellorizio in the local parish archive, in the possession of Nicholas G. Pappas.

2. Liakos, 'Eisagogi: to 1922 kai Emis', 12.

3. KMS, Pontus, Giatzimahmud: Haralambos Gerasimidis.

4. KMS, Pontus, Salamur: Yannis Papadopoulos.

5. KMS, Ionia, Nymphaio: Giorgos Bambourakis.

6. KMS, Ionia, Ahmetli: Thomas Stefanidis.

7. Eleni Papagaroufali, 'Town Twinning in Greece: Reconstructing Local Histories through Translocal Sensory-Affective Performances', *History and Anthropology*, 16 (2005), 338.

8. Dimitris Zaravelas, *Petrines Mnimes: Odoporiko stis hamenes patrides* (Athens and Ioannina, 1991), 40.

9. Or, 'Palaea Fokeia', as it is transliterated in Papagaroufali, 'Town Twinning in Greece', 336.

10. Papagaroufali, 'Town Twinning in Greece', 341–2.

11. Barbaros Tanc, 'Where Local Trumps National: Christian Orthodox and Muslim Refugees since Lausanne', *Balkanologie*, 1–2 (2001). www.balkanologie.revues.org/index732.html. Website accessed 14 January 2012.

12. Papagaroufali, 'Town Twinning in Greece', 345.

13. Anderson, *Imagined Communities*, 3.

Bibliography

Abbott, G. F., *Macedonian Folklore* (Cambridge, 1903).

Adamantidis, B., 'Ta Teleftea eti tis Ellinikis Koinotitas Prousas', *Mikrasiatika Chronika*, 4 (1948), 97–8.

Adanir, Fikret, 'Non-Muslims in the Ottoman Army and the Ottoman Defeat in the Balkan War of 1912–1913', in G. Suny, F. Göçek, and N. Naimark (eds), *A Question of Genocide: Armenians and Turks at the End of the Ottoman Empire* (New York, 2011).

Aksakal, Mustafa, *The Ottoman Road to War in 1914: The Ottoman Empire and the First World War* (Cambridge, 2008).

Akşin, Sina, *Turkey: From Empire to Revolutionary Republic* (New York, 2007).

Aktar, Ayhan, 'Homogenising the Nation, Turkifying the Economy: The Turkish Experience of the Population Exchange Reconsidered', in Renée Hirschon (ed.), *Crossing the Aegean: An Appraisal of the 1923 Compulsory Population Exchange between Greece and Turkey* (New York, 2003).

Alexandris, Alexis, 'The Greek Census of Anatolia and Thrace (1910–1912): A Contribution to Ottoman Historical Demography', in Dimitri Gondicas and Charles Issawi (eds), *Ottoman Greeks in the Age of Nationalism* (Princeton, 1999).

Alexiadis, Minas, 'Aftobiographia kai Laographia: Kimena apo to Mikrasiatiko Horo', *Mikrasiatika Chronika*, 19 (1995), 56–78.

Alexiou, Margaret, *Ritual Lament in Greek Tradition* (Cambridge, 1974).

Alexiou, Petro, 'A Body Broken: A Critical Biography of Alekos Doukas (1900–1962)' (PhD thesis, Macquaire University, 2008).

Anagnostopoulou, Sia, *Mikra Asia, 19os ai.–1919: i Ellinorthodoxes koinotites apo to Millet ton Romion sto elliniko ethnos* (Athens, 1997).

Anagnostopoulou, Sia, 'Greek Diplomatic Authorities in Anatolia', in Evangelia Baltaand Matthias Kappler (eds), *Cries and Whispers in Karamanlidika Books* (Weisbaden, 2010).

Anastasiadi-Manousaki, Sofia, *Kappadokias Mnimes* (Athens, 2002).

Anderson, Benedict, *Imagined Communities: Reflections on the Origin and Spread of Nationalism*, 3rd ed, (London, 2006).

Andreadis, Christos G., 'I Vouleftikes Ekloges tou 1908 stin Tourkia kai o Pontos', *Archeion Pontou*, 43 (1990/1), 8–26.

Arhigeni, Dimitri I., *Martyries apo ti Maikrasiatiki Katastrophi* (Athens, 1973).

Augustinos, Gerasimos, *Consciousness and History: Nationalist Critics of Greek Society, 1897–1914* (Boulder, CO, 1977).

Augustinos, Gerasimos, *The Greeks of Asia Minor: Confession, Community, and Ethnicity in the Nineteenth Century* (Kent, OH, 1992).

Baer, Marc, *The Dönme Jewish Converts, Muslim Revolution and Secular Turks* (Stanford, CA, 2009).

Balivet, Michel, 'Culture ouverte et echanges inter-religieux dans les villes ottomans due XIV* siecle', in Elizabeth Zahariadou (ed.), *The Ottoman Emirate (1300–1389)* (Rethymnon, 1993).

Balta, Evangelia, 'Periodisation et Typologie de la production des livres Karamanlis', *Deltio*, 12 (1997–8), 129–53.

Barkey, Karen, *Empire of Difference: The Ottomans in Comparative Perspective* (Cambridge, 2008).

Bayly, Christopher A., *The Birth of the Modern World 1780–1914: Global Connections and Comparisons* (Oxford, 2004).

Bayly, C. A., and Fawaz, Leila (eds), *Modernity and Culture: from the Mediterranean to the Indian Ocean* (New York, 2002).

Benz, Ernst, *The Eastern Orthodox Church: Its Life and Thought* (New York, 1963).

Bestemen, Catherine, and Gusterson, Hugh, (eds), *Why America's Top Pundits are Wrong: Anthropologists Talk Back* (Berkeley, CA, 2005).

Biondich, Mark, *The Balkans: Revolution, War, and Political Violence since 1878* (Oxford 2011).

Bjørnlund, Matthias, 'The 1914 Cleansing of Aegean Greeks as a Case of Violent Turkification', *Journal of Genocide Research*, 10.1 (2008), 41–57.

Bloxham, Donald, *The Great Game of Genocide: Imperialism, Nationalism, and the Destruction of the Ottoman Armenians* (Oxford, 2005).

Bloxham, Donald, 'The Great Unweaving: The Removal of Peoples in Europe, 1875–1949', in Richard Bessel and Claudia B. Haake (eds), *Removing Peoples: Forced Removal in the Modern World* (Oxford, 2009).

Blunt, J.E., *The People of Turkey*, vol. 2 (London, 1878).

Bonnett, Alastair, *Left in the Past: Radicalism and the Politics of Nostalgia* (New York, 2010).

Bouras, Catherine, 'The Greek Millet in Turkish Politics: Greeks in the Ottoman Parliament (1908–1918)', in Dimitri Gondicas and Charles Issawi (eds), *Ottoman Greeks in the Age of Nationalism* (Princeton, 1999).

Bowman, Glen, 'A Death Revisited: Solidarity and Dissonance in a Muslim-Christian Palestinian Village', in Ussama Makdisi and Paul A. Silverstein (eds), *Memory and Violence in the Middle East and North Africa* (Bloomington and Indianapolis, 2006).

Bowman, Glen, 'Orthodox-Muslim Interactions at Mixed Shrines in Macedonia', in Chris Hann and Hermann Goltz, (eds), *Eastern Christians in Anthropological Perspective* (Berkeley, CA, 2010).

Boyn, Svetlana, *The Future of Nostalgia* (New York, 2001).

Braudel, Fernand, *The Mediterranean and the Mediterranean World in the Age of Philip II*, vol. 1 (London, 1972).

Braudel, Fernand, *Civilization and Capitalism, 15th–18th Centuries*, vol. 1: *The Structures of Everyday Life: The Limits of the Possible* (London, 1981).

Brass, Paul, *The Production of Hindu-Muslim Violence in India* (Seattle, 2005).

Bravos, Thanasis, 'Ellinismos kai (Neo)Tourkiki Antilipsi peri Mionotiton, 1912–1922', *Mikrasiatika Chronika*, 22 (2007), 51–82.

Brewer, David, *Greece, the Hidden Centuries: Turkish Rule from the Fall of Constantinople to Greek Independence* (London, 2010).

Bringa, Tone, *Being Muslim the Bosnian Way: Identity and Community in a Central Bosnian Village* (Princeton, 1995).

——'Haunted about the Imaginations of the Past: Robert Kaplan's *Balkan Ghosts*', in Catherine Bestemen and Hugh Gusterson (eds), *Why America's Top Pundits are Wrong: Anthropologists Talk Back* (Berkeley, CA, 2005).

Brown, Peter, 'The Saint as Exemplar in Late Antiquity', *Representations*, 2 (1983), 1–25.

Brubaker, Rogers, 'Aftermaths of Empire and the Unmixing of Peoples', in Karen Barkey and Mark von Hagen (eds), *After Empire: Multiethnic Societies and Nation-Building: The Soviet Union and the Russian, Ottoman, and Habsburg Empires* (Boulder, CO, 1997).

Bryer, Anthony, 'The Pontic Greeks before Diaspora', *Journal of Refugee Studies*, 4 (1991), 315–34.

Burbank, Jane and Cooper, Frederick, *Empires in World History* (Princeton, 2010).

Burnaby, Fred, *On Horseback through Asia Minor* (London, 1877).

Campos, Michelle U., *Ottoman Brothers: Muslims, Christians, and Jews in Early Twentieth-Century Palestine* (Stanford, CA, 2011).

Caraveli, Anna, '"The Symbolic Village": Community Born in Performance', *Journal of American Folklore*, 98 (1985), 259–86.

Carmichael, Cathie, *Ethnic Cleansing in the Balkans: Nationalism and the Destruction of Tradition* (London and New York, 2002).

Childs, J. W., *Across Asia Minor on Foot* (Edinburgh and London, 1917).

Clark, Bruce, *Twice a Stranger: How Mass Expulsion Forged Modern Greece and Turkey* (Cambridge, MA, 2009).

Clay, Christopher, 'Labour Migration and Economic Conditions in Nineteenth-Century Anatolia', *Middle Eastern Studies*, 34.4 (1998), 1–32.

Clogg, Richard, 'Benjamin Barker's Journal of a tour in Thrace (1823)', *Anatolica: Studies in the Greek East in the 18th and 19th Centuries* (Brookfield, VT 1996).

——'Some Karamanlidika Inscriptions from the Monastery of the Zoodokhos Pigi, Balikli, Istanbul', in *Anatolica: Studies in the Greek East in the 18th and 19th Centuries* (Brookfield, VT, 1996).

——*Anatolica: Studies in the Greek East in the eighteenth and nineteenth centuries* (Brookfield, VT 1996).

——'A Millet within a Millet: The Karamanlides', in D. Gondicas and C. Issawi (eds), *The Ottoman Greeks in the Age of Nationalism: Politics, Economy, and Society in the Nineteenth Century* (Princeton, 1999).

Colakis, Marianthe, 'Images of the Turk in Greek Fiction of the Asia Minor Disaster', *Journal of Modern Greek Studies*, 4.2 (1986), 99–106.

Collins, Randall, *Macrohistory: Essays in Sociology of the Long Run* (Stanford, CA, 1999).

Cooper, Frederick, *Colonialism in Question: Theory, Knowledge, History* (Berkeley, CA, 2005).

—— with Brubaker, Rogers, 'Identity', in Frederick Cooper, *Colonialism in Question: Theory, Knowledge, History* (Berkeley, CA, 2005).

Courcouli, Maria, 'Le partage des lieux saints comme tradition méditerranéenne', in Dionigi Albera and Maria Couroucli (eds), *Religions traversées: Lieux saints partagés entre chrétiens, musulmans et juifs en Mediterranée* (Arles, 2009).

—— 'Saint George l'Anatolien, maitre des frontieres', in Dionigi Albera and Maria Couroucli (eds), *Religions traversées: Lieux saints partagés entre chrétiens, musulmans et juifs en Mediterranée* (Arles, 2009).

—— 'Empire Dust: The Web of Relations in Saint George's Festivals on Princes Island in Istanbul', in Chris Hann and Hermann Goltz (eds), *Eastern Christians in Anthropological Perspective* (Berkeley, CA, 2010).

Cowan, Jane, *Dance and the Body Politic in Northern Greece* (Princeton, 1990).

Corkalo, Dinka, Ajdukovic, Dean, Weinstein, Harvey M., Stover, Eric, Djipa, Dino, and Biro, Miklos, 'Neighbors Again? Intercommunity Relations after Ethnic Cleansing', in Eric Stover and Harvey M. Weinstein (eds), *My Neighbor, My Enemy: Justice and Community in the Aftermath of Mass Atrocity* (Cambridge, 2004).

Creed, Gerald W., 'Reconsidering Community', in Creed (ed.), *The Seductions of Community: Emancipations, Oppressions, Quandaries* (Santa Fe, NM, 2006).

Danforth, Loring, *The Death Rituals of Rural Greece* (Princeton, 1982).

—— and Riki Van Boeschoten, *Children of the Greek Civil War: Refugees and the Politics of Memory* (Chicago, 2012).

Davis, Natalie Zemon, 'Some Tasks and Themes in the Study of Popular Religion', in Charles Trinkaus and Heiko A. Oberman (eds), *The Pursuit of Holiness in Late Medieval and Renaissance Religion* (Leiden, 1974).

Davison, Roderic H., *Reform in the Ottoman Empire 1856–1876* (Princeton, 1963).

Dawkins, R.M., *Modern Greek in Asia Minor: A Study of the Dialects of Silli, Cappadocia and Pharasa, with Grammar, Texts, Translations and Glossary* (Cambridge, 1916).

Deringil, Selim, *The Well-Protected Domains: Ideology and the Legitimation of Power in the Ottoman Empire, 1876–1909* (London, 1999).

—— ' "There is no Compulsion in Religion": On Conversion and Apostasy in the Late Ottoman Empire: 1839–1856', *Comparative Studies in History and Society*, 3 (2000), 547–75.

Deschamps, Gaston, *Sur les routes d'Asie* (Paris, 1894).

Detoraki, Theochari, 'I Ekklisia tis Kritis kata tin Tourkokratia (1645–1898)', in Nikolas M. Panagiotakis (ed.), *Kriti: Istoria kai Politismos* (Heraklion, 1988).

Doukas, Stratis, *A Prisoner of War's Story*, trans. Petro Alexiou, with introduction by Dimitris Tziovas (Birmingham, 1999).

Doumanis, Nicholas, *Myth and Memory in the Mediterranean: Remembering Fascism's Empire* (London, 1997).

Du Boulay, Juliet, *Cosmos, Life, and Liturgy in a Greek Orthodox Village* (Limni, Evia, 2009).

Dursteler, Eric. R., *Venetians in Constantinople: Nation, Identity, and Coexistence in the Early Modern Mediterranean* (Baltimore, 2006).

Dwight, H. G., *Constantinople: Old and New* (New York, 1915).

Edib, Halidé, *The Turkish Ordeal* (New York, 1928).

Eley, Geoff, *A Crooked Line: From Cultural History to the History of Society* (Ann Arbor, MI, 2008).

——and Suny, Ronald Grigor, 'Introduction: From the Moment of Social History to the Work of Cultural Representation', in G. Eley and R. G. Suny (eds), *Becoming National: A Reader* (New York, 1996).

Elliadi, M., *Crete: Past and Present* (London, 1933).

Ellinikos Odigos: Idioktisia Eterias (Athens [1920], 1992).

Elliott, Charles Boileau, *Travels in the Three Great Empires of Austria, Russia and Turkey*, vol. 2 (London, 1838).

Epstein, Steven A., *Purity Lost: Transgressing Boundaries in the Eastern Mediterranean, 1000–1400* (Baltimore, 2006).

Erhan, Çagri, *Greek Occupation of Izmir and Adjoining Territories* (Ankara, 1999).

Exertzoglou, Charis, *Ethniki Taftotita stin Konstantinoupoli ton 19 eona: O Ellinikos Filologikos Syllogos Kostantinoupoleos, 1861–1912* (Athens, 1996).

——'I Ellinoorthodoxes Koinotites tis Othomanikis Aftokratorias (190s eonas—arches 20 ou)', in A. Liakos (ed), *To 1922 kai i Prosfiges:mia nea matia* (Athens, 2011).

——'I Istoria tis Prosfigikis Mnimis', in Antonis Liakos (ed.) *To 1922 kai Prosfiges: mia nea matia* (Athens, 2011).

I Exodos, vol. A, *Martyries apo tis eparchies ton Ditikon Paralion tis Mikrasias*, (ed), F. D. Apostolopoulou, (Athens, 1980).

I Exodos, vol. B, *Martyries apo tis eparchies tis Kentrikis kai Notias Mikrasias*, (eds), Paschalis Kitromilides and Yanni Mourelou, (Athens, 1982).

Farrar Jnr, L. L., McGuire, Kiernan, and Thompson, John E., 'Dog in the Night: The Limits of European Nationalism, 1789–1895', *Nations and Nationalism*, 4 (1998), 547–68.

Fentress, James and Wickham, Chris, *Social Memory* (Oxford, 1992).

Findley, Carter Vaughn, 'The Tanzimat', in Reşat Kasaba (ed.), *The Cambridge History of Turkey*, vol. 4: *Turkey and the Modern World* (Cambridge, 2008).

——*Turkey, Islam, Nationalism, and Modernity: A History 1789–2007* (New Haven, CT, 2011).

Garnett, Lucy Mary Jane, *The Women of Turkey and their Folklore* (London, 1893).

——*Turkey of the Ottomans* (London, 1911).

——*Mysticism and Magic in Turkey: An Account of the Religious Doctrines, Monastic Organisation and Ecstatic Powers of the Dervish Orders* (New York, 1912).

——*Turkey under the Ottomans* (New York, 1914).

Gaudefroy-Demombynes, Maurice, *Les Institutions Musulmanes* (Paris, 1921).

Gellner, Ernest, *Nations and Nationalism* (Oxford, 1983).

Georgelin, Hervé, *Le fin de Smyrne: Du cosmopolitisme aux nationalismes* (Paris, 2005).

Georgelin, Hervé, 'Perception of the other's fate: what Greek Orthodox refugees from the Ottoman Empire reported about the Destruction of Ottoman Armenians', *Journal of Genocide Research*, 10.1 (2008), 59-76.

Georgourdi, Stella, 'Sanctified Slaughter in Modern Greece', in Marcel Detienne and J.-P. Vernant (eds), *Cuisine of Sacrifice among the Greeks* (Chicago, 1998).

Gingeras, Ryan, *Sorrowful Shores: Violence, Ethnicity, and the End of the Ottoman Empire, 1912–1923* (Oxford, 2009).

Gladstone, William, *The Bulgarian Horrors and the Question of the East* (London, 1876).

Göçek, Fatma Müge, *Rise of the Bourgeoisie, Demise of Empire: Ottoman Westernization and Social Change* (New York, 1996).

Goffman, Daniel, *The Ottoman Empire and Early Modern Europe* (Cambridge, 2002).

Goldhagen, Daniel, *Hitler's Willing Executioners* (New York, 1997).

Gosden, Chris, *Archaeology and Colonialism: Cultural Contact from 5000 BC to the Present* (Cambridge, 2004).

Kouligka, Basili, *Kios 1912–1922: Skorpies Mnimes* (Athens and Ioannina, 1993).

Greene, Molly, *A Shared World: Christians and Muslims in the Early Modern Mediterranean* (Princeton, 2000).

Gross, Jan T., *Neighbors: The Destruction of the Jewish Community in Jedwabne, Poland* (Princeton, 2002).

Guha, Ranajit, *Domination without Hegemony: History and Power in Colonial India* (Cambridge, MA, 1997).

Halo, Thea, *Not Even My Name* (New York, 2000).

Hanioğlu, M. Sükrü, *Preparation for a Revolution: The Young Turks 1902–1908* (Oxford, 2001).

——'Turkish Nationalism and the Young Turks, 1889–1908', in Fatma Müge Göçek (ed.), *Social Constructions of Nationalism in the Middle East* (Albany, NY, 2002).

——*A Brief History of the Late Ottoman Empire* (Princeton, 2008).

Hart, Laurie Kain, *Time, Religion, and Social Experience in Rural Greece* (Lanham, MD, 1992).

Hasluck, Frederick W., *Letters on Religion and Folklore* (London, 1926).

——*Christianity and Islam under the Sultans*, ed. Margaret Hasluck (Oxford, 1929).

Hatzibeis, Stamatis, 'I Krini (Cesme) kai i Periohi tis', *Mikrasiatika Chronika*, 11 (1961), 227–45.

Hadziiossif, Christos, 'Class Structure and Class Antagonism in Late Nineteenth Century Greece', in Philip Carabott (ed.), *Greek Society in the Making, 1863–1913* (London, 1997).

Hadziiossif, Christos, 'To prosfigiko sok, i statheres kai i metavoles tis Ellinikis oikonmias', in Christos Hadziiossif (ed.), *Istoria tis Ellados tou 20ou aiona 1922–1940: O Mesopolemos* (Athens, 2002).

——*Sinasos: Istoria enos topou horis Istoria* (Herakleion, Crete, 2005).

——'The Ambivalence of Turkish in a Greek-Speaking Community of Central Anatolia', in Evangelia Balta and Matthias Kappler (eds), *Cries and Whispers in Karamanlidika Books* (Weisbaden, 2010).

Hayden, Robert, 'Antagonistic Tolerance: Competitive Sharing of Religious Sites in South Asia and the Balkans', *Current Anthropology*, 43.2 (2002), 205–31.

Hegel, G. W. F., *Lectures on the Philosophy of World History: Introduction*, trans. by H. B. Nisbet (Cambridge, 1974).

Herzfeld, Michael, *Ours Once More: Folklore, Ideology and the Making of Modern Greece* (Austin, TX, 1983).

——*Poetics of Manhood: Contest and Identity in a Cretan Mountain Village* (Princeton, 1985).

——*Anthropology through the Looking Glass: Critical Ethnography in the Margins of Europe* (Cambridge, 1987).

——*A Place in History: Social and Monumental Time in a Cretan Town* (Princeton, 1991).

——*Cultural Intimacy: Social Poetics in the Nation-State* (London and New York, 1997).

Hirschon, Renée, *Heirs of the Greek Catastrophe: The Social Life of Asia Minor Refugees in Piraeus*, 2nd edn (New York and London, 1998).

——'We got on well with the Turks', in David Shankland (ed.), *Archaeology, Anthropology and Heritage in the Balkans and Anatolia: The Life and Times of F. W. Hasluck, 1878–1920*, vol.2, (Istanbul, 2004).

Hodgson, Marshall, *The Venture into Islam*, vol. 1: *The Classical Age of Islam* (Chicago, 1977).

Hondros, Kiriakos M., *I Mikra Asia tin Dodekanision* (Rhodes, 2009).

Horden, Peregrine and Purcell, Nicholas, *The Corrupting Sea: A Study of Mediterranean History* (Oxford, 2000).

Horrocks, Geoffrey, *Greek: A History of the Language and its Speakers*, 2nd edn (Oxford, 2010).

Huntington, Samuel P., *The Clash of Civilizations and the Making of the New World Order* (New York, 1996).

Husain, Adnan, and Fleming, K. E. (eds), *A Faithful Sea: The Religious Cultures of the Mediterranean, 1200–1700* (London, 2007).

Ipek, Nedim, and Çağlayan, K. Tuncer, 'The Emigration from the Ottoman Empire to America', in A.Deniz Balgamiş and Kemal H. Karpat (eds), *Turkish Migration to the United States: From Ottoman Times to the Present* (Madison, WI, 2008).

Ivanov, Sergey A., *Holy Fools in Byzantium and Beyond* (Oxford, 2006).

Jenkins, R. J. H., 'Richard MacGillivray Dawkins, 1871–1955', *Proceedings of the British Academy*, 41 (1955), 373–88.

Judson, Pieter, *Guardians of the Nation: Activists on the Language Frontiers of Imperial Austria* (Cambridge, MA, 2007).

Just, Roger, 'Triumph of the Ethnos', in M. Chapman, E. Tonkin, and M. Macdonald (eds), *History and Ethnicity* (London, 1989).

Kafadar, Cemal, *Between Two Worlds: The Construction of the Ottoman State* (Berkeley, CA, 1995).

Kaldellis, Anthony, *Hellenism in Byzantium: The Transformation of Greek Identity and the Reception of the Classical Tradition* (Cambridge, 2007).

Kallivrettakis, Leonidas, 'A Century of Revolutions: The Cretan Question between European and Near Eastern Politics', Paschalis Kitromilides (ed.), *Eleftherios Venizelos: The Trials of Statesmanship* (Edinburgh, 2008).

Kalfoglous, Ioannis, *Istoriki Geographia tis Mikrasiatikis Hersonisou* (Istanbul, 1899, repr. Athens, 2002).

Kapoli, Evi, 'Archive of Oral Tradition of the Centre for Asia Minor Studies: Its Formation and its Contribution to Research', *Ateliers du LESC*, 32 (2008) (www. http://ateliers.revues.org/1143) accessed 12 January 2012.

Karpat, Kemal, 'The Transformation of the Ottoman State, 1789–1908', *International Journal of Middle Eastern Studies*, 1 (1972), 243–81.

Karpat, Kemal, *Ottoman Population 1830–1914: Demographic and Social Characteristics* (Madison, WI, 1985).

Karatza, Eleni, S., *Kappadokia: O Telefteos Ellinismos tis Periferias Askeri Gelveri (Karbalis)* (Athens, 1985).

Kayali, Hasan, 'The Struggle for Independence', in Reşat Kasaba (ed.), *The Cambridge History of Turkey*, vol. 4, *Turkey in the Modern World* (Cambridge, 2008).

Kaztaridi, Ioannis F., *I Exodos ton Ellinon tou Kars tis Armenias (1919–21)* (Athens, 1996).

Kechriotis, Vangelis, 'Greek-Orthodox, Ottoman Greeks or Just Greeks? Theories of Coexistence in the Aftermath of the Young Turk Revolution', *Etudes Balkaniques*, 1 (2005), 51–72.

Kentro Mikrasiatikon Spoudon, *Telefteos Ellinismos tis Mikras Asias* (Athens, 1974).

Keyder, Çağlar, 'The Ottoman Empire', in Karen Barkey and Mark von Hagen (eds), *After Empire: Multiethnic Societies and Nation-building: The Soviet Union and The Russian, Ottoman, and Habsburg Empires* (Boulder, CO, 1997).

Kieser, Hans-Likas, 'Aveliliki as Song and Dialogue: The village Sage Meluli Baba', in D. Shankland (ed.), *Archaeology, Anthropology and Heritage in the Balkans and Anatolia: The Life and Times of F.W. Hasluck, 1878–1920* (Istanbul, 2004).

Kırlı, Biray Kolluoğlu, 'Forgetting the Smyrna Fire', *History Workshop Journal*, 60 (2005), 25–55.

Kitromilides, Paschalis, and Alexandris, Alexis, 'Ethnic Survival, Nationalism and Forced Migration: The historical demography of the Greek community of Asia Minor at the close of the Ottoman Era', *Deltio: Kentro Mikrasiatikon Spoudon*, 3 (1984–85), 9–44.

Köker, Tolga, with Keskiner, Leyla, 'Lessons of Refugeehood: The Experience of Forced Migrants in Turkey', in Renée Hirschon (ed.), *Across the Aegean: An Appraisal of the 1923 Compulsory Population Exchange between Greece and Turkey* (New York, 2003).

Kokkolios, Vangelis, 'Galanadiotes kai Glinadiotes stin Poli kai stin Smyrni (O Kokolios ki o geros Smyrnios, O Avantis)', in N. A. Kefallianidis (ed.), *Mnimes apo tin Anatoli: Anekdota, Imerologia, Tragoudia, Eggrafa* (Athens, 1988).

Kokosalakis, Nikos, 'The Political Significance of Popular Religion in Greece', *Archives des sciences sociales des religions* 64 (1987), 40.

Kolluoglu, Birayand Toksöz, Meltem (eds), *Cities of the Mediterranean: From the Ottomans to the Present Day* (London, 2010).

Kontogiorgi, Elisabeth, *Population Exchange in Greek Macedonia* (Oxford, 2006).

Kontogiannis, Pantelis, *Geografia tis Mikra Asias* (Athens, 1921).

Korobeinikov, D. A., 'Raiders and Neighbours: The Turks (1040–1304)', in Jonathan Shepard (ed.), *The Cambridge History of the Byzantine Empire* (Cambridge, 2008).

Koufopoulou, Sofia, 'Muslim Cretans in Turkey: The Reformulation of Ethnic Identity', in Renée Hirschon (ed.), *Crossing the Aegean: An Appraisal of the 1923 Compulsory Population Exchange between Greece and Turkey* (New York, 2003).

Kouloucheris, Iakovos, *I Amisos kai ta pathi tis* (Thessaloniki, 1991).

Kymlicka, Will, *Multicultural Citizenship: A Liberal Theory of Minority Rights* (Oxford, 1995).

Ladas, Stephen, *The Exchange of Minorities: Bulgaria, Greece and Turkey* (New York, 1932).

Laitin, David D., *Nations, States, and Violence* (Oxford, 2007).

Lawson, John Cuthbert, *Modern Greek Folklore and Ancient Greek Religion* (Cambridge, 1910).

Le Goff, Jacques, *The Birth of Purgatory* (Chicago, 1984).

Liakos, Antonis, 'Introduction: to 1922 kai Emis', in Antonis Liakos (ed.), *To 1922 kai i Prosfiges: mia nea matia* (Athens, 2011).

Lianidis, Simos, '*Nekrika kai Tafika sti Santa tou Pontou*', *Archeion Pontiaka*, 26 (1964), 159-76.

Lieven, Dominic, *Empire: The Russian Empire and its Rivals from the Sixteenth Century to the Present* (London, 2002).

Lindholm, Charles, *The Islamic Middle East: Tradition and Change*, 2nd edn (Oxford, 2002).

Lowenthal, David, *The Past is a Foreign Country* (Cambridge, 1985).

Lüdtke, Alf (ed.), *The History of Everyday Life: Reconstructing Everyday Experiences and Ways of Life* (Princeton, 1995).

Macfie, A. L., *The End of the Ottoman Empire, 1908–1923* (London, 1998).

Mackridge, Peter, 'The Myth of Asia Minor Greek Fiction', in Renée Hirschon (ed.), *Across the Aegean: An Appraisal of the 1923 Compulsory Population Exchange between Greece and Turkey* (New York, 2003).

Macmillan, James F., 'War', in Donald Bloxham and Robert Gerwarth (eds), *Political Violence in the Twentieth Century* (Cambridge, 2011).

Makdisi, Ussama, *The Culture of Sectarianism: Community, History and Violence in Nineteenth-Century Ottoman Lebanon* (Berkeley, CA, 2000).

Makris, Ippokratis K., 'I Katiki tis Syzikinis Hersonisou', *Mikrasiatika Chronika*, 11 (1961), 211–26.

Mango, Andrew, *Atatürk: The Biography of the Founder of Modern Turkey* (New York, 1999).

Mansel, Philip, *Levant: Splendour and Catastrophe on the Mediterranean* (London, 2010).

Manomi, Kiriaki, and Istikopoulou, Lida, *Somatiaki Organosi tou Ellinismou sti Mikra Asia (1861–1922)* (Athens, 2006).

Masters, Bruce, *Christians and Jews in the Ottoman Arab World: The Roots of Sectarianism* (Cambridge, 2001).

Mavrogordatos, George Th., *Stillborn Republic: Social Coalitions and Party Strategies in Greece, 1922–1936* (Berkeley, CA, 1983).

Mavri Biblos: Diogmon kai Martyrion tou en Tourkia Ellinismou 1914–1918, (ed.) Ecumenical Patriarchate, (Istanbul, 1919).

Mazower, Mark, *Salonica, City of Ghosts: Christians, Muslims and Jews, 1630–1950* (London, 2004).

McCarthy, Justin, *Death in Exile: The Ethnic Cleansing of Ottoman Muslims, 1821–1922* (Princeton, 1996).

McGowan, Bruce, 'The Age of the Ayans, 1699–1812', in H. Inalcik and Donald Quataert (eds), *An Economic and Social History of the Ottoman Empire* (Cambridge, 1994).

McNeill, William H., *Polyethnicity and National Unity in World History* (Toronto, 1986).

Melikoff, Irene, 'Hasluck's study of the Bektashis and its Contemporary Significance', in D. Shankland (ed.), *Archaeology, Anthropology and Heritage in the Balkans and Anatolia: The Life and Times of F.W. Hasluck, 1870–1920*, vol. 1 (Istanbul, 2004).

Melville, Herman, *The Writings of Herman Melville, Northwestern Newberry Edition: Journals*, ed. Howard C. Horsford, with Lynn Horth (Chicago, 1989).

Melman, Billie, *Women's Orients: English Women and the Middle East, 1718–1918: Sexuality, Religion and Work* (Ann Arbor, MI, 1992).

Meslin, Michel, 'Le phenomene *religieux populaire*', in B. Lacroix and P. Boglioni (eds), *Les Religions populaire. Colloque international, 1970* (Quebec, 1972), 5–15.

Milioris, Nikos, 'To Ellinika horia tis periochis Vouron Mikras Asias', *Mikrasiatika Chronika*, 14 (1970), 177–225.

Millas, Hercules, 'History Textbooks in Greece and Turkey', *History Workshop Journal* 31 (1991), 21–33.

Millas, Iraklis, 'Toukokratia: History and the Image of Turks in Greek Literature', *South European Society and Politics*, 11 (2006), 47–60.

Milton, Giles, *Paradise Lost: Smyrna 1922: The Destruction of Islam's City of Tolerance* (London, 2008).

Mitchell, Timothy, *Colonising Egypt* (Berkeley, CA, 1988).

Monroe, W. S., *Turkey and the Turks: An Account of the Lands, the Peoples, and the Institutions of the Ottoman Empire* (London, 1908).

Moses, A. Dirk, 'Genocide and Settler Society in Australian History' in A. Dirk Moses (ed.), *Genocide and Settler Society: Frontier Violence and Stolen Indigenous Children in Australian History* (New York, 2004).

Mourelis, Y., 'The 1914 Persecutions and the First Attempt at an Exchange of Minorities between Greece and Turkey', *Balkan Studies*, 26 (1985), 388–413.

Muir, Edward, 'Introduction: Observing Trifles', in E. Muir and G. Ruggiero (eds), *Microhistory and the Lost Peoples of Europe* (Baltimore, 1991).

Multu, Servet, 'Late Ottoman Population and its Ethnic Distribution', *Nifusbilim-Dergisi/Turkish Journal of Population Studies*, 25 (2003), 3–38.

Myrivilis, Stratis, *Panagia i Gorgona*, (Athens, 1956).

Naimark, Norman M., *Fires of Hatred: Ethnic Cleansing in Twentieth-Century Europe* (Cambridge, MA, 2001).

Neyzi, Leyla, 'Remembering Smyrna/Izmir: Shared History, Shared Trauma', *History and Memory*, 20.2 (2008), 106–27.

Nobuyoshi, Fujinami, 'The Patriarchal Crisis of 1910 and Constitutional Logic: Ottoman Greeks' Dual Role in the Second Constitutional Politics', *Journal of Modern Greek Studies*, 27 (2009), 1–30.

Orla-Bukowska, Annamaria, 'Maintaining Borders, Crossing Borders: Social Relationships and the Shtetl', in Antony Polonsky (ed.), *Polin: Studies in Polish Jewry*, vol. 17, *The Shtetl: Myth and Reality* (2004), 171–95.

Osil, Ayşe, 'Anamesa stin Aftokratoria kai tin Demokratia: I Periodos 1918-1922 stin Tourkiki Istoriographia', in Antonis Liakos (ed.), *To 1922 kai i Prosfiges: mia nea matia* (Athens, 2011).

Palairet, Michael, *The Balkan Economies c.1800–1914: Evolution without Development* (Cambridge, 1997).

Pallis, A. A., 'Philetikes Metanastefsis sta Valkania kai i Diogmi tou Ellinismou (1912–1924), *Deltion*, 1 (1977), 79–81.

Pandiri, Thalia, 'Driven out of Eden', in Peter Isaac Rose (ed.), *The Dispossessed: An Anatomy of Exile* (Boston, 2004).

Papagaroufali, Eleni, 'Town Twinning in Greece: Reconstructing Local Histories through Translocal Sensory-Affective Performances', *History and Anthropology*, 16.3 (2005), 335–47.

Papailias, Penelope, *Genres of Recollection: Archival Poetics and Modern Greece* (New York, 2005).

Papataxiarchis, Euthymios, 'Friends of the Heart' in Peter Loizos and Euthymios-Papataxiarchis (eds), *Gender and Kinship in Modern Greece* (Princeton, 1991).

Pappas, Nicholas G., 'Concepts of Greekness: The Recorded Music of Anatolian Greeks after 1922', *Journal of Modern Greek Studies*, 17.2 (1999), 353–73.

Passerini, Luisa, 'Oral Memory of Fascism', in David Forgacs (ed.), *Rethinking Italian Fascism: Capitalism, Populism and Culture* (London, 1986).

——*Fascism in Popular Memory: The Cultural Experience of the Turin Working Class* (Cambridge, 1987).

Pears, Edwin, *Turkey and its People* (London, 1911).

Peleikis, Anja, 'The Making and Unmaking of Memories: The Case of a Multi Confessional Village in Lebanon', in Ussama Makdisi and Paul A. Silverstein (eds), *Memory and Violence in the Middle East and North Africa* (Bloomington and Indianapolis, 2006).

Pentzopoulos, Dimitri, *The Balkan Exchange of Minorities and Its Impact Upon Greece* (Paris, 1962).

Peronitis, Argiris P., 'Hazioustalar (Haciustalar): O Protomastoras Hatzi-Antonis kai i dio Mastori aderfia tou', *Mikrasiatika Chronika* 20 (1995), 197–260.

Persecution and Extermination of the Communities of Macri and Livissi (1914–1918) (Paris, 1919).

Petropoulou, Ioanna, 'I Ideologiki poria tis Melpo Merlier, to Kentro Mikrasiatikon Spoudon kai i sigkrotisi tou Archeiou Proiforikis Paradosis', in Al. Moutzouvi (ed.), *Martiries se ichitikes kai kinoumenes apotiposis os pigi tis Istorias* (Athens, 1998).

Philliou, Christine, *Biography of an Empire: Governing Ottomans in an Age of Revolution* (Berkeley, CA, 2011).

Pipes, Richar, *Russia under the Old Regime* (Harmondsworth, 1974).

Politis, Kosmas, *Stou Hatzifrangkou: Ta Saranta Chronia mias politias* (Athens, 1965).

Poutouridou, Margarita, 'The Of Valley and the Coming of Islam: The Case of the Greek-Speaking Muslims', *Deltion* 12 (1997–8), 62–7.

Pylarinos, Theodosis, 'To "Biblio" ton Ipotrophon tou Syllogou Mikrasiatikon "I Anatoli"', *Mikrasiatiko Chronika*, 21 (2002), 98–100.

Quataert, Donald, *Social Disintegration and Popular Resistance in the Ottoman Empire, 1881–1908: Reactions to European Penetration* (New York, 1983).

——'The Age of Reforms, 1812–1914', in Suraiya Faroqhi, Bruce McGowan, Donald Quataert and Şevket Pamuk (eds), *An Economic and Social History of the Ottoman Empire*, vol. 2, *1600–1914* (Cambridge, 1994).

——*The Ottoman Empire 1700–1922*, 2nd edn (Cambridge, 2005).

Ramsay, William Mitchell, *The Historical Geography of Asia Minor* (London, 1890).

——*Impressions of Turkey during Twelve Years' Wanderings* (London, 1897).

——*Pauline and Other Studies in Early Christian History* (London, 1906).

——*The Intermixture of Races in Asia Minor: Some of its Causes and Effects* (London, 1917).

Reynolds, Michael A., *Shattering Empires: The Clash and Collapse of the Ottoman and Russian Empires, 1908–1918* (Cambridge, 2011).

Renieri, Irini, ' "Xenophone Nevşehirlis...Greek Souled Neapolitans": The Persistent yet Hesitant Dissemination of the Greek Language in 1870s Nevshehir', in Evangelia Balta and Matthias Kappler (eds), *Cries and Whispers in Karamanlidika Books* (Weisbaden, 2010).

Rodrigue, Aron, 'Difference and Tolerance in the Ottoman Empire', *Stanford Humanities Review* (1995), 81–92.

Rogan, Eugene, *The Arabs: A History* (London, 2009).

Runciman, Steven, *The Great Church in Captivity: A Study of the Patriarchate of Constantinople from the Eve of the Turkish Conquest to the Greek War of Independence* (Cambridge, 1968).

Said, Edward, *Orientalism* (London, 1978).

Samouilidis, Christos, 'Kappadokia ethima kai doxasies gia to thanato kai ti zoi', *Mikrasiatika Chronika*, 17 (1981), 233–5.

Samouilidis, Christos, *Istoria tou Pontiakou Ellinismou* (Athens, 1985).

Sapountzakis, Charis, *Anthologia Pisidias* (Athens, 2000).

Sardar, Ziauddin, *Orientalism* (Buckingham and Philadelphia, 1999).

Savorianakis, Panagiotis, *Nisiotikes Koinotites sto Aigaio* (Athens, 2000).

Schaller, Dominik J., and Zimmerer, Jürgen, 'Late Ottoman Genocides: The Dissolution of the Ottoman Empire and Young Turkish Population and Extermination Policies—Introduction', *Journal of Genocide Research*, 10.1 (2008), 7–14.

Schwartz, Stuart B., *All Can Be Saved: Religious Tolerance and Salvation in the Iberian Atlantic World* (New Haven, CT, 2008).

Senisik, Pinar, 'Insights from the Cretan Revolt of 1897', *Journal of Modern Greek Studies*, 28 (2010), 27–47.

Seremetakis, Nadia, *The Last Word: Women, Death and Divination in Inner Mani* (Chicago, 1991).

Shevzov, Vera, 'Letting the People into Church: Reflections on Orthodoxy and Community in Late Imperial Russia', in Valerie A. Kivelson and Robert H. Greene (eds), *Orthodox Russia: Belief Under the Tsars* (University Park, PA, 2003).

——— *Russian Orthodoxy on the Eve of Revolution* (New York, 2007).

Simić, Andrei, 'Nationalism as folk ideology: The Case of the Former Yugoslavia' in Joel M. Halpern and David A. Kideckel (eds), *Neighbors at War: Anthropological Perspectives on Yugoslav Ethnicity, Culture and History* (University Park, PA, 2000).

Sinopoli, Carla, 'Imperial Integration and Imperial Subjects', in Susan Alcock et al. (eds), *Empires: Perspectives from Archaeology and History* (Cambridge, 2001).

Skopetea, Elli, *To Prototypo Vasilio kai i Megali Idea* (Athens, 1988).

Sluglett, Peter, (ed.), *The Urban Social History of the Middle East, 1750–1950* (Syracuse, NY, 2008).

Sotiriou, Dido, *Farewell Anatolia* (Athens, 1996).

Smynelis, Marie-Carmen, *Une societe hors de soi: Identités et relations sociales a Smyrne aux XVIIIᵉ et XIXᵉ siècles* (Paris, 2005).

Snyder, Timothy, *Bloodlands: Europe between Hitler and Stalin* (New York, 2010).

Soldatos, Christos, *I Ekpedeftiki kai Pnevmatiki Kinisi tou Ellinismou tis M. Asias (1800–1922)* 2 vols (Athens, 1989).

Stamatopoulos, Dimitris, 'I Mikrasiatiki Ekstratia: I Anthropo-geografia tis Katastrofis', in A. Liakos (ed.), *To 1922 kai i Prosfiges: mia nea matia* (Athens, 2011).

Stelaku, Vasso, 'Space and Identity: Two Cappadocian Settlements', in R. Hirschon (ed.), *Crossing the Aegean* (New York, 2003).

Stewart, Charles, *Demons and the Devil: Moral Imagination in Modern Greek Culture* (Princeton, 1991).

Stuart-Glennie, John S., 'Essays on the Science of Folklore, Greek Folkspeech, and the Survival of Paganism', in Lucy M. Garnett, *Greek Folk-Poesy* (London, 1896).

Sutton, David E., *Memories Cast in Stone: The Relevance of the Past in Everyday Life* (Oxford and New York, 1998).

—— *Remembrance of Repasts: An Anthropology of Food and Memory* (Oxford and New York, 2001).

Suny, G., Göçek, F., and Naimark, N. (eds), *A Question of Genocide: Armenians and Turks at the End of the Ottoman Empire* (New York, 2011).

Tanc, Barbaros, 'Where Local Trumps National: Christian Orthodox and Muslim Refugees since Lausanne', *Balkanologie*, 1–2 (2001) http://balkanologie.revues.org/index732.html (accessed 14 January 2012).

Thompson, E. P. *The Making of the English Working Class* (London, 1980).

—— *Customs in Common* (London, 1991).

Tilly, Charles, *Durable Inequality* (Berkeley, CA, 1998).

Todorova, Maria, *Imagining the Balkans* (Oxford, 1997).

Toksöz, Meltem, (eds), *Cities of the Mediterranean: from the Ottomans to the present day* (London, 2010).

Toynbee, Arnold J., *The Western Question in Greece and Turkey: A Study in the Contact of Civilizations* (London, 1922).

Trombley, Frank, 'The Christianisation of Rite in Byzantine Anatolia: F. W. Hasluck and Religious Continuity', in David Shankland (ed.), *Anthropology, Archaeology and Heritage in the Balkans and Anatolia: The Life and Times of F. W. Hasluck 1878–1920*, vol. 2 (Istanbul, 2004).

Tsing, Anna L., *In the Realm of the Diamond Queen* (Princeton, 1993).

Tziovas, Dimitris, 'Introduction', in Stratis Doukas, *A Prisoner of War's Story*, trans. Petro Alexiou, (Birmingham, 1999).

Ülker, Erol, '"Contextualizing Turkification": Nation-Building in the Late Ottoman Empire', *Nations and Nationalism*, 4 (2005), 613–36.

Üngör, Ugur Ümit, *The Making of Modern Turkey: Nation and State in Eastern Anatolia, 1913–1950* (Oxford, 2011).

Varshney, Ashutosh, *Ethnic Conflict and Civic Life: Hindus and Muslims in India* (New Haven, CT, 2002).

Venezis, Elias, *To Numero 31, 328*, 6th edn (Athens, 1972).

Von Hagen, Mark, 'The Russian Empire', in Karen Barkey and Mark von Hagen (eds), *After Empire: Multiethnic Societies and Nation-Building: The Soviet Union and the Russian, Ottoman, and Habsburg Empires* (Boulder, CO, 1997).

Vovelle, Michelle, *Ideologies and Mentalities* (Cambridge, 1990).

Vryonis Jnr, Speros, *The Decline of Medieval Hellenism in Asia Minor and the Process of Islamization from the Eleventh through to the Fifteenth Century* (Berkeley, CA, 1971).

Ware, Kallistos, *The Orthodox Way* (Crestwood, NY, 1995).

Wheatcroft, Andrew, *The Ottomans: Dissolving Images* (Harmonsworth, 1993).

White, A., 'Survivals of Primitive Religion among the People of Asia Minor', *Journals of the Transactions of the Victoria Institute*, 39 (1907), 146-66.

White, Richard, *The Middle Ground: Indians, Empires, and Republics in the Great Lakes Region, 1650–1815*, 2nd edn (Cambridge, 2010).

Wolf, Eric R., *Europe and the People without History* (Berkeley, CA, 1982).

Xenophanes, 1 (1896), 3–6 and 2 (1905).

Yapp, Malcolm, *The Making of the Modern Near East 1792–1923* (London, 1987).

Yiannakopoulos, Georgios A., 'The Reconstruction of a Destroyed Picture: The Oral History Archive of the Center for Asia Minor Studies', *Mediterranean Historical Review*, 8.2 (1993), 201–17.

Yıldırım, Onur, *Diplomacy and Displacement: Reconsidering the Turco-Greek Exchange of Populations, 1922–1934* (New York, 2006).

Zachariadou, E. A., 'Co-Existence and Religion', *Archivum Ottomanicum*, 5.15 (1997), 119-29.

——'À propos du syncrétisme Islamo-Chrétien dans les territoires Ottoman', in Gilles Veinstein (ed.), *Syncrétismes et hérésies dans l'Orient seljoukide et ottoman (XIVᵉ–XVIIIᵉ Siecle)* (Leuven, 2005).

Zaravelas, Dimitris, *Petrines Mnimes: Odoporikos stis hamenes patrides* (Athens and Ioannina, 1991).

Žižek, Slavoj, *Enjoy Your Symptom!: Jacques Lacan in Hollywood and Out* (London, 2001).

—— *Violence: Six Sideways Reflections* (London, 2008).

Zoupoulidis, Spyridon , 'I Eparchia Kolonias', *Xenophanes* (1910), 275–77.

Zürcher, Erik-Jan, 'The Ottoman Conscription System in Theory and Practice, 1844–1918', *International Review of Social History*, 43.3 (1998), 437–49.

Index

7184635